P9-CFI-349
3 2109 00098 6415
WITHDRAWAL

AN INDEX TO BIBLIOGRAPHIES, 1923–1932

NATHAN VAN PATTEN

AN INDEX TO BIBLIOGRAPHIES AND BIBLIOGRAPHICAL CONTRIBUTIONS

RELATING TO THE WORK OF AMERICAN AND BRITISH AUTHORS, 1923–1932

1934

Stanford University Press ◆ Stanford University, California
London: Humphrey Milford ◆ Oxford University Press

STANFORD UNIVERSITY PRESS
STANFORD UNIVERSITY, CALIFORNIA

LONDON: HUMPHREY MILFORD
OXFORD UNIVERSITY PRESS

THE BAKER AND TAYLOR COMPANY
55 FIFTH AVENUE, NEW YORK

ROBERT M. MCBRIDE & COMPANY
4 WEST SIXTEENTH STREET, NEW YORK

MARTINUS NIJHOFF
9 LANGE VOORHOUT, THE HAGUE

THE MARUZEN COMPANY
TOKYO, OSAKA, KYOTO, SENDAI

PRINTED AND BOUND IN THE UNITED STATES
OF AMERICA BY STANFORD UNIVERSITY PRESS

PREFACE

Three groups of potential users have been considered in the preparation of *An Index to Bibliographies and Bibliographical Contributions Relating to American and British Authors, 1923–1932:*

I. The collector of and the dealer in books by American and British authors.

II. The research worker in the fields of American and English literature.

III. The cataloguer and the reference librarian.

An effort has been made to draw with some precision the line between bibliography and criticism. In a broader and perhaps a better sense such a distinction should not be attempted. The scope of this work, however, has been deliberately limited to enumerative and descriptive bibliography, and only such books and journal contributions as have to do with books as books or which record the existence of previously unknown works of a particular author have been entered in the *Index.* Its purpose is to facilitate the acquisition of information concerning the printed and manuscript work of individual authors and data relating to the writing of an author's books, their printing, binding, paper, size, pagination, illustrations, variants, editions, issues, rarity, conditions, points, value, location, etc.

Critical works treating of books as literature and also biographies have been excluded unless a considerable amount of bibliographical material is to be found therein.

General bibliographies and bibliographical contributions to journals have not been noted in this *Index,* although a number of such works have been analyzed for pertinent data. A list of these is included in an Appendix, which also notes other general bibliographical publications supplementary to the purposes of the *Index.*

Some of the entries, particularly for contemporary authors, actually are rather trivial check-lists, but such material has been included as of some value in the absence of comprehensive bibliographies.

Important bio-bibliographies relating to individuals of other than literary fame, e.g., Cromwell, Lincoln, and Washington, although not strictly within the scope of the *Index,* have been noted.

Reviews of important bibliographical publications have been made a part of the entry covering the work reviewed. In the selection of such reviews preference has been given to contributions signed by well-known bibliographical scholars and giving additions or corrections.

Although many facsimiles of title-pages have been noted, no systematic effort has been made to record all such facsimiles published during the decade with which the *Index* is concerned. No pretense is made to comprehensiveness in this respect.

A few important bibliographies issued in the early part of 1933 have been included as immediately useful. These will be reprinted when a continuation of this *Index* can appear.

In the arrangement of entries, books and journal contributions relating to the works of a particular author precede those referring to single works. With a few exceptions, all entries have been made under the actual name of an author, with a cross-reference from a pseudonym if used.

The pagination of books is given only in the case of works largely devoted to bibliographical matters. Page variants in different editions of a republished work are indicated in parentheses.

When a volume covers parts of two or more years, the date of the last year only is given in the case of references to articles in journals. When a volume covers all of two or more years, the inclusive dates are given.

The fragmentary information available concerning the works of many American and British authors is made apparent by the publication of an index of this character.

NATHAN VAN PATTEN

STANFORD UNIVERSITY, CALIFORNIA
June 21, 1933

CONTENTS

AN INDEX TO BIBLIOGRAPHIES AND BIBLIOGRAPHICAL CONTRIBUTIONS RELATING TO THE WORK OF AMERICAN AND BRITISH AUTHORS, 1923-1932

Abbott, Jacob, 1803–1879
FULLERTON, BRADFORD M. Selective bibliography, p. 3.

Abbott, John S. C., 1805–1877
FULLERTON, BRADFORD M. Selective bibliography, p. 3.

Abercrombie, Lascelles, 1881——
GAWSWORTH, JOHN, *pseud.,* (T. Fytton Armstrong). Ten contemporaries: notes toward their definitive bibliography. First series. London, Benn, 1932.

Adams, Abigail, 1744–1818
FULLERTON, BRADFORD M. Selective bibliography, p. 4.

Adams, Arthur Henry, 1872——
SERLE, PERCIVAL. Bibliography of Australasian poetry, pp. 1–2.

Adams, Charles Follen, 1842–1918
FULLERTON, BRADFORD M. Selective bibliography, p. 4.

Adams, Francis William Lauderdale, 1862–1893
SERLE, PERCIVAL. Bibliography of Australasian poetry, p. 2.

Adams, Henry, 1838–1918
FULLERTON, BRADFORD M. Selective bibliography, p. 5.
JOHNSON, MERLE. American first editions, pp. 3–4 (3–4). The check-list in the 1929 edition was compiled by Vrest Orton.

Adams, Nicholas
See Bodrugan, Nicholas.

Adams, William Taylor, 1822–1897
FULLERTON, BRADFORD M. Selective bibliography, pp. 5–6.

Addison, Joseph, 1672–1719
S., G. A bibliographical note on the 1726 edition of Addison's works. *Modern philology,* 23 : 361, 1926.
Letter from Italy, 1709.
ANDERSON, P. B. Addison's *Letter from Italy. Modern language review,* 27 : 318, 1932.

Ade, George, 1866——
JOHNSON, MERLE. American first editions, pp. 5–6 (5–7). The check-list in the 1929 edition was compiled by J. B. McGee.
McGEE, J. B. American first editions: George Ade, 1866——. *Publishers' weekly,* 103 : 583, 1923.

Adeler, Max, *pseud.*
See Clark, Charles Heber.

Adrian IV, (*Pope*), *d.* 1159.
ALMEDINGEN, MARTHA E. VON. The English pope. (Adrian IV.) London, Heath, Cranton, ltd., 1925. Bibliography, pp. 199–200.

Aiken, Conrad Potter, 1889——
JOHNSON, MERLE. American first editions, pp. 7 (8–9). The check-list in the 1929 edition was compiled by Alfred C. Potter.

Ainsworth, William Harrison, 1805–1882
CARTER, JOHN. Binding variants in English publishing, 1820–1900. London, Constable, 1932.
LOCKE, HAROLD. A bibliographical catalogue of the published novels and ballads of William Harrison Ainsworth. London, E. Mathews, 1925. 68 pp.

Akenside, Mark, 1721–1770
WILLIAMS, IOLO A. Seven XVIIIth century bibliographies. London, Dulau, 1924, pp. 75–97.

Akhurst, William Mower

SERLE, PERCIVAL. Bibliography of Australasian poetry, p. 3.

Alabaster, William, 1561–1640

Roxana, 1632.

HUNTINGTON LIBRARY (San Marino, California). Tudor drama . . . (San Marino, California), 1932. Facsimile of title-page.

Alcott, Amos Bronson, 1799–1888

FULLERTON, BRADFORD M. Selective bibliography, pp. 6–7.

Alcott, Louisa May, 1832–1886

FULLERTON, BRADFORD M. Selective bibliography, pp. 7–8.

GULLIVER, LUCILE. Louisa May Alcott, a bibliography . . . with an appreciation by Cornelia Meigs. Boston, Little, Brown and co., 1932. 71 pp.

JOHNSON, MERLE. American first editions, pp. (10–12).

JOHNSON, MERLE. American first editions: Louisa May Alcott, 1832–1886. *Publishers' weekly,* 116: 1965–66, 1929.

Little women, 1868–1869.

CURLE, RICHARD. Collecting American first editions, p. 204.

WINTERICH, JOHN T. Romantic stories of books. Second series. *Little women. Publishers' weekly,* 120: 607–11, 1931. Facsimile of title-page.

Aldington, Richard, 1892——

SCHWARTZ, H. WARREN. Check-lists of twentieth-century authors. Second series. Milwaukee, Wis., Casanova booksellers, 1933.

Aldrich, Anne Reeve, 1866–1892

FULLERTON, BRADFORD M. Selective bibliography, p. 8.

Aldrich, Thomas Bailey, 1836–1907

FULLERTON, BRADFORD M. Selective bibliography, pp. 8–9.

JOHNSON, MERLE. American first editions, pp. 8–10 (13–16). The check-list in the 1929 edition was compiled by Vrest Orton.

Story of a bad boy, 1870.

CURLE, RICHARD. Collecting American first editions, p. 204.

Alger, Horatio, 1834–1899

FULLERTON, BRADFORD M. Selective bibliography, pp. 9–10.

Alken, Henry Thomas, 1784–1851

SAWYER and DARTON. English books, v. 2, pp. 223–34.

Allen, Elizabeth Ann (Chase, Akers), 1832–1911

FULLERTON, BRADFORD M. Selective bibliography, pp. 10–11.

Allen, Ethan, 1737–1789

PELL, JOHN. Ethan Allen. Boston, Houghton Mifflin co., 1929. "Bibliography and key to chronology and notes," pp. 271–79.

Reason the only oracle of man, 1784.

GOHDES, CLARENCE. Ethan Allen and his *magnum opus. Open court,* 43 : 129–51, 1929.

Allen, Ira, 1751–1814

WILBUR, JAMES B. Ira Allen. Founder of Vermont. 1751–1814. Boston, Houghton Mifflin co., 1928. 2 v. Bibliography, v. 2, pp. 527–31.

Allen, James Lane, 1849–1925

FULLERTON, BRADFORD M. Selective bibliography, pp. 11–12.

JOHNSON, MERLE. American first editions, pp. 11–12 (17–18). The check-list in the 1929 edition was compiled by Vrest Orton.

TOWNSEND, JOHN W. James Lane Allen, a personal note. With illustrations and a bibliography. Louisville, Ky., Courier-Journal, 1928. 149 pp., facsimiles.

Allen, Leslie Holdsworth, 1879——
SERLE, PERCIVAL. Bibliography of Australasian poetry, p. 4.

Allen, Paul, 1775–1826
FULLERTON, BRADFORD M. Selective bibliography, p. 12.

Allen, Samantha, *pseud.*
See Holley, Marietta.

Allston, Washington, 1779–1843
FULLERTON, BRADFORD M. Selective bibliography, pp. 12–13.

Altsheler, Joseph A., 1862–1919
OVERTON, GRANT. Cargoes for Crusoes. New York, Appleton, [1923], pp. 246–48.

Anderson, Andrew
SERLE, PERCIVAL. Bibliography of Australasian poetry, p. 6.

Anderson, John, 1815–1895
CRONE, JOHN S. Bibliography of John Anderson. *Irish book lover,* 14: [19]–20, 1924.

Anderson, Sherwood, 1876——
JESSUP, MARY E. A check-list of the writings of Sherwood Anderson. *American collector,* 5: 157–58, 1928.

JOHNSON, MERLE. American first editions, pp. 13–14 (19–20). The check-list in the 1929 edition was compiled by Aaron Manley.

MANLEY, AARON. American first editions: Sherwood Anderson, 1876——. *Publishers' weekly,* 103: 251, 1923.

Anderton, James
See Anderton, Lawrence.

Anderton, Lawrence, 1575–1643
HAWKES, ARTHUR J. The Birchley Hall secret press. *Library,* s. 4, 8: [137]–83, 1928. Bibliography of the press, pp. 160–83.

Andrews, Jane, 1835–1887
FULLERTON, BRADFORD M. Selective bibliography, pp. 13–14.

Anstey, Christopher, 1724–1805
WILLIAMS, IOLO A. Bibliography of Christopher Anstey. *London Mercury,* 11: 300–302, 414–17, 526–28, 643–44; 12: 194, 300–301, 1925.

Anstey, F., *pseud.*
See Guthrie, Thomas Anstey.

Arblay, Frances (Burney) d', 1752–1840
SAWYER and DARTON. English books, v. 1, p. 308.

Archer, William, 1856–1924
ARCHER, CHARLES. William Archer: life, work, and friendships. New Haven, Yale university press, 1931. Bibliographic appendix, pp. [419]–34. *Ibid.,* London, G. Allen & Unwin, 1931.

Arlen, Michael, 1895——
OVERTON, GRANT. Cargoes for Crusoes. New York, Appleton, [1923], p. 276.

Armstrong, John, 1709–1779
WILLIAMS, IOLO A. Bibliography of John Armstrong. *London Mercury,* 10: 76–77, 1924.
WILLIAMS, IOLO A. Seven XVIIIth century bibliographies. London, Dulau, 1924, pp. 17–38.

Arnold, Matthew, 1822–1888
CARTER, JOHN. Binding variants in English publishing, 1820–1900. London, Constable, 1932.

Arnold, William Harris, 1854–1923
NEWTON, A. EDWARD. This book-collecting game. Boston, Little, Brown and co., 1928, pp. 186–89.

Arp, Bill, *pseud.*
See Smith, Charles Henry.

Arthur, (*King of Britain*)

PARRY, JOHN J., *ed.* Bibliography of critical Arthurian legend, 1922–1929. New York, Modern language association of America, 1931. 59 pp.

Arthur, Henry

SERLE, PERCIVAL. Bibliography of Australasian poetry, pp. 8–9.

Arthur, Timothy Shay, 1809–1855

FULLERTON, BRADFORD M. Selective bibliography, p. 14.

Asquith, Herbert George, (*Lord Oxford and Asquith*), 1852–1928

SPENDER, JOHN A., and ASQUITH, CECIL. Life of Herbert Asquith . . . London, Hutchinson, [1932]. List of some of Asquith's published writings, addresses, and speeches, v. 2, p. 338.

Atherton, Gertrude (Franklin, Horn), 1857——

JOHNSON, MERLE. American first editions, pp. 15–16 (21–22).

JOHNSON, MERLE. American first editions: Gertrude Franklin Atherton, 1857——. *Publishers' weekly,* 104: 612, 1923.

Atkinson, Evelyn John Rupert, 1881——

SERLE, PERCIVAL. Bibliography of Australasian poetry, p. 9.

Audubon, John James, 1780–1851

The catfish of old Kentucky. *The month at Goodspeed's,* 3: 259–64, 1932. Refers to a manuscript.

Birds of America.

WINTERICH, JOHN T. Books and the man. New York, Greenberg, 1929, pp. 141–54. Facsimile of wrapper of first American edition.

Austen, Jane, 1775–1817

APPERSON, G. L. A Jane Austen dictionary. London, Palmer, 1932. 151 pp.

CHAPMAN, ROBERT W. Jane Austen and her publishers. *London Mercury,* 22: 337–42, 1930.

EDMONDS, JEAN L. Jane Austen: biography and criticism, a bibliography. *Bulletin of bibliography,* 12: 129–34, 150–55, 1925.

JOHNSON, REGINALD B. Jane Austen, her life, her work, her family, and her critics ... London, Dent, [1930]. Appendix E. List of writings and time-table of work. *Ibid.,* New York, Dutton, 1931.

KEYNES, GEOFFREY. Jane Austen: a bibliography ... London, Nonesuch press, 1929. xxv+282 pp., facsimiles. Contents: 1, original editions; 2, first American editions; 3, French translations; 4, collected editions; 5, Spanish translations; 6, letters; 7, miscellaneous writings; 8, biography and criticism; 9, books from Jane Austen's library.

SADLEIR, MICHAEL. The Northanger novels: a footnote to Jane Austen. [Oxford, Oxford university press], 1927. (English association. *Pamphlets,* no. 68.) 23+[8] pp., facsimiles.

THOMSON, CLARA L. Jane Austen: a survey. London, Horace Marshall, 1930. Bibliography, pp. 291–97.

Austin, Jane (Goodwin), 1831–1894

FULLERTON, BRADFORD M. Selective bibliography, p. 15.

Austin, William, 1778–1841

FULLERTON, BRADFORD M. Selective bibliography, pp. 15–17.

Bacheller, Irving Addison, 1859——

JOHNSON, MERLE. American first editions, pp. (23–24).

JOHNSON, MERLE. American first editions. Irving (Addison) Bacheller, 1859——. *Publishers' weekly,* 120: 2654, 1931.

Bacon, Francis, (*Viscount St. Albans*), 1561–1626
SAWYER and DARTON. English books, v. 1, pp. 177–79.
STEEL, BYRON, *pseud.*, (Francis Steegmüller). Sir Francis Bacon: the first modern mind. Garden City, Doubleday, Doran & co., 1930. Annotated bibliography, pp. 193–208.
STURT, MARY. Francis Bacon, a biography. New York, W. Morrow & co., 1932. Bibliography, pp. 243–44.

Essayes, London, 1597.
SAWYER and DARTON. English books, v. 1, p. [178]. Facsimile of title-page.

Essayes, London, 1625.
MAGGS BROTHERS. Catalogue no. 550. London, 1931. Facsimile of title-page, opp. p. 40.

Novum organum, London, 1620.
MAGGS BROTHERS. Catalogue no. 550. London, 1931. Facsimile of title-page, opp. p. 41.

Use of the law.
COLE, GEORGE W. Bibliographical pitfalls — linked books. Bibliographical society of America. *Papers,* 18: 12–30, 1925.

Baker, Ray Stannard, 1870——
JOHNSON, MERLE. American first editions: Ray Stannard Baker, 1870——. *Publishers' weekly,* 103: 1820, 1923.

Baker, William Mumford, 1825–1883
FULLERTON, BRADFORD M. Selective bibliography, p. 17.

Baldwin, Edward, *pseud.*
SAWYER and DARTON. English books, v. 2, p. 123.

Baldwin, Joseph Glover, 1815–1864
FULLERTON, BRADFORD M. Selective bibliography, pp. 17–18.

Baldwin, William, *fl.* 1547
SAWYER and DARTON. English books, v. 1, pp. 113–14.

Bale, John, 1495–1563

GREG, WALTER W. Notes on some early plays. *Library,* s. 4, 12: [44]–56, 1932. Refers to Bale's plays on the baptism and the temptation.

Bangs, John Kendrick, 1862–1922

BANGS, FRANCIS H. John Kendrick Bangs, humorist of the nineties. Yale university library. *Bulletin,* 7: 53–76, 1933. Contains a bibliography of Bangs's works, 1886–1920.

FULLERTON, BRADFORD M. Selective bibliography, p. 18.

Barclay, Alexander, 1475(?)–1552

SAWYER and DARTON. English books, v. 1, pp. 59–60.

WHITE, BEATRICE. A note on Alexander Barclay. *Modern language review,* 26: 169–70, 1931. Refers to two unique editions of Barclay's poems in the Huntington library.

Ship of fools, 1570.

SAWYER and DARTON. English books, v. 2, p. 148. Facsimile of title-page (London, 1570).

See also Brant, Sebastian.

Baring, Maurice, 1874——

CHAUNDY, LESLIE. A bibliography of the first editions of Maurice Baring. With poems by Maurice Baring and an introductory note on Maurice Baring by Desmond McCarthy. London, Dulau, 1925. 48 pp. Review by Iolo A. Williams, *London Mercury,* 12: 642–43, 1925.

Barker, James Nelson, 1784–1858

MUSSER, PAUL H. James Nelson Barker, 1784–1858; with a reprint of his comedy, *Tears and smiles.* Philadelphia, 1929. (Thesis, University of Pennsylvania.) Bibliography, pp. 211–23.

Barksted, William, *fl.* 1611

SAWYER and DARTON. English books, v. 1, p. 92.

Barlow, Joel, 1754–1812

ARMSTRONG, T. P. Raleigh and the *Columbiad. Notes and queries,* 162: 15, 1932.

Barnum, Frances (Courtenay, Baylor), 1848–1920

FULLERTON, BRADFORD M. Selective bibliography, pp. 19–20.

Barnum, Phineas Taylor, 1810–1891

WERNER, MORRIS R. Barnum. New York, Harcourt, Brace and co., 1923. Bibliography, pp. 373–76.

Barr, Amelia Edith (Huddleston), 1831–1919

FULLERTON, BRADFORD M. Selective bibliography, pp. 20–21.

Barrie, James Matthew, (*Sir*), 1860——

AMERICAN ART ASSOCIATION. Sales catalogue. First editions, letters, and mss. of Barrie, Dickens, Galsworthy, Shaw, Trollope ... from the library of Thomas Hatton. New York, 1929.

BLOCK, ANDREW. ... Sir J. M. Barrie, his first editions: points and values ... London, Foyle, [1933]. xiv+48 pp. (First editions and their values, no. 3.)

CUTLER, BRADLEY D. Sir James M. Barrie, a bibliography with full collations of the American unauthorized editions. New York, Greenberg, [1931]. 242 pp. Contents: a note on the American pirated editions; bibliography; collected editions; prefaces and introductions; books about James M. Barrie; prices and price trends; Canadian editions.

CUTLER and STILES. Modern British authors, pp. 7–11.

GARLAND, HERBERT. A bibliography of the writings of Sir James Matthew Barrie ... London, Bookman's journal, 1928. 146 pp.

Richard Savage, 1891.

See entry under Savage, Richard.

Bastard, Thomas, 1566–1618

Chrestoleros, London, 1598.

SAWYER and DARTON. English books, v. 1, pp. 3–4. Facsimile of title-page.

Bates, Arlo, 1850–1918

FULLERTON, BRADFORD M. Selective bibliography, p. 21.

Bates, Herbert Ernest, 1905——

GAWSWORTH, JOHN, *pseud.,* (T. Fytton Armstrong). Ten contemporaries: notes toward their definitive bibliography. Second series. London, Joiner & Steele, 1932.

Baughan, Blanche Edith, 1870——

SERLE, PERCIVAL. Bibliography of Australasian poetry, pp. 16–17.

Baxter, Richard, 1615–1691

MATTHEWS, ARNOLD G. The works of Richard Baxter: an annotated list . . . [London, Wyman & sons, 1932]. 52 pp.

NEWTON, A. EDWARD. This book-collecting game, p. 77.

Bayldon, Arthur Albert Dawson, 1865——

SERLE, PERCIVAL. Bibliography of Australasian poetry, p. 17.

Beadle, Erastus Flavel, 1821–1894

PEARSON, EDMUND L. Dime novels or following an old trail in popular literature. Boston, Little, Brown and co., 1929. Bibliography, pp. 271–72.

ROBINSON, HENRY M. Mr. Beadle's books. *Bookman* (New York), 69: 18–24, 1929.

Beadle, Irwin

See Beadle, Erastus Flavel.

Beale, Anne

SPARKE, ARCHIBALD. (List of the works of Anne Beale.) *Notes and queries,* 153: 213, 1927.

Beardsley, Aubrey Vincent, 1872–1898

First Edition Club. A bibliographical catalogue, pp. 1–2.

McFall, Haldane. Aubrey Beardsley: the man and his work. London, Lane, [1928]. xiv+109 pp.

Beauchamp, Kathleen

See Murry, Katherine Middleton.

Beaumont, Francis, 1584–1616

A new allusion to Shakespeare in a hitherto unknown poem by Francis Beaumont, in a newly discovered ms. commonplace book. *Daily telegraph* (London), February 3, 1928.

Weigle, Frederic H. The adaptations of Beaumont and Fletcher's comedies. 1932. (Thesis, University of Chicago.) Typewritten.

Comedies and tragedies, 1647.

Maggs Brothers. Catalogue no. 550. London, 1931. Facsimile of title-page, opp. p. 56.

Beckford, Peter, 1740–1811

Sawyer and Darton. English books, v. 2, p. 221.

Beckford, William, 1759–1844

Chapman, Guy, and Hodgkin, J. A bibliography of William Beckford of Fonthill . . . London, Constable, 1930. 127 pp. Contents: published books; attributed books; unpublished prose writings; verses; music; portraits of William Beckford; addenda, *Vathek.* Review by R. E. Gathorne-Hardy, *Book-collector's quarterly,* no. 1, December 1930–February 1931, pp. 59–63.

Grimsditch, Herbert B. William Beckford's minor works. *London Mercury,* 14: 599–605, 1926.

May, Marcel. La jeunesse de William Beckford et la genèse de son *Vathek.* Paris, Presses universitaires, 1928. 437 pp.

Beddoes, Thomas Lovell, 1803–1849
RUDER, BARNAT B. Beddoes editions. *Saturday review of literature,* 5: 665, 1929.

Beebe, Charles William, 1877——
JOHNSON, MERLE. American first editions, pp. 17 (25–26).

Beecher, Henry Ward, 1813–1887
FULLERTON, BRADFORD M. Selective bibliography, pp. 21–22.
HIBBEN, PAXTON. Henry Ward Beecher; an American portrait. New York, Doran, [1927]. Sources, pp. 357–67.

Beer, Thomas, 1889——
JOHNSON, MERLE. American first editions, p. (27).

Beerbohm, Max, 1872——
CUTLER and STILES. Modern British authors, pp. 12–13.

Beers, Ethel Lynn, 1827–1879
FULLERTON, BRADFORD M. Selective bibliography, pp. 22–23.

Beers, Ethelinda, *pseud.*
See Beers, Ethel Lynn.

Behn, Aphra (Amis), 1640–1689
Emperor of the Moon, 1687.
BENNETT, R. E. A bibliographical correction. *Review of English studies,* 3: 450–51, 1927.
Oroonoko, 1688.
JOHNSON, EDWIN D. Aphra Behn's *Oroonoko. Journal of Negro history,* 10: 334–42, 1925.

Belknap, Jeremy, 1744–1798
FULLERTON, BRADFORD M. Selective bibliography, pp. 22–23.
Foresters, 1792.
TAYLOR, LILLIAN G. The way of the best-seller. *Colophon,* part 6, 1931. Facsimile of title-page.

Bell, Acton, *pseud.*
See Brontë, Anne.

Bell, Currer, *pseud.*
See Brontë, Charlotte.

Bell, Ellis, *pseud.*
See Brontë, Emily Jane.

Bell, John, 1745–1831
MORISON, STANLEY. John Bell, 1745–1831. Bookseller, printer, publisher, typefounder, journalist, etc. Cambridge, 1930. Review by A. F. Johnson, *Book-collector's quarterly,* no. 1, December 1930–February 1931, pp. 36–40.

Bellamy, Edward, 1850–1898
FULLERTON, BRADFORD M. Selective bibliography, pp. 23–24.

Belloc, Hilaire, 1870——
NICHOLLS, NORAH. The first editions of Hilaire Belloc. *Bookman* (London), 81 : 62, 126–27, 1931.

Benét, Stephen Vincent, 1898——
JOHNSON, MERLE. American first editions, pp. (28–29).

Bennett, Arnold, 1867——
NICHOLLS, NORAH. Arnold Bennett: some bibliographical points. *Bookman* (London), 80: 62, 128–29, 1931.
OVERTON, GRANT. Authors of the day. New York, Doran, [1924], pp. 291–93.

Bennett, John, 1865——
FULLERTON, BRADFORD M. Selective bibliography, p. 24.

Bensley, Thomas, *d.* 1833
See Bulmer, William.

Benson, Stella, 1892——

Gawsworth, John, *pseud.,* (T. Fytton Armstrong). Ten contemporaries: notes toward their definitive bibliography. Second series. London, Joiner & Steele, 1932.

Bentham, Jeremy, 1748–1832

Kayser, Elmer L. The grand social enterprise; a study of Jeremy Bentham in his relation to liberal nationalism . . . New York, Columbia university press, 1932. Bibliography, pp. 94–103.

Beowulf

Chambers, Raymond W. Beowulf: an introduction to the study of the poem with a discussion of the stories of Offa and Finn. Cambridge, Cambridge university press, 1932. Second edition. Bibliography of Beowulf and Finnsburg, pp. [507]–37; additions to the bibliography to 1930, p. [538].

Haber, Tom B. Comparative study of the Beowulf and the Aeneid . . . Princeton, N.J., Princeton university press, 1931. Select bibliography, [135]–41. (Thesis, Ohio state university.)

Klaeber, Friedrich, *ed.* Beowulf and the fight at Finnsburg, edited with an introduction, bibliography, notes, glossary, and appendices . . . Boston, Heath, 1928.

Beresford, John Davys, 1873——

First Edition Club. A bibliographical catalogue, pp. [3]–15.

Berkeley, George, 1685–1753

Querist.

Meyerstein, E. H. W. The first London edition of *The querist. Times literary supplement,* May 20, 1926, p. 339.

Berlin, Irving, 1888——

WOOLLCOTT, ALEXANDER. The story of Irving Berlin. New York, Putnam, 1925. "Words and music by Irving Berlin, 1907–1909," pp. 225–37.

Berners, Juliana, *b.* 1388(?)

See Markham, Gervase.

Bickerstaff, Isaac, *d.* 1812(?)

MACMILLAN, ETHEL. The plays of Isaac Bickerstaff in America. *Philological quarterly,* 5: 58–69, 1926.

Bierce, Ambrose Gwinett, 1842–1914

A collection of Bierce letters. *University of California chronicle,* 34: 3–48, 1932.

FULLERTON, BRADFORD M. Selective bibliography, pp. 24–25.

JOHNSON, MERLE. American first editions, pp. 19–20 (30–32).

STARRETT, VINCENT. Ambrose Bierce: a bibliography. Philadelphia, Centaur book shop, 1929. 118 pp. Review, *American literature,* 1: 439, 1930.

TUFTS, JAMES. American first editions: Ambrose Bierce, 1842–1914. *Publishers' weekly,* 104: 1290, 1923.

Monk and the hangman's daughter.

MONAGHAN, FRANK. Ambrose Bierce and the authorship of *The monk and the hangman's daughter. American literature,* 2: 357–59, 1931.

Billings, Josh, *pseud.*

See Shaw, Henry Wheeler.

Bird, Robert Montgomery, 1808–1854

FULLERTON, BRADFORD M. Selective bibliography, pp. 25–26.

Blacker, Beaver Henry, 1821–1890

CRONE, JOHN S. Bibliography of Beaver Henry Blacker. *Irish book lover,* 14: [3]–5, 1924.

Blackmore, Richard Doddridge, 1825–1900

Lorna Doone.

BERNBAUM, ERNEST. On Blackmore and *Lorna Doone.* A selected bibliography with brief comments. *Library journal,* 50: 537–38, 1925.

Blair, Robert, 1699–1746

Grave, 1743.

NEWTON, A. EDWARD. This book-collecting game. Boston, Little, Brown and co., 1928, p. 89.

Blake, William, 1757–1827

BURDETT, OSBERT. William Blake. London, Macmillan, 1926. Bibliography, pp. v–vi.

BURLINGTON FINE ARTS CLUB. Catalogue Blake centenary exhibition. London, privately printed, 1927. 63 pp., 49 plates.

DAMON, S. FOSTER. Some American references to Blake before 1863. *Modern language notes,* 45: 365–70, 1930.

DAMON, S. FOSTER. William Blake, his philosophy and symbols. Boston, Houghton Mifflin co., 1924. Bibliography, pp. 478–79.

JAKAGU. A Japanese and English bibliography of William Blake. Tokyo, [1929]. 724 pp. Descriptions in English and Japanese.

MABBOTT, THOMAS O. More American references to Blake before 1863. *Modern language notes,* 47: 87–88, 1932.

NEWTON, A. EDWARD. This book-collecting game. Boston, Little, Brown and co., 1928, pp. 23, 25, 28, 268.

SAWYER and DARTON. English books, v. 1, p. 259; v. 2, pp. 75, 95, 130–31, 169–72, 177.

French revolution, 1791.

SAWYER and DARTON. English books, v. 2, p. 77. Facsimile of title-page.

Milton, 1804.

DAMON, S. FOSTER. A note on the discovery of a new page of poetry in William Blake's *Milton.* Boston, privately printed for the Club of odd volumes, 1925. 14 pp., facsimiles.

Poetical sketches, 1783.

AMERICAN ART ASSOCIATION. Sales catalogue. Rare books from the library of the late Willis Vickery. New York, 1933. Facsimile of title-page, p. 3.

Songs of innocence and experience, 1789.

AMERICAN ART ASSOCIATION. Sales catalogue. Rare books from the library of the late Willis Vickery. New York, 1933. Facsimile of title-page, p. 4.

Bleecker, Ann Eliza (Schuyler), 1752–1783

FULLERTON, BRADFORD M. Selective bibliography, pp. 26–27.

Blewett, Jean, 1862——

PIERCE, LORNE. Outline of Canadian literature, p. 96.

Blocksidge, William, 1887(?)——

SERLE, PERCIVAL. Bibliography of Australasian poetry, pp. 21–22.

Blome, Richard

See Ogilby, John.

Bodenham, John, *fl.* 1600.

SAWYER and DARTON. English books, v. 1, pp. 83–85.

Bodrugan, Nicholas

Epitome, London, 1548.

MAGGS BROTHERS. Catalogue no. 550. London, 1931. Facsimile of title-page, opp. p. 569.

Boker, George Henry, 1823–1890

Bradley, Edward S. George Henry Boker: poet and patriot ... Philadelphia, University of Pennsylvania press, 1927. A chronological list of his writings, pp. 343–49; bibliographies, pp. 350–55.

Fullerton, Bradford M. Selective bibliography, pp. 27–28.

Bolton, Herbert Eugene, 1870——

Ross, Mary. Writings and cartography of Herbert Eugene Bolton. 8 pp. (Reprinted from *New Spain and the West.*)

Borrow, George Henry, 1803–1881

Sawyer and Darton. English books, v. 2, pp. 321–22.

Stephen, George A. Borrow House museum: life of George Borrow and his Norwich home. Norwich, 1927. Bibliography.

Lavengro, 1851.

Sawyer and Darton. English books, v. 2, p. 323. Facsimile of title-page.

Boswell, James, 1740–1795

Boswell and Shakespeare problems. *Times literary supplement,* May 16, 1929, p. 408.

Chapman, Robert W. Boswell's archives. *Essays and studies by members of the English association.* Oxford, 1932, v. 17, pp. 33–43.

Chapman, Robert W. Boswell's proof sheets. *London Mercury,* 15: 50–58, 171–80, 1927.

Grolier Club. Catalogue of an exhibition of the private papers from Malahide castle. New York, privately printed, 1930.

Pottle, Frederick A. Boswellian myths. *Notes and queries,* 149: 4–6, 21–22, 41–42, 120, 1925.

Pottle, Frederick A. Boswellian notes. *Notes and queries,* 149: 113–14, 131–32, 184–86, 222, 1925.

POTTLE, FREDERICK A. Boswelliana: two attributions. *Notes and queries,* 147: 281, 375, 1925.

POTTLE, FREDERICK A. The literary career of James Boswell, esq.; being the bibliographical materials for a life of Boswell. Oxford, Clarendon press, 1929. xliv+335 pp.

POTTLE, FREDERICK A., and POTTLE, MARION S. The private papers of James Boswell from Malahide castle: a catalogue. London, Oxford university press, 1931. xxv+229 pp.

British essays in favour of the brave Corsicans, 1769.

ELKIN MATHEWS, LTD. Catalogue no. 23. London, 1929. Facsimile of title-page.

Corsica, 1768.

SAWYER and DARTON. English books, v. 2, p. 323. Facsimile of title-page.

Essence of the Douglas cause, 1767.

AMERICAN ART ASSOCIATION. Sales catalogue. Library of Frank Irving Fletcher. New York, 1932. Facsimile of title-page, p. 15.

Life of Johnson, 1791.

LYDENBERG, HARRY M. How many issues are there of the first edition of Boswell's *Life of Johnson*? New York public library. *Bulletin,* 31: 826–27, 1927.

Proofsheets of Boswell's *Johnson. Times literary supplement,* January 17, 1924.

North Britain extraordinary.

POTTLE, FREDERICK A. A *North Britain extraordinary. Notes and queries,* 147: 259–61, 403–4, 1925.

Observations on "The minor."

POTTLE, FREDERICK A. *Observations on "The minor."* New York public library. *Bulletin,* 29: 3–6, 1925.

Tour of the Hebrides, 1786.

CHAPMAN, ROBERT W. Cancels in Boswell's *Hebrides. Bodleian quarterly record,* 4: 124, 1924.

Boyesen, Hjalmar Hjorth, 1848–1895

FULLERTON, BRADFORD M. Selective bibliography, p. 28.

Boyle, Robert, 1627–1691

FULTON, T. F. A bibliography of the Honourable Robert Boyle, F.R.S. Oxford bibliographical society. *Proceedings and papers,* 3, part 1, 1931. (Separate edition, London, Oxford university press, 1931.) Reviews by Alfred W. Pollard, *Library,* s. 4, 13 : 108–11, 1933 ; and G. L. Keynes, *Bodleian quarterly review,* 7 : 149–50, 1932.

Bracken, Thomas, 1843–1898

SERLE, PERCIVAL. Bibliography of Australasian poetry, pp. 25–26.

Brackenridge, Hugh Henry, 1748–1816

ANDREWS, J. C. "The Pittsburgh gazette," a pioneer newspaper. *Western Pennsylvania historical magazine,* 15: 293–307, 1932.

FULLERTON, BRADFORD M. Selective bibliography, pp. 28–29.

JOHNSON, MERLE. American first editions, pp. (34–35).

NEWLIN, CLAUDE M. The life and writings of Hugh Henry Brackenridge. Princeton, N.J., Princeton university press, 1932. Bibliography, pp. [309]–22.

NEWLIN, CLAUDE M. The writings of Hugh Henry Brackenridge. *Western Pennsylvania historical magazine,* 10: 224–56, 1927.

Bradford, Ebenezer, 1746–1801

FULLERTON, BRADFORD M. Selective bibliography, pp. 29–30.

Bradford, Gamaliel, 1863–1932

JOHNSON, MERLE. American first editions, pp. 21–22 (36–37). The check-list in the 1929 edition was compiled by Alfred C. Potter.

RICHARDS, GERTRUDE R. B. The life and "lives" of Gamaliel Bradford. *Books,* 8: 4, April 24, 1932.

Bradford, Roark, 1863–1932
JOHNSON, MERLE. American first editions, pp. (36–37).

Bradley, Henry, 1845–1923
BRADLEY, HENRY. Collected papers . . . with a memoir by Robert Bridges. Oxford, Clarendon press, 1928. Full bibliography of Bradley's reviews and articles, pp. [259]–79.

Bradstreet, Anne (Dudley), 1612–1672
NEWTON, A. EDWARD. This book-collecting game, p. 80.

Tenth muse, London, 1650.

WALDMAN, MILTON. Americana. New York, Holt, 1925. Facsimile of title-page, opp. p. 240.

Brady, Edwin James, 1869——
SERLE, PERCIVAL. Bibliography of Australasian poetry, p. 26.

Brainard, John Gardner Calkins, 1796–1828
FULLERTON, BRADFORD M. Selective bibliography, pp. 30–31.

Brandt, Sebastian
See Brant, Sebastian.

Branner, John Casper, 1850–1922
PENROSE, RICHARD A. F. Memorial to John Casper Branner. Geological society of America. *Bulletin,* 36: 15–44, 1925. Bibliography, pp. 23–44.

Brant, Sebastian, 1458–1521

Ship of fools.

POMPEN, AURELIUS. The English versions of *The ship of fools* . . . London, Longmans, Green and co., 1925. List of works consulted, pp. xi–xiv; a full list of the different versions of *The ship of fools,* pp. 14–19.

Breakspere, Nicholas
See Adrian IV (*Pope*).

Breckenridge, William Clark, 1869–1927

BRECKENRIDGE, JAMES M. William Clark Breckenridge, historical research writer and bibliographer of Missouriana; his life, lineage and writings. St. Louis, 1932. Bibliography, pp. 249–349.

Brennan, Christopher John, 1870——

SERLE, PERCIVAL. Bibliography of Australasian poetry, p. 26.

Brereley, John

See Anderton, Lawrence.

Brereton, John le Gay, (*The older*)

SERLE, PERCIVAL. Bibliography of Australasian poetry, p. 27.

Brereton, John le Gay, (*The younger*), 1871——

SERLE, PERCIVAL. Bibliography of Australasian poetry, p. 28.

Brewer, Thomas, *fl.* 1624

SAWYER and DARTON. English books, v. 2, p. 161.

Merry devil of Edmonton, London, 1631.

SAWYER and DARTON. English books, v. 2, p. 160. Facsimile of title-page.

Bridges, Robert Seymour, 1844–1930

SAWYER and DARTON. English books, v. 2, p. 366.

Bridgewater, Benjamin

HOWELL, A. C. John Dunton and an imitation of the *Religio medici. Studies in philology,* 29: 442–62, 1932. Refers to *Religio bibliopolae,* London, 1691.

Briggs, Charles Frederick, 1804–1877

FULLERTON, BRADFORD M. Selective bibliography, pp. 30–31.

Broke, Arthur, *d.* 1563

SAWYER and DARTON. English books, v. 1, pp. 103–4.

Brome, Alexander, 1620–1666

SAWYER and DARTON. English books, v. 2, p. 154.

Bromfield, Louis, 1896——

JOHNSON, MERLE. American first editions, pp. (39–40).

Brontë, Anne, 1820–1849
See Brontë, Charlotte.

Brontë, Charlotte, 1816–1855

Brontë Society. Catalogue of the Bonnell collection in the Brontë parsonage museum. Haworth, 1932. 90 pp., 2 facsimiles.

Brontë Society. *Transactions.* Bradford (England), 1898——.

Cook, Davidson. Brontë manuscripts in the law collection. *Bookman* (London), 69: 100–104, 1925.

Cook, Davidson. Miniature magazines of Charlotte Brontë. With unpublished poems from an original ms. in the Ashley library. *Bookman* (London), 71: 162–65, 1927.

Haldane, Elizabeth S. The Brontës and their biographers. *Nineteenth century,* 112: 752–64, 1932.

Malham-Dembleby, J. Alleged Brontë manuscript explained. *Times literary supplement,* October 15, 1931. Refers to "Early reminiscences."

Sawyer and Darton. English books, v. 2, pp. 295–96, 326–28.

Wise, Thomas J. A Brontë library, a catalogue of printed books, manuscripts, and autograph letters by the members of the Brontë family . . . London, privately printed, 1925. xxiii+82 pp., facsimiles. Contents: 1, the writings of Charlotte Brontë; 2, the writings of Emily Jane Brontë; 3, the writings of Anne Brontë; 4, the writings of the Rev. Patrick Brontë; 5, the writings of Patrick Branwell Brontë; 6, Bronteana.

Jane Eyre, 1847.

Newton, A. Edward. This book-collecting game. Boston, Little, Brown and co., 1928. "A fine three-decker, 'Jane Eyre,' " ill., p. 367.

Sawyer and Darton. English books, v. 2, p. [327]. Facsimile of title-page.

Brontë, Patrick

See Brontë, Charlotte.

Brontë, Patrick Branwell

See Brontë, Charlotte.

Brontë, Emily Jane, 1818–1848

WILSON, ROMER, *pseud.,* (O'Brien, Florence Roma Muir Wilson). The life and private history of Emily Jane Brontë. New York, Boni, 1928. xii+292 pp. English edition with title, *All alone, the life* (etc.). London, Chatto & Windus, 1928.

See also Brontë, Charlotte.

Brooke, Henry, 1703(?)–1783

SAWYER and DARTON. English books, v. 1, pp. 312, 343.

Brooke, Rupert, 1887–1915

CUTLER and STILES. Modern British authors, pp. 14–15.

FIRST EDITION CLUB. A bibliographical catalogue, p. 16.

POTTER, RICHARD M. G. Rupert Brooke: a bibliographical note on his works published in book form, 1911–1919. Hartford, Conn., 1923. 28 pp.

SAWYER and DARTON. English books, v. 2, p. 366.

Brooks, Maria (Gowen), 1795–1845

FULLERTON, BRADFORD M. Selective bibliography, p. 31.

Brooks, Noah, 1830–1903

FULLERTON, BRADFORD M. Selective bibliography, p. 32.

Broome, William, 1689–1745

SAWYER and DARTON. English books, v. 1, pp. 268–69.

Brown, Alice, 1857——

FULLERTON, BRADFORD M. Selective bibliography, pp. 32–33.

JOHNSON, MERLE. American first editions, pp. 23–24 (32–33).

LATHAM, HAROLD S. American first editions: Alice Brown, 1857——. *Publishers' weekly,* 104: 719, 1923.

Brown, Charles Brockden, 1771–1810

FULLERTON, BRADFORD M. Selective bibliography, pp. 33–34.

JOHNSON, MERLE. American first editions, p. (44).

JOHNSON, MERLE. American first editions. Charles Brockden Brown: 1771–1810. *Publishers' weekly,* 121 : 2422, 1932.

NEWTON, A. EDWARD. This book-collecting game. Boston, Little, Brown and co., 1928, p. 275.

Edgar Huntley, 1801.

CURLE, RICHARD. Collecting American first editions, p. 201.

Ormond, 1799.

CURLE, RICHARD. Collecting American first editions, p. 201.

Wieland, 1798.

CURLE, RICHARD. Collecting American first editions, p. 201.

Brown, John, 1800–1859

WARREN, ROBERT P. John Brown: the making of a martyr. New York, Payson & Clarke, 1929. Bibliographical note, pp. 441–62.

Brown, William Hill, 1765–1793

ELLIS, MILTON. The author of the first American novel. *American literature,* 4: 359–68, 1933. Refers to the *Powder of sympathy,* attributed to Mrs. Sarah W. Morton.

FULLERTON, BRADFORD M. Selective bibliography, p. 316.

Browne, Charles Farrar, 1834–1867

FULLERTON, BRADFORD M. Selective bibliography, pp. 34–35.

Browne, Edward, 1644–1708

KEYNES, GEOFFREY. A bibliography of Sir Thomas Browne ... Cambridge, Cambridge university press, 1924, pp. 221–29.

Browne, Hablot Knight, 1815–1882

SAWYER and DARTON. English books, v. 2, pp. 172, 174, 207, 227–28, 230, 248, 250, 259, 261, 263, 274, 282, 289, 297, 308, 311–12.

Browne, Thomas, (*Sir*), 1605–1682

KEYNES, GEOFFREY. A bibliography of Sir Thomas Browne, kt., M.D. Cambridge, Cambridge university press, 1924. vii+255 pp., facsimiles. Review by Alfred W. Pollard, *Library,* s. 4, 5: 184–87, 1925.

KEYNES, GEOFFREY. The earliest compositions of Sir Thomas Browne. *Times literary supplement,* February 25, 1932, p. 134.

LEROY, O. A French bibliography of Sir Thomas Browne. London, Harrap, 1931. 97 pp.

MUNRO, T. K. Surreptitious editions of Sir Thomas Browne. Glasgow bibliographical society. *Records,* 7: 44–61, 1923.

SAWYER and DARTON. English books, v. 1, pp. 211–13.

STEPHEN, GEORGE A. A catalogue of works by and about Sir Thomas Browne, in the Norwich public libraries. Norwich, 1925. 4 pp.

Christian morals, Halle, 1723.

KEYNES, GEOFFREY. An unrecorded edition of Browne's *Christian morals. Library,* s. 4, 10: [418]–20, 1930. Facsimile of title-page, p. 418.

See also Bridgewater, Benjamin.

Browne, William, 1591–1643(?)

SAWYER and DARTON. English books, v. 2, pp. 203, 205–6.

Britannia's pastorals, 1613(?)–1616.

TILLOTSON, GEOFFREY. Towards a text of Browne's *Britannia's pastorals. Library,* s. 4, 11: [193]–202, 1931.

Brownell, Henry Howell, 1820–1872

FULLERTON, BRADFORD M. Selective bibliography, pp. 35–36.

Browning, Elizabeth (Barrett), 1806–1861

SAWYER and DARTON. English books, v. 2, pp. 108, 317.

See also Browning, Robert.

Browning, Robert, 1812–1889

ARMSTRONG, A. JOSEPH. Baylor university's Browning collection and other Browning interests. *Baylor bulletin,* 30: 51, 1927.

ARMSTRONG, A. JOSEPH. Robert Browning through French eyes. *Baylor university interests,* s. 3, pp. 9–45, [1932]. Contents include, IV, French Browningiana in Baylor university library.

CARTER, JOHN. Binding variants in English publishing, 1820–1900. London, Constable, 1932.

SAWYER and DARTON. English books, v. 1, p. 148; v. 2, pp. 108, 308, 316.

WENGER, CHRISTIAN N. Aesthetics of Robert Browning. Ann Arbor, Mich., Wahr, 1924. (Thesis, University of Michigan.) Bibliography, pp. 266–72.

WISE, THOMAS J. A Browning library. A catalogue of printed books, manuscripts, and autograph letters by Robert and Elizabeth Barrett Browning . . . London, privately printed, 1929. xxxii+126 pp., facsimiles. Contents: 1, the writings of Robert Browning; 2, the writings of Elizabeth Barrett Browning; 3, Browningiana.

Bryan, William Jennings, 1860–1925

HIBBEN, PAXTON. The peerless leader, William Jennings Bryan ... New York, Farrar and Rinehart, [1929]. Bibliography, pp. 409–19.

Bryant, William Cullen, 1794–1878

AMERICAN ART ASSOCIATION. Sales catalogue. Stephen H. Wakeman collection. New York, 1924. Items 1–155.

FULLERTON, BRADFORD M. Selective bibliography, pp. 36–37.

JOHNSON, MERLE. American first editions, pp. 36–37 (45–48).

Embargo, Boston, 1808.

AMERICAN ART ASSOCIATION. Sales catalogue. Stephen H. Wakeman collection. New York, 1924. Facsimile of title-page.

CURLE, RICHARD. Collecting American first editions, pp. 180–81, 193–95.

Forest hymn, [1860].

CURLE, RICHARD. Collecting American first editions, p. 209.

Fountain, 1842.

CURLE, RICHARD. Collecting American first editions, p. 58.

Hymns, 1864.

CURLE, RICHARD. Collecting American first editions, p. 199.

Letters of a traveller, 1850.

CURLE, RICHARD. Collecting American first editions, p. 209.

Oration, delivered at Stockbridge, Stockbridge, 1820.

CURLE, RICHARD. Collecting American first editions, p. 207.

Poems, 1821.

AMERICAN ART ASSOCIATION. Sales catalogue. Stephen H. Wakeman collection. New York, 1924. Facsimile of title-page.

CURLE, RICHARD. Collecting American first editions, pp. 58, 66, 172–73.

Popular considerations on homeopathia, 1841.
CURLE, RICHARD. Collecting American first editions, pp. 208–9.

Song of the sower, 1871.
CURLE, RICHARD. Collecting American first editions, p. 60.

Thirty poems, 1864.
CURLE, RICHARD. Collecting American first editions, pp. 144–45.

White-footed deer, 1844.
AMERICAN ART ASSOCIATION. Sales catalogue. Stephen H. Wakeman collection. New York, 1924. Facsimile of title-page.
CURLE, RICHARD. Collecting American first editions, p. 59.

Buck, George, (*Sir*), *d.* 1623
GREG, WALTER W. Three manuscripts by Sir George Buck. *Library,* s. 4, 12: [307]–21, 1932.

Bulmer, William, 1757–1830
MARROT, HAROLD V. William Bulmer, Thomas Bensley: a study in transition. London, Fleuron, ltd., 1930. 80 pp., facsimiles. Review, *Library,* s. 4, 11: 235–36, 1931.

Bumpstead, Helion, *pseud.*
See Wall, Arnold.

Bunbury, Henry William, 1750–1811
SAWYER and DARTON. English books, v. 2, pp. 178, 198.

Bundey, Ellen Milne
SERLE, PERCIVAL. Bibliography of Australasian poetry, p. 31.

Bunner, Henry Cuyler, 1855–1896
FULLERTON, BRADFORD M. Selective bibliography, p. 38.
JOHNSON, MERLE. American first editions, pp. 29–30 (49–50). The check-list in the 1929 edition was compiled by Vrest Orton.

Buntline, Ned, *pseud.*
See Judson, Edward L. C.

Bunyan, John, 1628–1688

Harris, J. Rendel. A further note on the fictitious Bunyan books. John Rylands library. *Bulletin,* 13 : 123–27, 1929.

Harrison, Frank M. A bibliography of the works of John Bunyan. London, Oxford university press, 1932. (Supplement to the Bibliographical society. *Transactions,* no. 6) xxviii+83 pp.

Sawyer and Darton. English books, v. 1, pp. 11, 19, 179–84; v. 2, pp. 115, 130, 241.

Waterston, David. A "unique" Bunyan. *Times literary supplement,* May 5, 1927, p. 318.

Book for boys and girls, 1686.

Hodgson, J. E. Bunyan's *Book for boys and girls. Times literary supplement,* November 4, 1926, p. 770.

Sawyer and Darton. English books, v. 1, p. 183. Facsimile of title-page.

Pilgrim's progress, 1678.

Greg, Walter W. The "issues" of *The pilgrim's progress. Times literary supplement,* August 19, 1926, p. 549.

McCombs, Charles F. The pilgrim's progress. John Bunyan, his life and times. 1628–1928. New York public library. *Bulletin,* 32 : 786–809, 1928. Refers to an exhibition of books, prints, and photographs. Part 1, John Bunyan, his life and times; part 2, *The pilgrim's progress,* early English editions, early collected editions, early American editions, abridgements and adaptations, translations into forty-one languages, poetical versions, illustrations, and illustrated editions, etc.

Sawyer and Darton. English books, v. 1, p. 180. Facsimile of title-page.

TROXELL, GILBERT M. An unrecorded *Pilgrim's progress. Colophon,* part 1, 1930.

WHAREY, JAMES B., *ed.* The pilgrim's progress from this world to that which is to come, by John Bunyan. Oxford, Clarendon press, 1928. Bibliographical introduction giving a history of the editions issued in England between 1678 and 1688. Facsimiles of title-pages. Bibliography, pp. 335–41.

WINTERICH, JOHN T. Books and the man. New York, Greenberg, 1929, pp. 123–40. Facsimile of title-page.

Burgess, Frank Gelett, 1866——

JOHNSON, MERLE. American first editions, pp. 31–32 (51–52). The check-list in the 1929 edition was compiled by Vrest Orton.

Burke, Edmund, 1729–1797

SAWYER and DARTON. English books, v. 1, p. 318.

Burke, Thomas, 1887——

GAWSWORTH, JOHN, *pseud.,* (T. Fytton Armstrong). Ten contemporaries: notes toward their definitive bibliography. Second series. London, Joiner & Steele, 1932.

Burn, David William Murray, 1862——

SERLE, PERCIVAL. Bibliography of Australasian poetry, p. 32.

Burne-Jones, Edward Coley, (*Sir*), 1833–1898

SAWYER and DARTON. English books, v. 2, pp. 372, 377.

Burnet, Gilbert, 1643–1715

SAWYER and DARTON. English books, v. 2, p. 201.

Burnett, Frances (Hodgson), 1849–1924

FULLERTON, BRADFORD M. Selective bibliography, p. 39.

Burney, Charles, 1726–1814

Roberts, W. Wright. Charles and Fanny Burney in the light of the new Thrale correspondence in the John Rylands library. John Rylands library. *Bulletin,* 16: 115–36, 1932. Bibliographical footnotes.

Burney, Frances

See Arblay, Frances (Burney) d'.

Burns, Robert, 1759–1796

Burns in the auction-room, 1929–1930. *Burns chronicle and club directory,* s. 2, v. 6, 1931.

Painter, Anna M. American editions of the poems of Burns before 1800. *Library,* s. 4, 12: [434]–56, 1932.

Ross, John D. Burns handbook. Stirling, Eneas Mackay, 1931. 378 pp.

Ross, John D. Robert Burns and his rhyming friends. With bibliographical and biographical notes and a glossary by George F. Black. Stirling, Eneas Mackay, 1929. 117 pp.

Sawyer and Darton. English books, v. 1, pp. 227, 237; v. 2, pp. 4, 22, 27–34.

Old bacchanal.

Cook, Davidson. Burns's *Old bacchanal* found at last. *Bookman* (London), 67: 202–4, 1925.

Poems, Kilmarnock, 1786.

Sawyer and Darton. English books, v. 2, p. [29]. Facsimile of title-page.

Starrett, Vincent. Pennywise and book foolish. New York, Covici Friede, 1929. Facsimile of title-page, p. 42.

Winterich, John T. Books and the man. New York, Greenberg, 1929, pp. 155–69. Facsimile of title-page.

Burrough, Edward, 1634–1662

Declaration of the sad and great persecution and martyrdom.

WALDMAN, MILTON. Americana. New York, Holt, 1925. Facsimile of title-page. *Ibid.,* London, Dulau, 1925.

Burroughs, John, 1837–1921

BARRUS, CLARA. Life and letters of John Burroughs. Boston, Houghton Mifflin co., 1925. List of books, v. 2, p. 426.

FULLERTON, BRADFORD M. Selective bibliography, pp. 39–40.

HIER, FREDERICK P., JR. The end of a literary mystery. *American Mercury,* 1 : 471–78, 1924. Refers to Walt Whitman's part in the writing of *Notes on Walt Whitman as poet and person.*

JOHNSON, MERLE. American first editions, pp. 33–35 (53–55). The check-list in the 1929 edition was compiled by Francis H. Allen.

Burton, Richard Francis, (*Sir*), 1821–1890

PENZER, NORMAN. An annotated bibliography of Sir Richard Francis Burton . . . preface by T. Grenfell Baker . . . London, A. M. Philpot, 1923. xvi+351 pp.

SAWYER and DARTON. English books, v. 2, pp. 325–26.

Burton, Robert, 1577–1640

Burtoniana. Oxford bibliographical society. *Proceedings and papers,* 1, part 3, 216–21, 1925.

OSLER, WILLIAM, (*Sir*). Burton as a transmitter. Oxford bibliographical society. *Proceedings and papers,* 1, part 3, 222.

OSLER, WILLIAM, (*Sir*). Robert Burton — the man, his book, his library. Oxford bibliographical society. *Proceedings and papers,* 1, part 3, 163–90, 1925.

SAWYER and DARTON. English books, v. 1, pp. 27, 213.

See also Jordan-Smith, Paul, under *Anatomy of melancholy,* below.

Burton, Robert (*Continued*)

Anatomy of melancholy, 1621.

AMERICAN ART ASSOCIATION. Sales catalogue. Library of Frank Irving Fletcher. New York, 1932. Facsimile of title-page, p. 27.

BENSLY, EDWARD. Some alterations and errors in successive editions of the *Anatomy.* Oxford bibliographical society. *Proceedings and papers,* 1, part 3, 198–215, 1925.

DUFF GORDON, E., and MADAN, FALCONER. Notes on the bibliography of the Oxford editions of the *Anatomy.* Oxford bibliographical society. *Proceedings and papers,* 1, part 3, 191–97, 1925.

JACKSON, HOLBROOK. Rupert Burton, his book. *Book-collector's quarterly,* no. 1, December 1930–February 1931, pp. 9–92.

JORDAN-SMITH, PAUL. Bibliographia Burtoniana. A study of Robert Burton's *The anatomy of melancholy,* with a bibliography of Burton's writings. Stanford University, Stanford university press, 1931. xix+120 pp. Review by Holbrook Jackson, *Book-collector's quarterly,* no. 8, October–December 1932, pp. 35–38.

MAGGS BROTHERS. Catalogue no. 550. London, 1931. Facsimile of title-page of Oxford, 1621, edition.

MAGGS BROTHERS. Catalogue no. 555. London, 1931. Facsimile of title-page of Oxford, 1621, edition.

SAWYER and DARTON. English books, v. 1, p. [214]. Facsimile of title-page.

Bury, John Bagnell, 1861–1927

BAYNES, NORMAN H. A bibliography of J. B. Bury: compiled with a memoir . . . Cambridge, Cambridge university press, 1929. 184 pp. Review in *Library,* s. 4, 10: 478, 1930.

Buss, Robert William, 1804–1875

SAWYER and DARTON. English books, v. 2, pp. 179, 244, 258–59.

Butler, Howard Crosby, 1872–1922

Howard Crosby Butler, 1872–1922. Princeton, N.J., Princeton university press, 1923. Bibliography, pp. 87–106.

Butler, James

FULLERTON, BRADFORD M. Selective bibliography, p. 40.

Butler, Samuel, 1612–1680

LAMAR, RENÉ, *ed.* Samuel Butler satires and miscellaneous poetry and prose. Cambridge, Cambridge university press, 1928. Bibliography of works consulted.

SAWYER and DARTON. English books, v. 1, pp. 202–3.

Butler, Samuel, 1835–1902

HOPPÉ, A. J. A bibliography of the writings of Samuel Butler, (author of *Erewhon*), and of writings about him. With some letters from Samuel Butler to the Rev. F. G. Fleay, now first published. London, Bookman's journal, 1925. xv+184 pp. Review by Alfred W. Pollard, *Library,* s. 4, 9: 225–26, 1929; by Iolo A. Williams, *London Mercury,* 12: 525, 1925.

HOPPÉ, A. J. If Mr. Higgs came to Bond street. (The first editions of Samuel Butler.) *Bookman's journal,* 12: 74–75, 1925.

SAWYER and DARTON. English books, v. 2, p. 366.

STILLMAN, CLARA G. Samuel Butler, a mid-Victorian modern. New York, Viking, 1932. Bibliography, pp. 307–14.

Butler, William Allen, 1825–1902

FULLERTON, BRADFORD M. Selective bibliography, p. 41.

Bynner, Edwin Lasseter, 1842–1893

FULLERTON, BRADFORD M. Selective bibliography, p. 41.

Bynner, Witter, 1881——

JOHNSON, MERLE. American first editions, pp. 36 (56–57).

Byrd, William, 1674–1744
SAWYER and DARTON. English books, v. 1, p. 52.

Byrne, Brian Oswald Donn, 1889–1928
JOHNSON, MERLE. American first editions, pp. (58–59).

Byron, Anne Isabelle (Millbanks), (*Baroness*), 1792–1860
Remarks occasioned by Mr. Moore's notices of Lord Byron's life.
ELKIN MATHEWS, LTD. Byron and Byroniana. London, Elkin Mathews, 1930. Facsimile of title-page, p. [111].

Byron, George Gordon Noel, (*Sixth Baron*), 1788–1824
ÅMAN-NILSSON, G. Medora Leigh et apokryfisk blad. Lord Byron's historia. Stockholm, 1927.
Byron and Coleridge. *Times literary supplement,* June 27, 1929, p. 520.
Byron manuscripts. *Times literary supplement,* November 20, 1930, p. 996.
CHEW, SAMUEL C. Byron in England: his fame and after-fame. London, Murray, 1924. Bibliography, pp. 353–407. One of the most useful guides for the bibliography of Byron's works and of books about him.
DEBEER, E. S., and SETON, WALTER. Byroniana: The archives of the London Greek committee. *Nineteenth century,* 100: 396–412, 1926. (*Ibid.* Separate edition. London, 1926.)
ELKIN MATHEWS, LTD. Byron and Byroniana. A catalogue of books. London, Elkin Mathews, 1930. 125 pp. "Byron's separate works are listed in the chronological order of their appearance. After the later editions of these works come books closely associated with them, also in chronological order — e.g., following *Childe Harold* and *Don Juan* there are lists of continuations, imitations, criticisms, and defenses of these poems. Finally there are the translations in alphabetical order of the languages into which they were made." The catalogue contains 776 items.

First editions of Lord Byron. *London Mercury,* 11: 641, 1925.

KRUG, WERNER G. Lord Byron als dichterische Gestalt in England, Frankreich, Deutschland, und Amerika. Potsdam, Schneider, 1932. (Thesis, Giessen.) "Byron in English, French, German, and American literature: a bibliography," pp. 101–42.

LOVELACE, EDITH. A missing Byron ms. (*Beppo.*) *Times literary supplement,* January 23, 1930, p. 60.

MAUROIS, ANDRÉ. Byron . . . translated from the French by Hamish Miles. London, J. Cape, [1930]. "Sources," pp. 440–57.

PRAZ, MARIO. Recent Byron literature. *English studies* (Amsterdam), 12: 129–38, 1930.

ROSE, W. From Goethe to Byron: the development of Weltschmertz in German literature. New York, Dutton, 1924. Bibliography, pp. 207–11.

SAWYER and DARTON. English books, v. 2, pp. 67–75.

WISE, THOMAS J. A bibliography of the writings in verse and prose of George Gordon Noel, Baron Byron, with letters illustrating his life and work and particularly his attitude toward Keats. London, privately printed, 1932. 2 v. Facsimiles of title-pages and manuscripts.

WISE, THOMAS J. A Byron library, a catalogue of printed books, manuscripts and autograph letters by George Gordon Noel, Baron Byron . . . London, privately printed, 1928. xxvii+144 pp., facsimiles. Contents: part 1, the writings of Lord Byron; part 2, Byroniana.

Childe Harold, 1812.

McCARTHY, WILLIAM H. The printing of Canto IV of Byron's *Childe Harold.* A bibliographical study. Yale university library. *Gazette,* 1: 39–41, 1927.

Byron, George Gordon Noel (*Continued*)

Het beleg van Corinthe, Amsterdam, 1831.

ELKIN MATHEWS, LTD. Byron and Byroniana. London, Elkin Mathews, 1930. Facsimile of title-page, p. [32].

Manfred, 1817.

BUTTERWICK, J. C. A note on the first editions of *Manfred. Book-collector's quarterly,* no. 3, June–August, 1931, pp. 39–42.

Poems on various occasions, Newark, 1807.

ELKIN MATHEWS, LTD. Byron and Byroniana. London, Elkin Mathews, 1930. Facsimile of title-page, p. [xi].

Poems written by somebody, 1818.

ELKIN MATHEWS, LTD. Byron and Byroniana. London, Elkin Mathews, 1930. Facsimile of title-page, p. 89.

Poetical works, Philadelphia, 1813.

ELKIN MATHEWS, LTD. Byron and Byroniana. London, Elkin Mathews, 1930. Facsimile of title-page, p. [72].

Waltz, 1813.

SAWYER and DARTON. English books, v. 2, p. [73]. Facsimile of title-page.

See also Roby, George.

C. E.

Emaricdulfe, 1595.

SAWYER and DARTON. English books, v. 1, pp. 9–10.

Cabell, James Branch, 1879——

BRUSSELL, ISIDORE R. Bibliography of the writings of James Branch Cabell . . . Philadelphia, Centaur book shop, 1932. 126 pp.

CAPPON, LESTER J. Bibliography of Virginia history since 1865. University, Va., Institute for research in the social sciences, 1930.

HOLT, GUY. A bibliography of the writings of James Branch Cabell. Philadelphia, Centaur book shop, 1924. 73 pp.

JOHNSON, MERLE. American first editions, pp. 37–39 (60–63).

VAN DOREN, CARL. James Branch Cabell. New York, McBride, 1925. Revised edition, 1932. "The books of James Branch Cabell," pp. 87–89.

Cable, George Washington, 1844–1925

FULLERTON, BRADFORD M. Selective bibliography, p. 42.

JOHNSON, MERLE. American first editions, pp. 40–41 (64–65).

Caedmon, *fl.* 670

The Caedmon ms. of Anglo Saxon biblical poetry: *Junius XI* in the Bodleian library. Introduction by Sir Israel Gollancz. London, British academy, 1927.

KRAPP, GEORGE P., *ed.* The Junius manuscript. (The Anglo-Saxon poetic records.) New York, Columbia university press, 1931. Bibliography, pp. [xlv]–lviii.

Caius, John, 1510–1573

De antiquitate Cantebrigiensis academiae libri duo, 1574.

PLOMER, HENRY R. The 1574 edition of Dr. John Caius' *De antiquitate Cantebrigiensis academiae libri duo. Library,* s. 4, 7: [253]–68, 1927.

Caldecott, Randolph, 1846–1886

SAWYER and DARTON. English books, v. 2, pp. 131, 187.

Caldwell, Robert

SERLE, PERCIVAL. Bibliography of Australasian poetry, pp. 35–36.

Call, Frank Oliver, 1878——

PIERCE, LORNE. Outline of Canadian literature, p. 100.

Camden, William, 1551–1623

SAWYER and DARTON. English books, v. 2, pp. 101, 131.

Cameron, George Frederick, 1854–1885
PIERCE, LORNE. Outline of Canadian literature, pp. 69–70.

Campbell, William Wilfred, 1861–1919.
PIERCE, LORNE. Outline of Canadian literature, pp. 36, 76–78, 115–16.

Campion, Thomas, 1567–1620
HESSELSTINE, PHILIP. Two unpublished poems by Thomas Campion? *London Mercury,* 13 : 413–14, 1926.
SAWYER and DARTON. English books, v. 1, pp. 52, 89.

Canning, Elizabeth, 1734–1773
SAWYER and DARTON. English books, v. 1, pp. 272, 277.

Capell, Edward, 1713–1781
SAWYER and DARTON. English books, v. 1, p. 32.

Careless, John, *pseud.*
SAWYER and DARTON. English books, v. 2, p. 207.

Carew, Bampfylde Moore, 1693–1770
SAWYER and DARTON. English books, v. 1, pp. 223, 226.

Carew, Elizabeth, (*Lady*), *fl.* 1590
Tragedie of Marian, 1613.
MAGGS BROTHERS. Catalogue no. 550. London, 1931. Facsimile of title-page.

Carew, Richard, 1555–1620
SAWYER and DARTON. English books, v. 1, p. 201.

Carey, Alice, 1820–1871
FULLERTON, BRADFORD M. Selective bibliography, p. 46.

Carey, David, 1782–1824
SAWYER and DARTON. English books, v. 2, p. 197.

Carey, Elizabeth, (*Lady*)
See Carew, Elizabeth, (*Lady*).

Carey, Matthew, 1760–1839
FULLERTON, BRADFORD M. Selective bibliography, pp. 42–43.

Carey, Phoebe, 1824–1871
See Carey, Alice.

Carleton, Elizabeth (Hussey, Crane)
McCORKLE, JULIA N. A note concerning "Mistress Crane" and the Martin Marprelate controversy. *Library,* s. 4, 12: [276]–83, 1932.

Carleton, Will, 1845–1912
FULLERTON, BRADFORD M. Selective bibliography, pp. 43–44.

Carlyle, Thomas, 1795–1881
DYER, ISAAC W. A bibliography of the writings and ana of Thomas Carlyle. Portland, Me., Southworth press, 1928. xii+587 pp. *Ibid.,* London, Spurr & Swift, 1929.
NEFF, EMERY E. Carlyle. New York, Norton, [1932]. Introductory bibliography, pp. 271–71; bibliographical notes, pp. 273–76.
SAWYER and DARTON. English books, v. 2, pp. 270, 315.
WILSON, DAVID A. Carlyle. London, Paul, 1923–1924. 2 v. Bibliographical footnotes.

Carman, William Bliss, 1861–1929
FULLERTON, BRADFORD M. Selective bibliography, p. 44.
JOHNSON, MERLE. American first editions, pp. 42–45 (66–72). The check-list in the 1929 edition was compiled by Vrest Orton and R. H. Hathaway.
PIERCE, LORNE. Outline of Canadian literature, pp. 73–76, 133.
VAN PATTEN, NATHAN. Notes for a bibliography of Bliss Carman. Unpublished manuscript.
VAN PATTEN, NATHAN. Bliss Carman and the bibliophile. *Queen's quarterly,* 33: 202–5, 1925.

Carroll, Lewis, *pseud.*
See Dodgson, Charles Lutwidge.

Carruthers, William Alexander, 1806–1872(?)
FULLERTON, BRADFORD M. Selective bibliography, pp. 44–45.

Carryl, Charles Edward, 1842–1920
FULLERTON, BRADFORD M. Selective bibliography, pp. 45–46.

Carter, Frederick
GAWSWORTH, JOHN, *pseud.,* (T. Fytton Armstrong). Ten contemporaries: notes toward their definitive bibliography. Second series. London, Joiner & Steele, 1932.

Cary, John, 1754–1835
FORDHAM, HERBERT G., (*Sir*). John Cary: engraver, map, chart and print-seller, and globe maker. 1754–1835. A bibliography with an introduction and biographical notes. London, Cambridge university press, 1925. xxxiv+139 pp.

Caskoden, Edwin, *pseud.*
See Major, Charles.

Cather, Willa (Sibert), 1876——
CATHER, WILLA. My first novels (there were two). *Colophon,* part 6, 1931. 4 pp. Refers to *Alexander's bridge* and *O pioneers!*

JESSUP, MARY E. A bibliography of the writings of Willa Cather. *American collector,* 6: 67, 1928.

JOHNSON, MERLE. American first editions, pp. 46 (73–74). The check-list in the 1929 edition was compiled by David Moss.

MOSS, DAVID. American first editions: Willa Cather, 1876——. *Publishers' weekly,* 103: 321, 1923.

Catherwood, Mary (Hartwell), 1847–1902

FULLERTON, BRADFORD M. Selective bibliography, pp. 46–47.

Caustic, Christopher, *pseud.*

See Fessenden, Thomas Green.

Cawein, Madison Julius, 1865–1914

FULLERTON, BRADFORD M. Selective bibliography, p. 48.

ROTHERT, OTTO A. The story of a poet: Madison Cawein ... Filson club. *Publications,* no. 30, 1921. Bibliographical references, pp. 511–24; list of Cawein's books and index to poems, appendix.

Caxton, William, 1422(?)–1491

CROTCH, W. J. BLYTHE. Caxton documents. *Library,* s. 4, 7: [426]–55, 1927.

CROTCH, W. J. BLYTHE. Caxton on the continent. *Library,* s. 4, 7: [387]–401, 1927.

CROTCH, W. J. BLYTHE. Caxton's son-in-law. *Library,* s. 4, 9: [48]–52, 1929.

CROTCH, W. J. BLYTHE. Caxtoniana. *Library,* s. 4, 11: [103]–4, 1931.

HITTMAIER, R. William Caxton, Englands erster Drucker und Verleger. Innsbruck, Wagner, 1931. 53 pp.

MARCHAM, FRANK. Caxton's son-in-law. *Library,* s. 4, 9: [325], 1929.

POLLARD, ALFRED W. The new Caxton indulgence. *Library,* s. 4, 9: [86]–89, 1929.

SAWYER and DARTON. English books, v. 1, pp. 13, 38–39, 41, 43, 45, 48–49; v. 2, pp. 150, 370.

Dictes or sayings of the philosophers, 1477.

SAWYER and DARTON. English books, v. 1, frontispiece. Facsimile of title-page.

Game of playe of chesse, ca. 1483.

SAWYER and DARTON. English books, v. 1, p. [47]. Facsimile of a page.

Chambers, Anne

Poems, 1764.

SAWYER and DARTON. English books, v. 2, p. [368]. Facsimile of title-page.

Chambers, Robert William, 1865——

OVERTON, GRANT. Authors of the day. New York, Doran, [1924], pp. 376–79.

Channing, Edward, 1856–1931

ROBINSON, GEORGE W. Bibliography of Edward Channing. With an introduction by Lawrence Shaw Mayo. Cambridge, Harvard university press, 1932. 29 pp.

Channing, William Ellery, 1780–1842

FULLERTON, BRADFORD M. Selective bibliography, pp. 48–49.

Chapman, George, 1559–1634

SAWYER and DARTON. English books, v. 1, pp. 106, 135–36.

Eastward hoe, 1605.

BRETTLE, R. E. *Eastward hoe,* 1605. By Chapman, Jonson, and Marston. Bibliography and circumstances of production. *Library,* s. 4, 9: [287]–302, 1929.

GREG, WALTER W. *Eastward hoe,* 1605. Note. *Library,* s. 4, 9: [303]–4, 1929.

Iliad, 1598.

SAMUEL, HOWARD. Chapman's *Iliad. Times literary supplement,* March 24, 1932, p. 230.

SAWYER and DARTON. English books, v. 1, p. [107]. Facsimile of title-page.

May-day, 1611.

MAGGS BROTHERS. Catalogue no. 493. Shakespeare and Shakespeareana. London, 1927. Facsimile of title-page, opp. p. 201.

Chapman, William, 1850–1917

PIERCE, LORNE. Outline of Canadian literature, pp. 57–58.

Charles II, (*King*), 1630–1685

HORROX, WILLIAM A. Bibliography of the literature relating to the escape and preservation of King Charles II after the battle of Worcester. Aberdeen, Aberdeen university press, 1924. 64 pp. Review, *Times literary supplement,* May 15, 1924, p. 308.

Chase, Elizabeth Ann (Akers)

See Allen, Elizabeth Ann (Chase, Akers)

Chatterton, Thomas, 1752–1770

MABBOTT, THOMAS O. A new poem by Chatterton. *Modern language notes,* 39: 226–29, 1924. "Elegy Oct 29" from a manuscript in the Columbia university library.

Chaucer, Geoffrey, 1340–1400

BRUSENDORFF, AAGE. The Chaucer tradition. London, Oxford university press, 1925.

CHAUCER SOCIETY. *Publications,* s. 1. London, 1868——.

CHAUCER SOCIETY. *Publications,* s. 2. London, 1869——.

FRENCH, ROBERT D. A Chaucer handbook. New York, Crofts, 1927. 934 pp.

GREG, WALTÈR W. The early printed editions of the *Canterbury tales.* Modern language association of America. *Publications,* 39: 737–61, 1924.

GRIFFITH, D. DUDLEY. A bibliography of Chaucer, 1908–1924. Seattle, Wash., University of Washington press, 1926. (University of Washington. *Publications in language and literature.*) 148 pp.

HAMMOND, ELEANOR P. Chaucer, a bibliographical manual. New York, P. Smith, 1933. 597 pp. (A reprint.)

KASE, C. ROBERT. Observations on the changing position of groups G and DE in the mss. of the *Canterbury tales,* (in) Three Chaucer studies. London, Oxford university press, 1932. 89 pp.

Chaucer, Geoffrey (*Continued*)

KOCH, J. Der gegenwärtige Stand der Chaucerforschung. *Anglia,* 1925. "A most exhaustive account of everything worthy of note that has been written on the poet since 1908."—*The year's work in English studies,* v. 6, p. 94, 1925.

POLLARD, ALFRED W. Chaucer. London, Macmillan, 1931. 136 pp.

RICKERT, EDITH. Are there more Chaucer manuscripts? *Times literary supplement,* December 17, 1931, p. 1028.

SPURGEON, CAROLINE F. E. Five hundred years of Chaucer criticism and allusion, 1357–1900. Cambridge, Cambridge university press, 1925. 3 v. Review, *The year's work in English studies,* v. 6, pp. 93–95, 1925.

TATLOCK, JOHN S. P., and KENNEDY, ARTHUR G. Concordance to the complete works of Geoffrey Chaucer and to the *Romaunt of the rose.* Washington, Carnegie institution, 1927.

Chesebrough, Caroline, 1825–1873

FULLERTON, BRADFORD M. Selective bibliography, pp. 49–50.

Chesterton, Gilbert Keith, 1873——

FIRST EDITION CLUB. A bibliographical catalogue, pp. [17]–42.

Child, Lydia Maria (Francis), 1802–1880

FULLERTON, BRADFORD M. Selective bibliography, pp. 50–51.

Chivers, Thomas Holley, 1807–1858

CAMPBELL, KILLIS. A bit of Chiversian mystification. University of Texas. *Studies in English,* no. 10, pp. 152–54, 1930. Refers to the poem, "The departed," in the *Broadway journal* (July 12, 1845) attributed to Poe by Chivers and here suggested to be actually the work of the latter.

DAMON, S. FOSTER. Thomas Holley Chivers, friend of Poe . . . New York, Harper, 1930. xxix+305 pp., facsimiles. Bibliography of Chivers' books and pamphlets, pp. 283–86; selected bibliography of articles on Chivers, pp. 287–88.

FULLERTON, BRADFORD M. Selective bibliography, pp. 51–52.

MABBOTT, THOMAS O. Collation of a book by T. H. Chivers. *Notes and queries,* 159–258, 1930.

Chopin, Kate, 1851–1904

FULLERTON, BRADFORD M. Selective bibliography, pp. 52–53.

RANKIN, DANIEL S. Kate Chopin and her Creole stories. Philadelphia, 1932. (Thesis, University of Pennsylvania.) Bibliography, pp. 296–307.

Churchill, Charles, 1731–1764

WILLIAMS, IOLO A. Seven XVIIIth century bibliographies. London, Dulau, 1924, pp. 181–205.

Churchill, Winston, 1871——

FULLERTON, BRADFORD M. Selective bibliography, p. 53.

JOHNSON, MERLE. American first editions, p. (75).

JOHNSON, MERLE. American first editions: Winston Churchill, 1871——. *Publishers' weekly,* 119:327, 1931.

Churchyard, Thomas, 1520(?)–1604

BYRNE, M. S. Thomas Churchyard's spelling. *Library,* s. 4, 4: [243]–48, 1924.

Cibber, Colley, 1671–1757

CROISSANT, DE WITT C. A note on *The egoist: or Colley upon Cibber,* 1743. *Philological quarterly,* 3:76–77, 1924. Suggests that Cibber himself was the author.

Clark, Charles Heber, 1841–1915

FULLERTON, BRADFORD M. Selective bibliography, p. 54.

Clark, Lewis Gaylord, 1810–1873
FULLERTON, BRADFORD M. Selective bibliography, p. 54.

Clark, Willis Gaylord, 1810–1841
FULLERTON, BRADFORD M. Selective bibliography, p. 55.

Clarke, Marcus Andrew Hislop, 1846–1881
SERLE, PERCIVAL. Bibliography of Australasian poetry, pp. 41–42.

Clarke, Rebecca Sophia, 1833–1906
FULLERTON, BRADFORD M. Selective bibliography, pp. 55–56.

Cleland, Thomas Maitland, 1880——
HAMILL, ALFRED E. Decorative work [of T. M. Cleland]: a record and review. With a biographical and critical introduction . . . New York, Pynson, 1929.

Clemens, Samuel Langhorne, 1835–1910
BLISS, WALTER. Twainiana notes from annotations. Edited with an introduction by Frances M. Edwards. Hartford, Conn., 1930. 7+24 pp.
BRASHEAR, MINNIE M. Mark Twain juvenilia. *American literature,* 2: 25–53, 1931.
FULLERTON, BRADFORD M. Selective bibliography, pp. 56–59.
JOHNSON, MERLE. American first editions, pp. 215–18 (76–81).
POTTER, JOHN K. Samuel L. Clemens: first editions and values. Chicago, Black archer press, 1932. 83 pp.

Celebrated jumping frog, 1867.
AMERICAN ART ASSOCIATION. Sales catalogue. Library of Frank Irving Fletcher. New York, 1932. Facsimile of title-page, p. 50.
CURLE, RICHARD. Collecting American first editions, p. 14.

Connecticut Yankee, 1889.
CURLE, RICHARD. Collecting American first editions, p. 210.

Huckleberry Finn, 1885.

CURLE, RICHARD. Collecting American first editions, pp. 152, 187, 205–6.

KEMBLE, E. M. Illustrating *Huckleberry Finn. Colophon,* part 1, 1930.

UNDERHILL, IRVING S. An inquiry into *Huckleberry Finn. Colophon,* part 6, 1931.

Innocents abroad, 1869.

CURLE, RICHARD. Collecting American first editions, p. 6.

WINTERICH, JOHN T. Books and the man. New York, Greenberg, 1929, pp. 170–92. Facsimile of title-page.

Life on the Mississippi, 1883.

CURLE, RICHARD. Collecting American first editions, pp. 6–7.

Prince and the pauper, 1881 and 1882.

CURLE, RICHARD. Collecting American first editions, p. 187.

1601, 1882.

CURLE, RICHARD. Collecting American first editions, p. 208.

1601. By Mark Twain. Foreword by C. E. S. Wood. San Francisco, Grabhorn, 1925. 36 pp.

Tom Sawyer, 1876.

CURLE, RICHARD. Collecting American first editions, pp. 205–6.

Cliffton, William, 1772–1799

FULLERTON, BRADFORD M. Selective bibliography, pp. 59–60.

Cobb, Irvin Shrewsbury, 1876——

JOHNSON, MERLE. American first editions, pp. 47–49 (82–85).

MAURICE, ARTHUR B. Irvin S. Cobb. *Bookman* (New York), 69: 588–89, 1929. Refers to the circumstances connected with the publication of Cobb's various stories.

OVERTON, GRANT. Authors of the day. New York, Doran, [1924], pp. 310–11.

Cobb, Sylvanus, Jr., 1823–1887
FULLERTON, BRADFORD M. Selective bibliography, pp. 60–61.

Coffin, Charles Carleton, 1823–1896
FULLERTON, BRADFORD M. Selective bibliography, p. 61.

Coleman, Helena, 1860——
PIERCE, LORNE. Outline of Canadian literature, p. 93.

Coleridge, Hartley, 1796–1849
HARTMAN, HERBERT. Hartley Coleridge: poet's son and poet. London, Oxford university press, 1931. Bibliography, pp. [196]–200. "It is provided with a good index and a scholarly bibliography. Let one small but interesting item be added: Coleridge, Hartley. *Life of Andrew Marvell,* Hull, 1853."—Arthur Beatty in his review, *Modern language review,* 27: 488–90, 1932.

Coleridge, Samuel Taylor, 1772–1834
CENTRAL PUBLIC LIBRARY, HAMPSTEAD, ENGLAND. Catalogue of the Coleridge and Wordsworth books and mss. London, 1929.
CHARPENTIER, JOHN. Coleridge: the sublime somnambulist. New York, Dodd, Mead and co., 1929. Brief bibliography.
GRIGGS, EARL L. Notes on a proposed edition of the correspondence of Samuel Taylor Coleridge. Michigan academy. *Papers,* 12: 293–99, 1929.
KOSZUL, A. Coleridgiana. *Revue Anglo-Americaine,* pp. 247–53, 327–35, 1930.
RAYSOR, THOMAS M. Unpublished fragments in aesthetics by S. T. Coleridge. *Studies in philology,* 22: 529–37, 1925.
WRIGHT, G. W. A sonnet by Coleridge? *Notes and queries,* 152: 115–16, 1927. Refers to "To poverty" in Joseph Cottle's *Selection of poems designed chiefly for schools and young people.*

Annual anthology, 1799.

AMERICAN ART ASSOCIATION. Sales catalogue. Library of Frank Irving Fletcher. New York, 1932. Facsimile of title-page, p. 53.

Prospectus for *The watchman.*

WINSHIP, GEORGE P. *Times literary supplement,* March 19, 1925.

See also Wordsworth, William.

Collier, John, 1901——

GAWSWORTH, JOHN, *pseud.,* (T. Fytton Armstrong). Ten contemporaries: notes toward their definitive bibliography. Second series. London, Joiner & Steele, 1932.

Collins, William, 1721–1759

MEYERSTEIN, E. H. W. A hitherto unpublished letter of William Collins. *London Mercury,* 11 : 169–74, 1925. Refers to a letter to John Gilbert Cooper acquired by the British museum.

WILLIAMS, IOLO A. Seven XVIIIth century bibliographies. London, Dulau, 1924, pp. 101–14.

Verses to Sir Thomas Hanmer, 1743.

MAGGS BROTHERS. Catalogue no. 550. London, 1931. Facsimile of title-page, opp. p. 136.

Collins, William Wilkie, 1824–1889

ELLIS, STEWART M. Wilkie Collins, Le Fanu, and others. London, Constable, 1931. Bibliographies at end of chapters.

FLOWER, DESMOND. Authors and copyright in the nineteenth century, with unpublished letters from Wilkie Collins. *Book-collector's quarterly,* no. 7, July–September, 1932, pp. 1–35.

Ms. letters. *Bodleian quarterly record,* 7 : 31, 1932.

Condell, Henry, d. 1627.

See Shakespeare, William (under Barnard, Etwell A. B.).

Congreve, William, 1670–1729

PROTOPOPESCO, DRAGOSH. Un classique moderne: sa vie, son oeuvre. Paris, La vie universitaire, 1924. Bibliography.

SAWYER and DARTON. English books, v. 1, p. 209.

TAYLOR, D. CRANE. William Congreve. London, Oxford university press, 1931. First editions of Congreve, pp. [231]–32; bibliography, pp. [233]–40.

Incognita, 1692.

NEWTON, A. EDWARD. This book-collecting game. Boston, Little, Brown and co., 1928. Facsimile of title-page, p. 6.

Connolly, James

RYAN, DESMOND. James Connolly, his life & writings ... with a preface by H. W. Nevinson. Dublin, Talbot press, 1924. "Bibliography and sources," pp. 133–34.

Connor, Ralph, *pseud.*

See Gordon, Charles William.

Conrad, Joseph, 1857–1924.

AMERICAN ART ASSOCIATION. Sales catalogue. Edward Garnett collection. Inscribed books and autograph material of Joseph Conrad and W. H. Hudson. New York, 1928.

AMERICAN ART ASSOCIATION. Sales catalogue. First editions, inscribed copies, and autograph letters of Joseph Conrad, property of Mrs. Ford Madox Hueffer; an important Kipling collection; the fine Poe collection of Mr. Joseph Jackson ... New York, 1928.

AMERICAN ART ASSOCIATION. Sales catalogue. Richard Curle['s] Conrad collection. New York, 1927.

Conrad books and manuscripts. *Times literary supplement,* February 26, 1925.

A Conrad collection. *Times literary supplement,* May 12, 1927. p. 340.

CURLE, RICHARD. Handlist of books . . . about Joseph Conrad. New York, Goldsmith, 1932.

CUTLER and STILES. Modern British authors, pp. 23–28.

HOPKINS, FREDERICK M. Curle sale of Conradiana. *Publishers' weekly,* 111 : 2186–88, 1927.

The J. B. Pinker collection of Conradiana. *Bookman's journal,* 11 : 190–91, 1925.

Joseph Conrad : a sketch with a bibliography. Garden City, Doubleday, Page & co., [1925]. 46 pp. Bibliography, pp. 40–46.

KEATING, GEORGE T. A Conrad memorial library. The collection of George T. Keating. Garden City, Doubleday, Doran and co., 1929. xvi+448 pp., facsimiles.

MÉGROZ, RODOLPHE L. Joseph Conrad's mind and method . . . London, Faber & Faber, [1931]. Bibliographical list of Conrad's works, pp. 249–56; Conradiana, pp. 257–62.

OVERTON, GRANT. American nights entertainment. New York, Appleton, 1923, pp. 87–90.

OVERTON, GRANT. Authors of the day. New York, Doran, [1924], pp. 53–56.

SARGENT, GEORGE H. Conrad manuscripts in America. (A list.) *Bookman's journal,* 9 : 137–39, 1924.

SAWYER and DARTON. English books, v. 2, pp. 332, 362–65.

SYMONS, ARTHUR. Notes on Joseph Conrad, with some unpublished letters. London, Myers, 1925.

WISE, THOMAS J. A Conrad library. A catalogue of printed books, manuscripts, and autograph letters by Joseph Conrad . . . London, privately printed, 1928. xvii+66 pp., facsimiles. Contents : The writings of Joseph Conrad ; Conradiana ; addendum—*To my brethren of the pen,* 1927.

Cook, James, 1728–1779

Public Library of New South Wales. Bibliography of Captain Charles Cook. Sydney, N.S.W. 172 pp.

Cooke, John Esten, 1830–1886

Fullerton, Bradford M. Selective bibliography, pp. 62–64.

Wegelin, Oscar. A bibliography of the separate writings of John Esten Cooke. *American collector,* 1:96–99, 1926.

Cooke, Philip Pendleton, 1816–1850

Fullerton, Bradford M. Selective bibliography, p. 64.

Cooke, Rose Terry, 1827–1892

Fullerton, Bradford M. Selective bibliography, pp. 64–66.

Coolbrith, Ina Donna, 1842–1928

Fullerton, Bradford M. Selective bibliography, p. 65.

Stevens, Ivalu D. A bibliography of Ina Donna Coolbrith. *News notes of California libraries,* 27: [105]–123, 1932.

Coolidge, Archibald Cary, 1866–1928

Coolidge, Harold J., and Lord, Robert H. Archibald Cary Coolidge. Life and letters. Boston, Houghton Mifflin co., 1932. Bibliography of his more important works, pp. 254–55.

Coolidge, Susan, *pseud.*

See Woolsey, Sarah Chauncey.

Cooper, Courtney Riley, 1886——

Overton, Grant. Cargoes for Crusoes. New York, Appleton, 1924, pp. 302–3.

Cooper, James Fenimore, 1789–1851

FOX, DIXON R., *ed.* New York: being an introduction to an unpublished manuscript entitled "The towns of Manhattan." New York, Payson, 1930. x+63 pp.

FULLERTON, BRADFORD M. Selective bibliography, pp. 65–69.

JOHNSON, MERLE. American first editions, pp. 50–53 (86–89).

LEISY, ERNEST E. The American novel (on American themes) before 1860; the early novels of James Fenimore Cooper (1821–1831). Urbana, Ill., 1926. 27 pp.

SPILLER, ROBERT E., and BLACKBURN, PHILIP C. A descriptive bibliography of the writings of James Fenimore Cooper. New York, Payson, 1932. "This, the first Cooper bibliography, is a close study of Cooper first editions in several languages. In addition to its numerous detailed listings, the volume contains new findings of the first importance to bibliophiles; also general introductory matter and a collection of letters to Cooper from publishers."—Publisher's announcement.

Deerslayer, 1841.

CURLE, RICHARD. Collecting American first editions, pp. 105, 124–25.

French governess, 1843.

CURLE, RICHARD. Collecting American first editions, p. 159.

Heidenmauer, 1832.

CURLE, RICHARD. Collecting American first editions, p. 209.

Cooper, James Fenimore (*Continued*)

Jack Tier, 1848.

CURLE, RICHARD. Collecting American first editions, p. 137.

Last of the Mohicans, 1826.

CURLE, RICHARD. Collecting American first editions, p. 62. Facsimile of title-page, opp. p. 62.

Letter to Gen. Lafayette, 1831 and 1832.

COOPER, JAMES FENIMORE. *Letter to Gen. Lafayette,* and related correspondence on the finance controversy, reproduced from the original Paris editions of 1831 and 1832. Bibliographical note by Robert E. Spiller. New York, Columbia university press, 1931. (Facsimile text society, Series I, Language and literature, v. 6.)

Lionel Lincoln, 1825.

CURLE, RICHARD. Collecting American first editions, pp. 122–24. Facsimiles of title-pages of v. 1 and 2, between pp. 122 and 123.

Manikins, 1835.

CURLE, RICHARD. Collecting American first editions, p. 209.

Mercedes of Castile, 1840.

CURLE, RICHARD. Collecting American first editions, pp. 125–26.

Mouchoir, 1843.

CURLE, RICHARD. Collecting American first editions, pp. 158–59.

Oak openings.

OAKLEY, KATE R. James Fenimore Cooper and *Oak openings. Michigan history magazine,* 16: 309–20, 1932.

Pathfinder, 1840.

CURLE, RICHARD. Collecting American first editions, p. 123.

Pilot, 1823.

CURLE, RICHARD. Collecting American first editions, p. 161.

Pioneers, 1823.

CURLE, RICHARD. Collecting American first editions, pp. 160–61.

Prairie, 1827.

CURLE, RICHARD. Collecting American first editions, p. 161.

Precaution, 1820.

CURLE, RICHARD. Collecting American first editions, p. 181.

Red rover, 1827 and 1828.

CURLE, RICHARD. Collecting American first editions, pp. 187.

Spy, 1821.

CURLE, RICHARD. Collecting American first editions, p. 207.

Water witch, 1830 and 1831.

CURLE, RICHARD. Collecting American first editions, p. 187.

Wing-and-wing, 1842.

CURLE, RICHARD. Collecting American first editions, p. 161.

Copland, Robert, *fl.* 1508–1547

WHITE, BEATRICE. Two tracts on marriage by Robert Copland. Huntington library. *Bulletin,* 1 : 205–7, 1931.

Copley, John Singleton, 1737–1885

Copley letters and manuscripts in the library. (Boston public library.) *More books,* s. 6, 5 : 202–5, 1930.

Coppard, Alfred Edgar, 1878——

COPPARD, ALFRED E. On first getting into print. *Colophon,* part 6, 1931. 8 pp.

SAUL, GEORGE B. A. E. Coppard: his life and his poetry to the publication of the "bibliography" (1931) . . . Philadelphia, 1932. (Thesis, University of Pennsylvania.) Bibliography, pp. [7]–14; "a bibliography of the poetry to July 1931," pp. 79–82.

SCHWARTZ, JACOB. The writings of Alfred Edgar Coppard: a bibliography. Foreword and notes by A. E. Coppard. London, Ulysses bookshop, 1931. 73 pp. Review, *Book-collector's quarterly,* no. 3, June–August, 1931, pp. 78–79.

Corvo, Frederick, (Styled *Baron*), *pseud.*

See Rolfe, Frederick William.

Coryate, Thomas, 1577(?)–1617

SAWYER and DARTON. English books, v. 1, pp. 100–101.

Cotton, John, 1585–1652

TUTTLE, JULIUS H. Writings of Rev. John Cotton. Bibliographical essays, a tribute to Wilberforce Eames.

Spiritual milk, 1656.

WALDMAN, MILTON. Americana. New York, Holt, 1925. Facsimile of title-page, opp. p. 158.

Cowley, Abraham, 1618–1667

LOISEAU, JEAN. Abraham Cowley, sa vie, son oeuvre. Paris, Henri Didier, 1931. Bibliography. 33 pp.

Poetical blossoms, 1673.

AMERICAN ART ASSOCIATION. Sales catalogue. Rare books from the library of the late Willis Vickery. New York, 1933. Facsimile of title-page, p. 12.

Cowper, William, 1731–1800

POVEY, KENNETH. Further notes for a bibliography of Cowper's letters. *Review of English studies,* 8: 316–19, 1932.

Cox, Palmer, 1840–1924

FULLERTON, BRADFORD M. Selective bibliography, p. 70.

Cox, William, *d.* 1851

FULLERTON, BRADFORD M. Selective bibliography, pp. 70–71.

Cozzens, Frederick Swartwout, 1818–1869

FULLERTON, BRADFORD M. Selective bibliography, p. 71.

Cranch, Christopher Pearse, 1813–1892

FULLERTON, BRADFORD M. Selective bibliography, pp. 71–72.

Crane, Stephen, 1871–1900

FOLLETT, WILSON. A note on Stephen Crane, 1871–1900. *Bookman* (New York), 68: 532–37, 1929.

FOLLETT, WILSON. The second twenty-eight years: a note on Stephen Crane, 1871–1900. Newark, N.J., Stephen Crane association, 1930. 22 pp.

FULLERTON, BRADFORD M. Selective bibliography, pp. 72–73.

HERZBERG, M. J. Stephen Crane and the Stephen Crane association. Newark, N.J., 1926. Bibliography.

JOHNSON, MERLE. American first editions, pp. 54–56 (90–92). The check-list in the 1929 edition was compiled by O. L. Griffith.

STARRETT, VINCENT. Stephen Crane: a bibliography. Philadelphia, Centaur book shop, 1926. 46 pp.

STARRETT, VINCENT. Stephen Crane: notes biographical and bibliographical. *Colophon,* part 3, 1931.

STOLPER, BENJAMIN J. R. Stephen Crane: a list of his writings and articles about him. Newark, N.J., Newark public library, 1930. 30 pp.

Crane, Walter, 1845–1915

MASSÉ, GERTRUDE C. E. Bibliography of first editions of books illustrated by Walter Crane. Preface by H. Summer. London, Chelsea publishing co., 1923. 64 pp.

Crawford, Francis Marion, 1854–1909

FULLERTON, BRADFORD M. Selective bibliography, pp. 73–74.

Crawford, Isabella Valancy, 1850–1887

PIERCE, LORNE. Outline of Canadian literature, pp. 67–69.

Crévecoeur, J. Hector, 1735–1813

FULLERTON, BRADFORD M. Selective bibliography, pp. 74–75.

Crockett, David, 1786–1836

FULLERTON, BRADFORD M. Selective bibliography, p. 75.

Cromwell, Oliver, 1599–1658

ABBOT, WILLIAM C. A bibliography of Oliver Cromwell. A list of printed materials relating to Oliver Cromwell . . . Cambridge, Harvard university press, 1929. xxviii +540 pp. Review by Alfred W. Pollard, *Library,* s. 4, 11 : 238–40, 1931.

Cross, Marian Evans Lewes, 1819–1880

Autograph manuscripts of George Eliot. *Times literary supplement,* April 24, 1930, p. 356.

CARTER, JOHN. Binding variants in English publishing, 1820–1900. London, Constable, 1932.

George Eliot and Dr. Chapman. *Times literary supplement,* September 11, 1930, p. 720.

MAGGS BROTHERS. Catalogue no. 555. London, 1931. pp. 67–68. Describes a collection of thirty-four autograph letters from George Eliot to Frederic Harrison.

MUDGE, ISADORA, and SEARS, MINNIE E. George Eliot dictionary . . . London, Routledge, 1924. xlvii+260 pp.

MUIR, PERCY H. A bibliography of the first editions of books by George Eliot (Mary Ann Evans) (1819–1880). Bibliographies of modern authors. Third series. London, Bookman's journal, 1931, pp. 41–58.

MUIR, PERCY H. George Eliot. *Bookman's journal,* supplement, pp. 1–58, 1927–1928.

PURDY, RICHARD L. Journals and letters of George Eliot. Yale university library. *Gazette,* 7 : 1–4, 1932.

Cross, Zora

SERLE, PERCIVAL. Bibliography of Australasian poetry, p. 48.

Cruikshank, George, 1792–1878

COHN, ALBERT M. George Cruikshank: a catalogue raisonné of the work executed during the years, 1806 to 1877, with some collations, notes, approximate values, facsimiles, and illustrations ... London, Bookman's journal, 1924. 391 pp.

SAWYER and DARTON. English books, v. 2, pp. 118, 131, 136, 141, 172–74, 183, 189, 193, 196–97, 234, 245, 254, 256, 287, 289, 305, 308, 310.

Hop o' my thumb.

SAWYER and DARTON. English books, v. 2, p. [137]. Facsimile of title-page.

Cummings, Edward Estlin, 1894–

JOHNSON, MERLE. American first editions, p. (92).

Cummins, Maria Susanna, 1827–1866

FULLERTON, BRADFORD M. Selective bibliography, p. 76.

Cunningham-Graham, Robert Bontine, 1852——

CHAUNDY, LESLIE. A bibliography of the first editions of R. B. Cunningham-Graham. London, Dulau, 1924. 16 pp. Reviews, *Bookman's journal,* 11 : 19, 1925; by Iolo A. Williams in *London Mercury,* 10 : 194, 1924.

Curll, Edmund, 1675–1747

STRAUS, RALPH. The unspeakable Curll, bookseller: to which is added a list of his books. London, Chapman and Hall, 1927.

Curtis, George William, 1824–1892
FULLERTON, BRADFORD M. Selective bibliography, pp. 76–77.

Cutter, Bloodgood Haviland, 1817–1906
WINTERICH, JOHN T. The life and works of Bloodgood Haviland Cutter. *Colophon,* part 2, 1930. 8 pp.

Daley, Victor James William Patrick, 1858–1905
SERLE, PERCIVAL. Bibliography of Australasian poetry, p. 50.

Damon, Samuel Foster, 1893——
DAMON, S. FOSTER. Astrolabe, infinities, and hypocrisies ... New York, Harper, 1927. Bibliographical note, 1 leaf following p. ix.

Dana, John Cotton, 1856–1929
CAHILL, E. C. The life and works of John Cotton Dana. *Americana,* 24 : 69–84, 1930.

Dana, Richard Henry, Sr., 1787–1879
FULLERTON, BRADFORD M. Selective bibliography, pp. 77–78.

Dana, Richard Henry, Jr., 1815–1882
FULLERTON, BRADFORD M. Selective bibliography, pp. 78–79.

Two years before the mast, 1840.

CURLE, RICHARD. Collecting American first editions, pp. 149–51, 204.

JOHNSON, MERLE. American first editions, pp. (94–95).

WINTERICH, JOHN T. Romantic stories of books. Second series, VIII : *Two years before the mast. Publishers' weekly,* 117 : 1581–85, 1930.

Daniel, Samuel, 1562–1619

SAWYER and DARTON. English books, v. 1, p. 89.

SELLERS, H. A bibliography of the works of Samuel Daniel. 1585–1623 ... Oxford bibliographical society. *Proceedings and papers,* 2: 29–54, 1928.

SELLERS, H. Supplementary note to a bibliography of Samuel Daniel. Oxford bibliographical society. *Proceedings and papers,* 2: 341–42, 1930.

D'Arusmont, Frances (Wright), 1795–1852

WATERMAN, WILLIAM R. Frances Wright. New York, Columbia university press, 1924. Bibliography, pp. 257–64. (Thesis, Columbia university.)

Darwin, Charles Robert, 1809–1882

Origin of species.

VICTORIUS, PAUL B. A sketch of *The origin of species. Colophon,* part 9, 1932. Refers to the early English and American editions.

Daunce, Edward

Prayse of nothing.

SARGENT, RALPH M. The authorship of *The prayse of nothing. Library,* s. 4, 12: [322]–31, 1932.

D'Avenant, William, (*Sir*), 1606–1668

SAWYER and DARTON. English books, v. 1, p. 210.

Davidson, John, 1857–1909

CUTLER and STILES. Modern British authors, pp. 29–30.

DAVIDSON, JOHN. Poems. New York, Modern library, 1924. Bibliography, 4 pp.

FIRST EDITION CLUB. A bibliographical catalogue, pp. 53–54.

STONEHILL, C. A., and STONEHILL, H. W. Bibliographies of modern authors. Second series. London, J. Castle, 1925.

Davies, Rhys, 1903——

GAWSWORTH, JOHN, *pseud.,* (T. Fytton Armstrong). Ten contemporaries: notes toward their definitive bibliography. First series. London, Benn, 1932.

Davies, William Henry, 1870——

LOOKER, SAMUEL J. W. H. Davies: his later bibliography. 1922–1928. *Bookman's journal,* 17: 10, 122–27, 1929.

MURPHY, GWENDOLEN. Bibliographies of modern authors. No. 3. W. H. Davies. *London Mercury,* 17: 76–80, 1928.

Davis, Jefferson, 1808–1889

WINSTON, ROBERT W. High stakes and hair trigger: the life of Jefferson Davis. New York, Holt, [1930]. Bibliography, pp. 289–95.

Davis, John, 1767–1816

FULLERTON, BRADFORD M. Selective bibliography, pp. 79–80.

Davis, Richard Harding, 1864–1916

FULLERTON, BRADFORD M. Selective bibliography, p. 80.

JOHNSON, MERLE. American first editions, pp. 57–59 (96–98). The check-list in the 1929 edition was compiled by H. C. Quinby.

QUINBY, HENRY C. Richard Harding Davis: a bibliography. New York, Dutton, [1924]. xxi+294 pp.

Davison, Francis, *ca.* 1575 to *ca.* 1619

SAWYER and DARTON. English books, v. 1, p. 81.

Dawes, Rufus, 1803–1859

FULLERTON, BRADFORD M. Selective bibliography, p. 81.

Dawks, Ichabod, 1661–1730

MORISON, STANLEY. Ichabod Dawks and his *News letter.* London, Cambridge university press, 1931. Review by Harry Carter, *Book-collector's quarterly,* no. 6, April–June, 1932.

Day, John, *fl.* 1606

Isle of Gulls, 1606.

GREG, WALTER W. The two issues of Day's *Isle of Gulls,* 1606. *Library,* s. 4, 3: [307]–9, 1923.

Day, Thomas, 1748–1789

Sandford and Merton, 1783, 1787, 1789.

NEWTON, A. EDWARD. This book-collecting game. Boston, Little, Brown and co., 1928, pp. 9, 45–54, 60. Facsimile of title-page.

Defoe, Daniel, 1661–1731

DOTTIN, PAUL. Daniel De Foe et ses romans. Paris, Les presses universitaires, 1924. 3 v. "Liste des oeuvres de De Foe," pp. [799]–849; "bibliographie critique," pp. [851]–77.

DOTTIN, PAUL. The life and strange and surprising adventures of Daniel Defoe. New York, Macaulay, [1929]. List of Defoe's works, pp. 267–304; biographies of Defoe, pp. 305–11.

HARASZTI, Z. A great Defoe library. *More books,* 1931.

Hermann Ullrich; a bibliography. *English studies,* 13: 87–89, 1931. A list of Ullrich's writings concerning Defoe.

NICHOLLS, NORAH. Some early editions of Defoe. *Bookman* (London), 80: 42–43, 1931.

SAWYER and DARTON. English books, v. 1, pp. 237–45.

WRIGHT, THOMAS. Life of Daniel Defoe . . . with a great deal of entirely new information . . . London, Farncombe, 1931. 427 pp.

Essay on projects, 1697.

JACOB, ERNST G. Daniel Defoe: *Essay on projects* (1697). Eine wirtschafts- und sozialgeschichte Studie. *Kölner analytische Arbeiten,* Bd. 9, Leipzig, 1929. 142 pp.

Defoe, Daniel (*Continued*)

Reasons humbly offered for a law to enact the castration of Popish ecclesiasticks, 1700.

Moore-Smith, G. C. An unrecognized work of Defoe's. *Review of English studies,* 5 : 64–66, 1929.

Robinson Crusoe, 1719.

Currie, Barton. Fishers of books. Boston, Little, Brown and co., 1929. Facsimile of title-page of first edition (1719), opp. p. 26.

Dix, E. R. McC. The first Dublin edition of *Robinson Crusoe. Times literary supplement,* October 13, 1927, pp. 715, 742.

The Dublin edition of *Robinson Crusoe. Times literary supplement,* September 29, 1927, p. 672.

Hutchins, Henry C. *Robinson Crusoe* and its printing, 1719–1731. A bibliographical study. With a foreword by A. Edward Newton. New York, Columbia university press, 1925. xix+201 pp. Reviews, *Times literary supplement,* October 22, 1925; (*cf.* R. B. McKerrow, *ibid.,* October 29, 1925); by Temple Scott, *Saturday review of literature,* 2 : 339, 1925).

Hutchins, Henry C. Two hitherto unrecorded editions of *Robinson Crusoe. Library,* s. 4, 7 : [58]–72, 1927.

Sawyer and Darton. English books, v. 1, p. 239. Facsimile of title-page of first edition (1719).

Winterich, John T. Books and the man. New York, Greenberg, 1929, pp. 18–36. Facsimile of title-page of first edition (1719).

De Forest, John William, 1826–1906

Fullerton, Bradford M. Selective bibliography, pp. 81–83.

Dekker, Thomas, 1570(?)–1641(?)

Gregg, Kate L. Thomas Dekker: a study in economic and social backgrounds. Seattle, Wash., University of Washington press (1924). (University of Washington. *Publications. Language and literature,* v. 2, no. 2.) Bibliography, pp. 111–12.

Sawyer and Darton. English books, v. 1, p. 133.

Bloodie banquet, 1604.

Oliphant, E. H. C. *The bloodie banquet.* A Dekker-Middleton play. *Times literary supplement,* December 17, 1925. (*Cf.* W. W. Greg, *ibid.,* December 24, 1925.)

Converted courtezan or the honest whore, 1604.

Baird, Matthew. The early editions of Thomas Dekker's *The converted courtezan or the honest whore. Library,* s. 4, 10: [52]–60, 1930. (*Cf.* Frank Marcham, *ibid.,* s. 4, 10: [339], 1930.)

Keep the widow waking.

Sisson, Charles. *Keep the widow waking.* A lost play by Dekker. *Library,* s. 4, 8: [39]–57, [233]–59, 1928.

Whole magnificent entertainment, 1604.

Maggs Brothers. Catalogue no. 493. Shakespeare and Shakespeareana. London, 1927. Facsimile of title-page, opp. p. 232.

Delafield, E. M., *pseud.*

See De La Pasture, Edmeé Elizabeth Monica.

De La Mare, Walter, 1873——

Cutler and Stiles. Modern British authors, pp. 31–33.

Mégroz, Rodolphe L. Walter de la Mare: a biographical study. London, Hodder & Stoughton, 1924. Books by Walter de la Mare with dates of first editions, pp. 287–88.

Murphy, Gwendolen. Bibliographies of modern authors. No. 1. Walter de la Mare. *London Mercury,* 15: 526–31, 635–39; 16: 70–73, 1927.

Deland, Margaret (Margaretta Wade Campbell), 1857——

FULLERTON, BRADFORD M. Selective bibliography, pp. 83–84.

JOHNSON, MERLE. American first editions, pp. (99–100).

JOHNSON, MERLE. American first editions: Margaret Deland, 1857——. *Publishers' weekly,* 120:2328–29, 1931.

De La Pasture, Edmeé Elizabeth Monica, 1890——

GAWSWORTH, JOHN, *pseud.,* (T. Fytton Armstrong). Ten contemporaries: notes toward their definitive bibliography. Second series. London, Joiner & Steele, 1932.

Deming, Philander, 1829–1915

FULLERTON, BRADFORD M. Selective bibliography, p. 84.

Dennis, Clarence James, 1876——

SERLE, PERCIVAL. Bibliography of Australasian poetry, pp. 53–54.

Denton, Daniel

Brief description of New York, 1670.

PALTSITS, VICTOR H. Daniel Denton's description of New York in 1670. New York public library. *Bulletin,* 28: 599–604, 1924. Includes a census of copies and a facsimile of title-page.

Derby, George Horatio, 1823–1861

FULLERTON, BRADFORD M. Selective bibliography, pp. 85–86.

De Vere, Edward, (*17th Earl of Oxford*), 1550–1604

ALLEN, P. The case of Edward de Vere, seventeenth Earl of Oxford as "Shakespeare." London, C. Palmer, 1931.

WARD, B. M. The seventeenth Earl of Oxford, 1550–1604, from contemporary documents. London, J. Murray, 1928. Review, *Library,* s. 4, 9:211–14, 1929.

Dewey, John, 1859——

Thomas, Milton H., and Schneider, Herbert W. A bibliography of John Dewey. New York, Columbia university press, 1930. 151 pp. Review, *American Mercury,* 21 : xlii, (October) 1930.

De Worde, Wynkyn, *d.* 1534

Leuze, Otto. Zwei unbekannte Drucke des Wynkyn de Worde (1506). *Zeitschrift für Bücherfreunde,* n.f., 22 : 101–4, 1930. Refers to Seissello, *Ad angliae regem Henricum VII oratio* (Westminster, 1506), and Gryphus, *Oratio ad angliae regem pro recessu suo* (Westminster, 1506).

Dexter, Timothy, 1748–1806

Pickle for the knowing ones, 1838.

Marquand, John P. Lord Timothy Dexter of Newburyport, Masstts. New York, Minton, Balch & co., 1925. Reprints the 1838 edition.

Dickens, Charles, 1812–1870

American Art Association. Sales catalogue. A Charles Dickens collection . . . the library of Frederick W. Lehmann. New York, 1930. First editions of Dickens, items 233–366.

American Art Association. Sales catalogue. Catalogue of the McCutcheon collection of Dickens and Thackeray. New York, 1931.

American Art Association. Sales catalogue. First editions, letters, and mss. of Barrie, Dickens, Galsworthy, Shaw, Trollope . . . from the library of Thomas Hatton. New York, 1929.

American Art Association. Sales catalogue. The renowned collection of the works of Charles Dickens formed by Mr. and Mrs. Edward C. Daoust. New York, 1929.

Carter, John. Binding variants in English publishing, 1820–1900. London, Constable, 1932.

Dickens, Charles (*Continued*)

CAVANAUGH, CORTES W. Charles Dickens, his life as traced by his works. New York public library. *Bulletin,* 33: 291–301, 1929.

CURRIE, BARTON. Fishers of books. Boston, Little, Brown and co., 1931, pp. 60–85. Refers to John Forster and the Dickens manuscripts.

DARWIN, BERNARD. The Dickens advertiser. A collection of the advertisements in the original parts of novels by Charles Dickens. London, Mathews and Marrot, 1930. vii+208 pp.

Dickens and Barrie manuscripts. *Times literary supplement,* June 26, 1930, p. 540.

Dickens and others. *Times literary supplement,* June 20, 1929, p. 500.

Dickens to his first publisher. *Dickensian,* 28: 193–96, 1932.

Dickensian: a magazine for Dickens' lovers . . . London, v. 19– , 1923——.

ECKEL, JOHN C. The first editions of the writings of Charles Dickens, their points and values; a bibliography . . . London, Maggs, 1932. xvi+272 pp., facsimiles.

EDGAR, HERMAN L., and VAIL, R. W. G. Early American editions of the works of Charles Dickens. New York public library. *Bulletin,* 33: 302–19, 1929.

FIRST EDITION CLUB. A bibliographical catalogue, p. 55.

HAYWARD, ARTHUR L. Dickens encyclopaedia. London, Routledge, 1931. 175 pp.

MAGGS BROTHERS. Catalogue no. 555. London, 1931, pp. 59–60. Describes a collection of twenty-four autograph letters on "The village coquettes" written to John P. Hullah.

MATZ, BERTRAM W. Writings wrongfully attributed to Dickens. *Dickensian,* 21: 122–27, 1925.

PALMER, CECIL. A unique Dickens collection (belonging to Bertram W. Matz). *Book notes,* 3:179–80, 192, 1925.

SAWYER and DARTON. English books, v. 2, pp. 239–92.

SAWYER, CHARLES J., and DARTON, FREDERICK H. Dickens and Barrabas, Forster intervening: a study based upon some hitherto unpublished letters. London, Sawyer, 1930.

SAWYER, CHARLES J., LTD. Charles Dickens' first and collected editions, autographs, personal relics. Catalogue no. 103. London, Sawyer, [1931].

SPENCER, WALTER T. Forty years in my bookshop. London, Constable, 1923. Dickensiana, pp. 89–152. Refers to rare editions, manuscripts, play-bills, etc.

WAGENKNECHT, EDWARD. The man Charles Dickens, a Victorian portrait, with an introduction by Gamaliel Bradford. Boston, Houghton Mifflin co., 1929. Bibliography, pp. 307–53.

WILKINS, WILLIAM G. Dickens in cartoon and caricature. Edited with an introduction by B. W. Matz. Boston, privately printed, 1924. (Bibliophile society. *Publications.*) 241 pp., 60 plates.

Battle of life, 1846.

NEW YORK PUBLIC LIBRARY. *Bulletin,* 33: opp. p. 298, 1929. Facsimile of title-page of first issue of first edition.

SAWYER and DARTON. English books, v. 2, p. [285]. Facsimile of title-page.

Chimes, 1845.

CURRIE, BARTON. Fishers of books. Boston, Little, Brown and co., 1931. Facsimile of title-page, p. 63.

Dickens, Charles (*Continued*)

Christmas carol, 1843.

JOHNSON, R. BRIMLEY. About *A Christmas carol. Dickensian,* 28: 7–10, 1932.

NEW YORK PUBLIC LIBRARY. *Bulletin,* 33: opp. p. 299, 1929. Facsimile of title-page.

OSBORNE, EDNA A. Variants of the *Christmas carol. Bookman* (London), 81: 192–94, 1931.

QUARITCH, BERNARD, LTD. Catalogue no. 472. London, 1933. Facsimile of title-page, p. 79.

SADLEIR, MICHAEL. *A Christmas carol. Times literary supplement,* January 28, 1932, p. 60.

SAWYER and DARTON. English books, v. 2, p. [288]. Facsimile of variants of Stave I.

Edwin Drood.

BECKER, MAY L. (Continuations of *Edwin Drood.*) *Saturday review of literature,* 1: 653, 1925.

JOHNSON, F. S. A notable *Drood* collection. *Dickensian,* 28: 231–34, 1932.

Mrs. Lirriper's lodgings, [1866].

SAWYER and DARTON. English books, v. 2, p. [288]. Facsimile of title-page.

Oliver Twist.

NEW YORK PUBLIC LIBRARY. *Bulletin,* 33, opp. p. 298, 1929. Facsimile of title-page of first American edition, Philadelphia, 1837.

Pickwick papers, 1845.

CURRIE, BARTON. Fishers of books. Boston, Little, Brown and co., 1931. Facsimile of title-page, p. 147.

DAVIS. *The posthumous papers of the Pickwick club:* some new bibliographical discoveries. London, Marks, 1929.

ECKEL, JOHN C. Prime Pickwicks in parts, census with complete collation, comparison, and comment . . . with foreword by A. Edward Newton. New York, E. H. Wells and co., 1928. 91 pp., facsimiles.

ROBBINS, FRANK E. Pickwickian chronology. Bibliographical society of America. *Papers,* 18: 1–11, 1925.

SAWYER and DARTON. English books, v. 2, p. [238]. Facsimile of wrapper of part I.

UHRSTRÖM, W. Pickwick notes. *Studier i modern språkvetenskap,* 11: 45–67, 1931. Bibliography, pp. 63–67.

WINTERICH, JOHN T. Books and the man. New York, Greenberg, 1929, pp. 37–61. Facsimile of the wrapper of part I.

Pickwick papers, Philadelphia, 1836.

AMERICAN ART ASSOCIATION. Sales catalogue. Library of Frank Irving Fletcher. New York, 1932. Facsimile of title-page, p. 67.

Strategems of bonanza.

SAWYER and DARTON. English books, v. 2, p. [251]. Facsimile of first page of unpublished manuscript.

Sunday under three heads, 1836.

SAWYER and DARTON. English books, v. 2, p. [281]. Facsimile of wrapper.

Village coquettes, 1837.

SPENCER, WALTER T. Forty years in my bookshop. London, Constable, 1923, p. [203]. Facsimile of title-page.

Dickinson, Emily, 1830–1886

FULLERTON, BRADFORD M. Selective bibliography, p. 86.

HAMPSON, ALFRED L. Emily Dickinson: a bibliography. Northampton, Mass., The Hampshire bookshop, 1930. 36 pp.

JOHNSON, MERLE. American first editions, pp. 60 (103–4). The check-list in the 1929 edition was compiled by Charles R. Green.

Dickinson, Emily (*Continued*)

Pollitt, Josephine. Emily Dickinson: the human background of poetry. New York, Harper, 1930. Sources, pp. 323–50.

Taggard, Genevieve. A Dickinson bibliography. *Saturday review of literature,* 7: 698, 1931. (A review.)

Taggard, Genevieve. The life and mind of Emily Dickinson. New York, Knopf, 1930. "Books used," pp. 341–44; "Notes on books about Emily Dickinson," pp. 351–56.

Todd, Mabel L. Emily Dickinson's literary debut. *Harper's magazine,* 160: 403–71, 1930.

Whicher, George F. Bibliography of Emily Dickinson, 1830–1886. Amherst, Mass., Jones library, 1930. Review, *Books,* 7: 31, April 12, 1931.

Whicher, George F. Emily Dickinson: a bibliography. Amherst, Mass., Jones library, 1931. Second edition.

Disraeli, Benjamin, (*Earl of Beaconsfield*), 1804–1881

Carter, John. Binding variants in English publishing, 1820–1900. London, Constable, 1932.

Dixon, Thomas, Jr., 1864——

Overton, Grant. Cargoes for Crusoes. New York, Appleton, [1924], pp. 248–49.

Dobson, Henry Austin, 1840–1921

Dobson, Alban. An Austin Dobson causerie. *Cornhill,* 58: 149–62, 1925.

Dobson, Alban. A bibliography of the first editions of published and privately printed books and pamphlets by Austin Dobson. With a preface by Sir Edmund Gosse. London, First edition club, 1925. xxii+88 pp.

Dodge, Mary Elizabeth (Mapes), 1836–1905

Fullerton, Bradford M. Selective bibliography, pp. 86–87.

Dodgson, Charles Lutwidge, 1832–1898

COLUMBIA UNIVERSITY. Catalogue of an exhibition at Columbia university to commemorate the 100th anniversary of the birth of Lewis Carroll, 1832–1898. New York, Columbia university press, 1932. 153 pp.

CUTLER and STILES. Modern British authors, pp. 16–22.

FISH, HELEN D. "1832–1932." *Saturday review of literature,* 8: 704, 1932. Refers to the "Lewis Carroll" exhibition at Columbia university.

HARRISON, E. Carrolliana. *Times literary supplement,* March 24, 1932, p. 217.

LEHMANN-HAUPT, H. Zum 100 Geburtstag von Lewis Carroll. Beilage für das *Philobiblon.* Vienna, 1932. 16 pp.

LIVINGSTON, FLORA V. The Harcourt Amory collection of Lewis Carroll in the Harvard college library. Cambridge, Mass., privately printed, 1932. ix+190 pp.

MADAN, FALCONER. The Lewis Carroll centenary in London, 1932, including a catalogue of the exhibition, with notes; an essay on Dodgson's illustrators by Harold Hartley; and additional literary pieces (chiefly unpublished) ... London, Bumpus, 1932. 140 pp., 6 plates.

PARRISH, M. L. A list of the writings of Lewis Carroll in the library at Dormy House, Pine Valley, New Jersey. Privately printed, 1928. viii+148 (i.e., 152) pp.

PARRY, EDWARD A., (*Sir*). The early writings of Lewis Carroll. *Cornhill,* 56: 455–68, 1924.

PARTINGTON, WILFRED. The untold tale of Lewis Carroll. *Bookman* (New York), 75: 78–80, 1932.

SAWYER and DARTON. English books, v. 1, pp. 16, 19; v. 2, pp. 116, 118, 371.

WATSON, E. H. LACON. Lewis Carroll and his centenary. *English review,* 54: 276–83, 1932.

WILLIAMS, SIDNEY H. A bibliography of the writings of Lewis Carroll (Charles Lutwidge Dodgson) ... London, Bookman's journal, 1924. xiii+142 pp.

Dodgson, Charles Lutwidge (*Continued*)

WILLIAMS, SIDNEY H., and MADAN, FALCONER. A handbook of the literature of the Rev. C. L. Dodgson (Lewis Carroll). London, Oxford university press, 1931. xxiv+336 pp. Review, Library association. *Record,* n.s., 2: 69–71, 1932.

Alice in wonderland, 1865.

LEHMANN-HAUPT, H. Zum 100 Geburtstag von Lewis Carroll. Beilage für das *Philobiblon.* Vienna, 1932. Facsimile of title-page, dated 1864, from the proof.

SAWYER and DARTON. English books, v. 2, p. [117]. Facsimile of title-page of 1865 edition, p. [112]; facsimile of title-page of 1866 edition, p. 117.

VAIL, R. W. G. *Alice in wonderland.* The manuscript and its story. New York public library. *Bulletin,* 32: 783, 1928.

Nursery "Alice," 1889.

AMERICAN ART ASSOCIATION. Sales catalogue. Library of Frank Irving Fletcher. New York, 1932. Facsimile of title-page, p. 42.

Wonderland postage-stamp case, 1888.

(*Wonderland postage-stamp case.*) *The month at Goodspeed's,* 2: 308–9, 1931. Facsimile of front of slip-case, p. 308.

Doesticks, Q. C. Philander, *pseud.*
See Thomson, Mortimer.

Dollard, James B., 1872——
PIERCE, LORNE. Outline of Canadian literature, p. 106.

Domett, Alfred, 1811–1887
SERLE, PERCIVAL. Bibliography of Australasian poetry, pp. 55–56.

Donne, John, 1573–1631

KEYNES, GEOFFREY. A bibliography of Dr. John Donne, Dean of St. Paul's. Cambridge, Cambridge university press, 1923. xiv+195 pp. Second edition. Review, *Book-collector's quarterly,* no. 7, July–September, 1932, pp. 85–89.

KEYNES, GEOFFREY. Donne, John. Devotions upon emergent occasions. Cambridge, Cambridge university press, 1923. Bibliography, pp. xxv–xxx.

SAWYER and DARTON. English books, v. 1, pp. 200–201.

SIMPSON, EVELYN M. S. A study of the prose works of John Donne. Oxford, Clarendon press, 1924. Chronological list of sermons, pp. 340–55; prose works attributed to Donne, pp. 356–59.

WILLIAMSON, GEORGE. The Donne tradition: a study in English poetry from Donne to the death of Cowley. Cambridge, Harvard university press, 1930. Seventeenth century editions of Donne's poetry, p. 253; bibliography, pp. 258–64.

Biathanatos.

DONNE, JOHN. Biathanatos. Reproduced from the first edition . . . Oxford, Blackwell, 1930. (Facsimile text society.) Bibliographical note by J. William Hebel. Facsimiles of title-pages of first edition (1644–1647?) and re-issue (1648).

Dos Passos, John Roderigo, 1896——

JOHNSON, MERLE. American first editions, pp. (103–4).

NEUSSE, WERNER. Die literarische Entwicklung von John Dos Passos. Geissen, 1931. Bibliography.

Doughty, Charles Montagu, 1843–1926

Arabia deserta, 1886.

FAIRLEY, BARKER. Doughty's *Arabia deserta. Times literary supplement,* May 2, 1929, p. 362.

ROBERTS, SYDNEY C. Doughty's *Arabia deserta. Times literary supplement,* May 2, 1929, p. 383.

Douglas, Gawin, 1474(?)–1522

Aeneid, 1553.

SAWYER and DARTON. English books, v. 1, p. 55. Facsimile of title-page.

Douglas, Norman, 1868——

CUTLER and STILES. Modern British authors, pp. 34–36.

FIRST EDITION CLUB. A bibliographical catalogue, pp. [57]–66.

MCDONALD, EDWARD D. A bibliography of the writings of Norman Douglas. Philadelphia, Centaur bookshop, 1927. 166 pp.

MCDONALD, EDWARD D. The early works of Norman Douglas. *Bookman* (New York), 66: 42–46, 1927.

STONEHILL, C. A. A bibliography of the writings of Norman Douglas. *Bookman's journal,* supplement, 1926. 7 pp.

South wind, 1917.

JESSUP, MARY E. A note on Norman Douglas' *South wind. American collector,* 5: 118–19, 1928.

Dowland, John, 1563(?)–1626

Second booke of songs or ayres.

DOWLING, MARGARET. The printing of John Dowland's *Second booke of songs or ayres. Library,* s. 4, 12: [365]–80, 1932.

Dowson, Ernest Christopher, 1867–1900

CUTLER and STILES. Modern British authors, pp. 37–38.

FIRST EDITION CLUB. A bibliographical catalogue, p. 67.

STONEHILL, C. A., and STONEHILL, H. W. Bibliographies of modern authors. Second series. London, J. Castle, 1925.

Doyle, Arthur Conan, (*Sir*), 1859–1930

CUTLER and STILES. Modern British authors, pp. 39–43.

LOCKE, HAROLD. A bibliographical catalogue of the writings of Sir Arthur Conan Doyle, 1879–1928. Turnbridge Wells, D. Webster, 1929. 84 pp.

ROBERTS, SYDNEY C. Doctor Watson, prolegomena to the study of Sherlock Holmes . . . London, Faber & Faber, [1931]. 32 pp. The bibliography relates to the imaginary works of Sherlock Holmes.

Drake, Benjamin, 1794–1841

FULLERTON, BRADFORD M. Selective bibliography, pp. 87–88.

Drake, Joseph Rodman, 1795–1820

FULLERTON, BRADFORD M. Selective bibliography, p. 88.

Drayton, Michael, 1563–1631

HEBEL, J. WILLIAM, *ed.* The works of Michael Drayton. Oxford, Blackwell, 1932. Bibliographies, v. 5.

Polybiblion, 1613–1622.

MAGGS BROTHERS. Catalogue no. 550. London, 1931. Facsimile of title-page, opp. p. 168.

Dreiser, Theodore, 1871——

JOHNSON, MERLE. American first editions, pp. 61–62 (105–8). The check-list in the 1929 edition was compiled by Vrest Orton and W. W. Lange.

MCDONALD, EDWARD D. Bibliography of the writings of Theodore Dreiser. Philadelphia, Centaur bookshop, 1928. 131 pp. Review, *American Mercury,* 13: lxxii, (April) 1928.

MCDONALD, EDWARD D. Dreiser before *Sister Carrie. Bookman* (New York), 67: 369–74, 1928.

ORTON, VREST. Dreiseriana: a book about his books. New York, Chocorua press, 1929. 93 pp.

ORTON, VREST. Notes to add to a bibliography of Theodore Dreiser. [New York], 1928.

Dreiser, Theodore (*Continued*)

RASCOE, BURTON. Theodore Dreiser. New York, McBride, 1925. Bibliography, p. 91.

WALDMAN, MILTON. Contemporary American authors: Theodore Dreiser. *London Mercury,* 14: 283–91, 1926.

Drinkwater, John, 1882——

CUTLER and STILES. Modern British authors, pp. 44–47.

Drummond, William Henry, 1854–1909

PIERCE, LORNE. Outline of Canadian literature, pp. 70–71.

Dryden, John, 1631–1700

BRUNNER, FRIEDA. John Dryden's Hymnen . . . Freiberg im Breisgau, K. Henn, 1931. xv+134 pp. "Literatur," pp. [ix]–xv.

Dryden first editions. *Times literary supplement,* April 7, 1927, p. 256.

The first collation of an interesting Dryden item. *Bookman's journal,* 12: 163–64, 1925.

HAM, ROSWELL G. An addition to the works of Dryden. *Times literary supplement,* October 8, 1931, p. 778.

NICHOLLS, NORAH. The early editions of John Dryden. *Bookman* (London), 79: 370–71, 1931.

NICHOLLS, NORAH. Some early editions of John Dryden. *Bookman* (London), 80: 266–67, 1931.

SAWYER and DARTON. English books, v. 1, pp. 189–93.

WISE, THOMAS J. A Dryden library. A catalogue of the plays, poems, and prose writings of John Dryden. London, privately printed, 1930. xxiv+89 pp., facsimiles. Contents: I, the writings of John Dryden; II, prologues, epilogues, etc., contributed to books by other writers; III, Drydeniana.

Annus mirabilis, 1667.

SAWYER and DARTON. English books, v. 1, p. [174]. Facsimile of title-page.

State of ignorance.

WHITING, GEORGE W. Dryden's abortive opera. *Times literary supplement,* December 24, 1932, p. 1041. Refers to a manuscript in the Huntington library.

Du Chaillu, Paul Belloni, 1831–1903

FULLERTON, BRADFORD M. Selective bibliography, pp. 88–89.

Dugdale, William, (*Sir*), 1605–1686

JENKINS, HERBERT M. Dr. Thomas' edition of Sir William Dugdale's *Antiquities of Worcestershire* . . . Stratford on Avon, Dugdale society, 1931. 20 pp.

Du Maurier, George Louis Palmella Busson, 1834–1896

FIRST EDITION CLUB. A bibliographical catalogue, p. 68.

Trilby, 1894.

WINTERICH, JOHN T. Books and the man. New York, Greenberg, 1929, pp. 102–21. Facsimiles of the title-pages of the first edition (London, 1894) and the first American edition (New York, 1894).

Dunbar, Paul Lawrence, 1872–1906

BURRIS, ANDREW M. Bibliography of the works of Paul Lawrence Dunbar, Negro poet and author, 1872–1906. *American collector,* 5 : 69–73, 1928.

FULLERTON, BRADFORD M. Selective bibliography, pp. 89–90.

JOHNSON, MERLE. American first editions, pp. (109–11).

Duncan, Sarah Jeannette, (Mrs. Everard Cotes), 1862–1922

PIERCE, LORNE. Outline of Canadian literature, pp. 169–70.

Dunne, Finley Peter, 1867——

FULLERTON, BRADFORD M. Selective bibliography, pp. 90–91.

JOHNSON, MERLE. American first editions, p. 63 (111).

Dunsany, Edward John Moreton Drax Plunkett, (*18th Baron*), 1878——
CUTLER and STILES. Modern British authors, pp. 48–49.
FIRST EDITION CLUB. A bibliographical catalogue, p. 69.

Dunton, John, 1659–1733
See Bridgewater, Benjamin.

Dwight, Timothy, 1752–1817
FULLERTON, BRADFORD M. Selective bibliography, p. 91.

Eastman, Mary (Henderson), 1818——
Aunt Phillis's cabin, 1852.
WINTERICH, JOHN T. Books and the man. New York, Greenberg, 1929, pp. 96–99. Facsimile of title-page.

Eaton, Arthur W. H., 1849——
PIERCE, LORNE. Outline of Canadian literature, p. 93.

Eddy, Isaac, 1777–1847
RUGG, HAROLD G. Isaac Eddy, printer-engraver, with a bibliography of Eddy publications. Bibliographical essays: a tribute to Wilberforce Eames.

Eddy, Mary Baker, 1821–1910
DAKIN, EDWIN F. Mrs. Eddy. The biography of a virginal mind. New York, Scribner, 1929. Bibliography, pp. 527–37. Includes Mrs. Eddy's books and periodicals as well as books, pamphlets, and periodical articles about her.

Eden, Richard, 1521(?)–1576
Decades of the new world, 1555.
MAGGS BROTHERS. Catalogue no. 555. London, 1931. Facsimile of title-page, p. 65.

Edwards, Harry Stilwell, 1855–1927
FULLERTON, BRADFORD M. Selective bibliography, p. 92.

Edwards, Richard, 1523(?)–1566
SAWYER and DARTON. English books, v. 1, p. 82.

Egan, Pierce, 1814–1880
Life in London, 1821.
SAWYER and DARTON. English books, v. 2, p. 195.

Egerton, George, *pseud.,* (Mary Chavelita Bright [Dunne] [Mrs. R. G. Bright])
GAWSWORTH, JOHN, *pseud.,* (T. Fytton Armstrong). Ten contemporaries: notes toward their definitive bibliography. First series. London, Benn, 1932.

Eggleston, Edward, 1837–1902
FULLERTON, BRADFORD M. Selective bibliography, pp. 92–93.
JOHNSON, MERLE. American first editions, pp. (112–14).

Eliot, Charles William, 1834–1926
ELIOT, CHARLES WILLIAM. A late harvest . . . Boston, Atlantic monthly press, 1924. Bibliography, 1914–1924, pp. 297–305.

Eliot, George, *pseud.*
See Cross, Marian Evans Lewes.

Eliot, John, 1604–1690
HARASZTI, Z. Eliot's Indian bible. *More books,* 4: 217–22, 1929.

Eliot, John Armstrong Blandford
SERLE, PERCIVAL. Bibliography of Australasian poetry, pp. 59–60.

Eliot, Thomas Stearns, 1888——
FRY, VARIAN. A bibliography of the writings of Thomas Stearns Eliot. *Hound & horn,* 1: 214–[218], 320–24, 1928.

Elliott, Sarah Barnwell, 1848–1928
FULLERTON, BRADFORD M. Selective bibliography, pp. 93–94.

Ellis, Edith, (Mrs. Havelock Ellis), 1861–1916
See Ellis, Havelock.

Ellis, Edward Sylvester, 1840–1916
FULLERTON, BRADFORD M. Selective bibliography, pp. 94–95.

Ellis, Havelock, 1859——
GOLDBERG, ISAAC. Havelock Ellis: biographical and critical survey ... New York, Simon and Shuster, 1926. Bibliography, pp. 349–51; bibliography of Mrs. Edith Ellis, p. 353.

Elyot, Thomas, (*Sir*), 1490(?)–1546
Castell of helth corrected, 1572.
MAGGS BROTHERS. Catalogue no. 550. London, 1931. Facsimile of title-page, opp. p. 456.

Embury, Emma Catharine (Manley), 1806–1863
FULLERTON, BRADFORD M. Selective bibliography, p. 95.

Emerson, Oliver Farrar, 1860–1927
NORTHUP, CLARK S. The writings of Oliver F. Emerson. (A bibliography.) Published as pages 27–32 of a reprint of O. F. Emerson's "More notes on 'Pearl'" from Modern language association of America. *Publications,* 42:807–32, 1930.

Emerson, Ralph Waldo, 1803–1882
AMERICAN ART ASSOCIATION. Sales catalogue. Stephen H. Wakeman collection. New York, 1924. Items 156–260.
JOHNSON, MERLE. American first editions, pp. 64–66 (115–18).
McDOWELL, TREMAINE. A freshman poem by Emerson. Modern language association. *Publications,* 45:326–29, 1930.

Concord discourse, 1835.

CURLE, RICHARD. Collecting American first editions, p. 172.

Conduct of life, 1860.

CURLE, RICHARD. Collecting American first editions, pp. 10, 22–26, 145.

Divinity college address, 1838.

CURLE, RICHARD. Collecting American first editions, p. 172.

English traits, 1856.

CURLE, RICHARD. Collecting American first editions, p. 11.

Essays, 1841.

CURLE, RICHARD. Collecting American first editions, pp. 147–48.

WINTERICH, JOHN T. Romantic stories of books. Second series. Emerson's *Essays. Publishers' weekly,* 118: 271–75, 1930.

Essays, second series, 1844.

CURLE, RICHARD. Collecting American first editions, p. 89.

Letter to the Second church, 1832.

AMERICAN ART ASSOCIATION. Sales catalogue. Stephen H. Wakeman collection. New York, 1924. Facsimile of title-page.

CURLE, RICHARD. Collecting American first editions, p. 207.

Letter to Whitman, 1855 or 1856.

CURLE, RICHARD. Collecting American first editions, p. 196.

Letters and social aims, 1876.

CURLE, RICHARD. Collecting American first editions, p. 209.

May-day, 1867.

CURLE, RICHARD. Collecting American first editions, pp. 90, 179.

Nature, 1836.

CURLE, RICHARD. Collecting American first editions, pp. 100, 143. Facsimile of title-page.

Emerson, Ralph Waldo (*Continued*)

Nature. Addresses and lectures, 1849.

CURLE, RICHARD. Collecting American first editions, p. 189.

Nature. An essay, 1845.

CURLE, RICHARD. Collecting American first editions, p. 189.

Phi Beta Kappa oration, 1837.

CURLE, RICHARD. Collecting American first editions, p. 172.

Poems, 1847.

CURLE, RICHARD. Collecting American first editions, pp. 50, 58, 64–66.

Representative men, 1850.

CURLE, RICHARD. Collecting American first editions, p. 10. Facsimile of title-page, between pp. 10 and 11.

Society and solitude, 1870.

CURLE, RICHARD. Collecting American first editions, p. 209.

English, Thomas Dunne, 1819–1902

FULLERTON, BRADFORD M. Selective bibliography, pp. 97–98.

HUNT, W. S. The story of a song ("Ben Bolt"). New Jersey historical society. *Proceedings,* 51 : 24–33, 1933.

Evans, George Essex, 1863–1909

SERLE, PERCIVAL. Bibliography of Australasian poetry, p. 62.

Evans, Lloyd

BOSANQUET, EUSTACE F. An early printed account book. *Library,* s. 4, 11 : [203]–11, 1931. Refers to *An almanacke and prognostication for the year MDLXXXII.*

Evelyn, John, 1620–1706

CRAWFORD, DAVID A. E. L. Gabriel Naudé and John Evelyn: with some notes on the Mazarinades. *Library,* s. 4, 12 : [381]–408, 1932.

KEYNES, GEOFFREY. John Evelyn as a bibliophil. *Library,* s. 4, 12 : [175]–93, 1932.

Exon, Edwin
SERLE, PERCIVAL. Bibliography of Australasian poetry, p. 63.

Fairfax, James Griffyth
SERLE, PERCIVAL. Bibliography of Australasian poetry, p. 64.

Faraday, Michael, 1791–1867
PRATT INSTITUTE FREE LIBRARY (Brooklyn, N.Y.). Michael Faraday, 1791–1867. Brooklyn, 1931. 13 pp. A selected list of books and periodical literature.

Farnol, Jeffery, 1878——
OVERTON, GRANT. Cargoes for Crusoes. New York, Appleton, [1924], p. 81.

Farquharson, Martha, *pseud.*
See Finley, Martha.

Farrell, John, 1851–1904
SERLE, PERCIVAL. Bibliography of Australasian poetry, p. 65.

Faulkner, William, 1897——
JOHNSON, MERLE. American first editions, pp. (119–20).
SMITH, M. J. Faulkner of Mississippi. *Bookman* (New York), 74: 411–17, 1931.

Fawcett, Edgar, 1847–1904
FULLERTON, BRADFORD M. Selective bibliography, p. 98.
JOHNSON, MERLE. American first editions, pp. 67–68 (121–23). The check-list in the 1929 edition was compiled by Vrest Orton.

Fay, Edwin Whitfield, 1865–1920
In memoriam, Edwin Whitfield Fay, 1865–1920 . . . Austin, Texas, University of Texas, 1924. (University of Texas. *Bulletin,* no. 2425.) Bibliography.

Fay, Theodore Sedgwick, 1807–1898
FULLERTON, BRADFORD M. Selective bibliography, pp. 98–99.

Ferber, Edna, 1887——
A complete bibliography of Edna Ferber's works. Garden City, Doubleday, Doran and co., 1928.
JOHNSON, MERLE. American first editions, pp. (124–25).

Ferguson, Adam, 1723–1816
LEHMANN, W. C. Adam Ferguson and the beginnings of modern sociology. New York, Columbia university press, 1931. Bibliography, pp. 259–62.

Ferguson, Dugald
SERLE, PERCIVAL. Bibliography of Australasian poetry, p. 66.

Ferguson, Samuel, (*Sir*), 1810–1886
DEERING, ARTHUR. Sir Samuel Ferguson, poet and antiquarian . . . Philadelphia, 1931. (Thesis, University of Pennsylvania.) Bibliography, pp. 139–45.

Fern, Fanny, *pseud.*
See Parton, Sarah Willis.

Ferrier, Susan, 1782–1854
MCKIRDIE, ISABELLE. The novels of Susan Ferrier. Chicago, 1932. (Thesis, University of Chicago.) Typewritten.

Fessenden, Thomas Green, 1771–1838
FULLERTON, BRADFORD M. Selective bibliography, pp. 99–100.

Field, Eugene, 1850–1895
FULLERTON, BRADFORD M. Selective bibliography, pp. 100–101.
JOHNSON, MERLE. American first editions, pp. 70–71 (126–28).

KELSOE, W. A. Eugene Field's St. Louis newspaper work. *Missouri historical review,* 27 : 78–79, 1932.

WASHINGTON UNIVERSITY LIBRARY (St. Louis, Mo.). Eugene Field manuscripts and memorabilia in the library of Washington university. St. Louis, Mo., 1927. 9 pp. Typewritten.

Field, Nathaniel, 1587–1633

GREG, WALTER W. Nathan Field and the Beaumont and Fletcher folio of 1679. *Review of English studies,* 3 : 337–38, 1927.

Amends for ladies, 1628.

MAGGS BROTHERS. Catalogue no. 493. Shakespeare and Shakespeareana. London, 1927. Facsimile of title-page, opp. p. 249.

Field, Richard, 1561–1625

KIRWOOD, ALBERT E. M. Richard Field, printer, 1589–1624. *Library,* s. 4, 12 : [1]–39, 1932.

Fielding, Henry, 1707–1754

BLANCHARD, FREDERIC T. Fielding the novelist: a study in historical criticism. New Haven, Yale university press, 1926.

CROSS, WILBUR L. The Fielding collection. Yale university library. *Gazette,* 1 : 31–34, 1927.

CROSS, WILBUR L. History of Henry Fielding. 1928. 3 v. Volume 3 contains a bibliography with collations, points, etc.

DIGEON, AURELIEN. The novels of Fielding. London, Routledge, 1925. Bibliographical notes, pp. 249–55.

SAWYER and DARTON. English books, v. 1, pp. 272–77.

VOORDE, FRANS PIETER VAN DER. Henry Fielding, critic and artist . . . 's Gravenhage, P. Westerbaan, 1931. (Proefschrift, Amsterdam.) List of books and articles consulted, pp. [226]–30.

Fielding, Henry (*Continued*)

Joseph Andrews, 1742.

CASTRO, J. PAUL DE, *ed.* Fielding, Henry. Joseph Andrews. Introduction and bibliographical notes. London, Scholartis press, 1929.

Masquerade, 1728.

CURRIE, BARTON. Fishers of books. Boston, Little, Brown and co., 1931, pp. 174–75. Facsimiles of title-pages of two issues.

Miser, ca. 1733.

Fielding's *Miser.* Huntington library. *Bulletin,* 1 : 211–13, 1931.

Tom Jones, 1749.

MAGGS BROTHERS. Catalogue no. 550. London, 1931. Facsimile of title-page, opp. p. 232.

MAGGS BROTHERS. Catalogue no. 555. London, 1931. Facsimile of title-page, p. 31.

SAWYER and DARTON. English books, v. 1, p. 275. Facsimile of title-page.

Fields, James Thomas, 1816–1881

FULLERTON, BRADFORD M. Selective bibliography, p. 101.

Filsinger, (*Mrs.*) **Ernest B.**

See Teasdale, Sara.

Filson, John, 1747(?)–1788

Filson's *Kentucke:* a facsimile reproduction of the original Wilmington edition of 1784, with paged critique, sketch of Filson's life, and bibliography. Edited by Willard Rouse Jillson. Louisville, Ky., 1929. (Filson club. *Publications,* no. 35.) Annotated bibliography, pp. [151]–67.

Finley, Martha, 1828–1909

FULLERTON, BRADFORD M. Selective bibliography, p. 102.

Firbank, Arthur Annesley Ronald, 1886–1926

CUTLER and STILES. Modern British authors, p. 50.

MUIR, PERCY H. A bibliography of the first editions of books by Arthur Annesley Ronald Firbank (1886–1926). Bibliographies of modern authors. Third series. London, Bookman's journal, 1931, pp. 1–8.

Firth, Charles Harding, (*Sir*), 1857——

Bibliography of the writings of Sir Charles Firth. London, Oxford university press, 1928. 45 pp.

Fitch, William Clyde, 1865–1909

MOSES, MONTROSE J., and GERSON, VIRGINIA. Clyde Fitch and his letters. Boston, Little, Brown and co., 1924. List of Fitch's plays, pp. 389–93.

FitzGerald, Edward, 1809–1883

Rubaiyat.

NICHOLLS, NORAH. Some early editions of Fitzgerald's Omar. *Bookman* (London), 79: 320–21, 1931.

POTTER, AMBROSE G. Bibliography of Omar Khayyam: with kindred matter in prose and verse pertaining thereto. London, Ingpen and Grant, 1929. xiv+314 pp.

WINTERICH, JOHN T. Books and the man. New York, Greenberg, 1929, pp. 326–42. Facsimiles of the title-pages of the first edition (London, 1859); second edition (London, 1868); first American edition (Columbus, Ohio, 1870) and so-called first American edition (Boston, 1878).

Flecker, James Elroy, 1884–1915

CUTLER and STILES. Modern British authors, pp. 51–52.

Fletcher, John, 1579–1625

See Beaumont, Francis.

Fletcher, Phineas, 1582–1650

SEATON, ETHEL, *ed.* Venus & Anchises (Britain's Ida) and other poems by Phineas Fletcher, edited from a Sion college manuscript ... London, Oxford university press, 1926.

Flint, Timothy, 1780–1840

FULLERTON, BRADFORD M. Selective bibliography, pp. 102–3.

Foote, Mary Hallock, 1847——

FULLERTON, BRADFORD M. Selective bibliography, pp. 103–4.

Foote, Samuel, 1720–1777

BELDEN, MARY M. The dramatic work of Samuel Foote. New Haven, Yale university press, 1929. Bibliography, pp. 196–206.

Ford, John, *fl.* 1639

LLOYD, BERTRAM. An inedited ms. of Ford's *Fames memorial. Review of English studies,* 1:93–95, 1925.

LLOYD, BERTRAM. An unprinted poem by John Ford(?). *Review of English studies,* 1:217–19, 1925.

Ford, Paul Leicester, 1865–1902

FULLERTON, BRADFORD M. Selective bibliography, p. 104.

JOHNSON, MERLE. American first editions, pp. 72–74 (129–31). The check-list in the 1929 edition was compiled by Vrest Orton.

Forester, Fanny, *pseud.*

See Judson, Emily Chubbock.

Forester, Frank, *pseud.*

See Herbert, Henry William.

Forman, Simon, 1552–1611

Bocke of plaies.

KLEIN, DAVID. Forman's *Bocke of plaies. Philological quarterly,* 11 : 385–95, 1932.

Foster, Hannah (Webster), 1759–1840

FULLERTON, BRADFORD M. Selective bibliography, p. 105.

Coquettes, 1797.

SHURTER, ROBERT L. Mrs. Hannah Webster Foster and the early American novel. *American literature,* 4 : 306–8, 1933. Refers particularly to *The coquette,* 1797.

TAYLOR, LILLIAN G. The way of the best-seller. *Colophon,* part 6, 1931. Facsimile of title-page.

Foster, Stephen Collins, 1826–1864

ADKINS, NELSON F. A note on the bibliography of Stephen C. Foster. *Notes and queries,* 163 : 331–32, 1932. Refers to Horace Waters's use of Foster's melodies.

Fox, George, 1624–1691

JONES, RUFUS M. Life and message of George Fox, 1624–1924 . . . New York, Macmillan, 1924. Bibliography, p. 31.

Fox, John William, Jr., 1862–1919

FULLERTON, BRADFORD M. Selective bibliography, pp. 105–6.

JOHNSON, MERLE. American first editions, p. (132).

Franklin, Benjamin, 1706–1790

ADAMS, R. G. And sold by Messrs. Franklin and Hall. *Pennsylvania magazine of history and biography,* 55 : 24–31, 1931.

EDDY, GEORGE S. A work book of the printing house of Benjamin Franklin and David Hall, 1759–1766. New York public library. *Bulletin,* 34 : 575–89, 1930.

FAY, BERNARD. Franklin the apostle of modern times. Boston, Little, Brown and co., 1929. Bibliography, pp. 517–33.

Franklin, Benjamin (*Continued*)

Franklin and Hall imprints. New York public library. *Bulletin,* 34: 719, 1930.

Autobiography.

(*Autobiography* of Benjamin Franklin.) *The month at Goodspeed's,* 2: 176–80, 1931. Facsimile of title-page of London edition of 1793.

WINTERICH, JOHN T. Books and the man. New York, Greenberg, 1929, pp. 343–56. Facsimile of title-page of first edition (Paris, 1791).

Cato major, 1744.

WALDMAN, MILTON. Americana. New York, Holt, 1925. Facsimile of title-page of Philadelphia edition of 1744, opp. p. 229.

Fraser, Claude Lovat, 1890–1921

MCFALL, HALDANE. The book of Claude Lovat Fraser. London, Dent, 1923.

MILLARD, CHRISTOPHER S. The printed work of Claude Lovat Fraser. London, Danielson, 1923. x+106 pp.

Frederic, Harold, 1856–1898

FULLERTON, BRADFORD M. Selective bibliography, p. 106.

Freeman, Mary Eleanor (Wilkins), 1862–1930

FULLERTON, BRADFORD M. Selective bibliography, p. 107.

JOHNSON, MERLE. American first editions, pp. (133–34).

French, Alice, 1850——

FULLERTON, BRADFORD M. Selective bibliography, pp. 107–8.

Freneau, Philip Morin, 1752–1832

AINSWORTH, E. G. An American translator of Ariosto: Philip Freneau. *American literature,* 4: 393–95, 1933. Refers to an expansion of *Orlando furioso,* VI, 22, published in 1788.

FULLERTON, BRADFORD M. Selective bibliography, pp. 108–9.

HALLENBECK, C. T. A note for future editors of Freneau's poems. *American literature,* 4: 391–93, 1933. Refers to errors in the printing of *Verses occasioned by General Washington's arrival.*

JOHNSON, MERLE. American first editions, pp. (135–36).

JOHNSON, MERLE. American first editions: Philip Freneau, 1752–1832. *Publishers' weekly,* 122: 213–14, 1932.

SMITH, FRANK. Philip Freneau and *The time-piece and literary companion. American literature,* 4: 270–87, 1933.

Frost, Robert Lee, 1875——

JOHNSON, MERLE. American first editions, pp. 75 (137–38). The check-list in the 1929 edition was compiled by Frederic G. Melcher.

MELCHER, FREDERIC G. American first editions: Robert Lee Frost, 1875——. *Publishers' weekly,* 103: 24, 1923.

Fuller, Henry Blake, 1857–1929

FULLERTON, BRADFORD M. Selective bibliography, pp. 109–10.

JOHNSON, MERLE. American first editions, p. 76 (139). The check-list in the 1929 edition was compiled by Vrest Orton.

OLYBRIUS, *pseud.* Henry B. Fuller: his pseudonym. *Notes and queries,* 113: 477, 1932. Refers to a short story, "Rosamond risks it," signed Hanley R. Fulton.

Fuller, Margaret, *pseud.*

See Ossoli, Sarah Margaret (Fuller) d'.

Gaines, Charles Kelsey, 1854——

Gorgo.

BROWN, W. ROLFE. *Gorgo:* a great historical novel. *South Atlantic quarterly,* 24: 179–90, 1925.

Gale, Zona, 1874——

JOHNSON, MERLE. American first editions, pp. 77 (140–41). The check-list in the 1929 edition was compiled by E. Jacoby van de Water.

OVERTON, GRANT. American nights entertainment. New York, Appleton, 1923, pp. 253–54.

OVERTON, GRANT. Authors of the day. New York, Doran, [1924], p. 143.

Gallagher, William Davis, 1808–1894

FULLERTON, BRADFORD M. Selective bibliography, pp. 110–11.

Galsworthy, John, 1867–1932

AMERICAN ART ASSOCIATION. Sales catalogue. First editions, letters, and mss. of Barrie, Dickens, Galsworthy, Shaw, Trollope . . . from the library of Thomas Hatton. New York, 1929.

CUTLER and STILES. Modern British authors, pp. 53–58.

FABES, GILBERT H. John Galsworthy. His first editions: points and values. London, Foyle, 1932.

FIRST EDITION CLUB. A bibliographical catalogue, pp. 70–[71].

MARROT, HAROLD V. A bibliography of the works of John Galsworthy. London, E. Mathews, 1928. xii+252 pp. Review by Alfred W. Pollard, *Library,* s. 4, 9: 418–21, 1929.

OVERTON, GRANT. American nights entertainment. New York, Appleton, 1923, pp. 30–33.

OVERTON, GRANT. Authors of the day. New York, Doran, [1924], pp. 28–31.

Galt, John, 1779–1839

LUMSDEN, HARRY. Bibliography of John Galt. Glasgow bibliographical society. Records, v. 9, 1931. Review, *Year's work in English studies,* 12: 316, 1931.

Garfield, James Abram, 1831–1881

SMITH, THEODORE C. The life and letters of James Abram Garfield. New York, Yale university press, 1925. 2 v. Bibliographical footnotes.

Garland, Hamlin, 1860——

FULLERTON, BRADFORD M. Selective bibliography, pp. 111–12.

HILL, EDWIN B. American first editions: Hamlin Garland, 1860——. *Publishers' weekly,* 103: 1270, 1923.

JOHNSON, MERLE. American first editions, pp. (142–44).

Garland, John de, *fl.* 1202–1252

Multorum vocabulorum equivicorum, 1505.

MAGGS BROTHERS. Catalogue no. 550. London, 1931. Facsimile of title-page, opp. p. 249.

Garth, Samuel, 1661–1719

FIRST EDITION CLUB. A bibliographical catalogue, p. 72.

Garvin, Amelia Beers (Warnock), 1878——

PIERCE, LORNE. Outline of Canadian literature, p. 100.

Gascoigne, George, *ca.* 1525–1577

SAWYER and DARTON. English books, v. 1, pp. 90–91.

Steele glas, [1576].

MAGGS BROTHERS. Catalogue no. 550. London, 1931. Facsimile of title-page, opp. p. 264.

Gaskell, Elizabeth Cleghorn (Stevenson), 1810–1865

SANDERS, GERALD DE W. Elizabeth Gaskell. New Haven, Yale university press, 1929. Bibliography by Clark S. Northup, pp. [163]–267.

Gay, John, 1685–1732

FIRST EDITION CLUB. A bibliographical catalogue, p. 75.

Gay, William, 1865–1897

SERLE, PERCIVAL. Bibliography of Australasian poetry, p. 73.

Gibbs, Cosmo Hamilton
See Hamilton, Cosmo.

Gibbs, George Fort, 1870——
OVERTON, GRANT. Cargoes for Crusoes. New York, Appleton, [1924], pp. 373–74.

Gibbs, Philip Hamilton, (*Sir*), 1877——
OVERTON, GRANT. Cargoes for Crusoes. New York, Appleton, [1924], pp. 26–27.

Gibson, Wilfred Wilson, 1878——
GAWSWORTH, JOHN, *pseud.,* (T. Fytton Armstrong). Ten contemporaries: notes toward their definitive bibliography. First series. London, Benn, 1932.

Gilbert, William Schwenck, (*Sir*), 1836–1911
DUBOIS, A. E. Additions to the bibliography of W. S. Gilbert's contributions to magazines. *Modern language notes,* 47: 308–14, 1932.
FIRST EDITION CLUB. A bibliographical catalogue, p. 73.
SEARLE, TOWNLEY. Sir William Schwenck Gilbert: a topsy-turvy adventure by . . . and an introduction by R. E. Swartout . . . London, Alexander-Ouseley, 1931. A bibliography of works by Gilbert (including the Gilbert and Sullivan operas), books illustrated by him, books and magazine articles about him, separate musical selections from the operas, etc. Review by John Carter, *Book-collector's quarterly,* part 4, October–December, 1931, pp. 61–64.

Gilder, Richard Watson, 1844–1909
FULLERTON, BRADFORD M. Selective bibliography, p. 112.

Gilman, Samuel, 1791–1858
Fair Harvard.
[*Fair Harvard*]. *The month at Goodspeed's,* 2: 300–302, 1931.

Gilpin, William, 1724–1804

TEMPLEMAN, WILLIAM D. Three anonymous works by William Gilpin. *Notes and queries,* 160: 112–14, 1931.

Gissing, George Robert, 1857–1903

CUTLER and STILES. Modern British authors, pp. 59–61.

MABBOTT, THOMAS O. A tale by Gissing identified. *Times literary supplement,* July 7, 1932, p. 499.

SCOTT, TEMPLE. Critical studies of the works of Charles Dickens by George Gissing: with an introduction and bibliography of Gissing by ... New York, Greenberg, 1924. Bibliography of George Gissing, pp. 161–65.

SWINNERTON, FRANK A. George Gissing, a critical study. New York, Doran, 1923. Bibliography, pp. [197]–200. Originally published in 1912.

Glasgow, Ellen (Anderson, Gholson), 1874——

CAPPON, LESTER J. Bibliography of Virginia history since 1865. University, Va., Institute for research in the social sciences, 1930.

FULLERTON, BRADFORD M. Selective bibliography, p. 113.

JOHNSON, MERLE. American first editions, pp. (145–46).

Goldsmith, Oliver, 1728–1774

BALDERSTON, KATHERINE C. A census of the manuscripts of Oliver Goldsmith. London, Oxford university press, 1927. 73 pp.

An exhibition in the Yale university library of the work of Oliver Goldsmith ... New Haven, Bibliographical press, 1928. 16 pp.

GOLDSMITH and JOHNSON. *Times literary supplement,* October 24, 1929, p. 852.

MCCARTHY, WILLIAM H. Goldsmith memorial exhibition. Yale university library. *Gazette,* 3: 63–64, 1929.

SAWYER and DARTON. English books, v. 1, pp. 319–27.

Goldsmith, Oliver (*Continued*)

SCOTT, TEMPLE. Oliver Goldsmith: biographically and bibliographically considered. Introduction by A. Edward Newton. New York, Bowling Green press, 1928. 361 pp. Based on the collection of W. M. Elkins.

SEITZ, R. W. Goldsmith and *A concise history of England. Notes and queries,* 153: 3–4, 1927.

SELLS, ARTHUR L. Les sources Françaises de Goldsmith. Paris, H. Champion, 1924. (Bibliothéque de la Revue de littérature comparée, v. 12.)

TUPPER, CAROLINE F. Essays erroneously attributed to Goldsmith. Modern language association of America. *Publications,* 39: 325–42, 1924.

WILLIAMS, IOLO A. (Bibliography of Oliver Goldsmith.) *London Mercury,* 10: 637–38, 1924; 11: 82–86, 1925.

WILLIAMS, IOLO A. Seven XVIIIth century bibliographies. London, Dulau, 1924, pp. 118–77.

Deserted village, 1770.

SAWYER and DARTON. English books, v. 1, p. 326. Facsimile of title-page.

Essays.

CRANE, RONALD S. Goldsmith's *Essays:* dates of original publications. *Notes and queries,* 153: 153, 1927.

Poems, 1775.

ELKIN, MATHEWS, LTD. Catalogue no. 23. London, 1929. Facsimile of title-page of Belfast edition of 1775.

Vicar of Wakefield, 1766.

MAGGS BROTHERS. Catalogue no. 550. London, 1931. Facsimile of title-page, opp. p. 265.

NEWTON, A. EDWARD. This book-collecting game, p. 13. Facsimile of title-page.

SAWYER and DARTON. English books, v. 1, p. 320. Facsimile of title-page.

STARRETT, VINCENT. Pennywise and book foolish. New York, Covici Friede, 1929. Facsimile of title-page.

WINTERICH, JOHN T. Books and the man. New York, Greenberg, 1929, pp. 193–211. Facsimile of title-page.

Goldsmith, Oliver, 1787–1861

PIERCE, LORNE. Outline of Canadian literature, pp. 62–63.

Goodrich, Samuel Griswold, 1793–1860

FULLERTON, BRADFORD M. Selective bibliography, pp. 113–14.

Goodwin, Jane Austin

See Austin, Jane (Goodwin).

Gordon, Adam Lindsay, 1833–1870

SERLE, PERCIVAL. Bibliography of Australasian poetry, pp. 77–79.

Gordon, Alexander, 1841–1931

McLACHLAN, H. Alexander Gordon . . . A biography with a bibliography. Manchester, University press, 1932. 207 pp.

Gordon, Charles William, 1860——

OVERTON, GRANT. American nights entertainment. New York, Appleton, 1923, pp. 187–88.

OVERTON, GRANT. Authors of the day. New York, Doran, [1924], pp. 109–10.

Gosse, Edmund William, (*Sir*), 1849–1931

CHARTERIS, EVAN. The life and letters of Sir Edmund Gosse. New York, Harper, 1931.

Gosson, Stephen, 1555–1624

SAWYER and DARTON. English books, v. 1, pp. 97–100.

Schoole of abuse, 1579.

SAWYER and DARTON. English books, v. 1, p. [99]. Facsimile of title-page.

Goulding, Francis Robert, 1810–1881

FULLERTON, BRADFORD M. Selective bibliography, pp. 114–15.

Grady, Henry Woodfin, 1851–1889

TERRELL, RUSSELL F. A study of the early journalistic writings of Henry W. Grady . . . Nashville, Tenn., 1927. (George Peabody college for teachers. *Contributions to education,* no. 39.) Bibliography, p. 177.

Grafton, Richard, *d.* 1572(?)

SISSON, CHARLES J. Grafton and the London Grey Friars. *Library,* s. 4, 11: [121]–49, 1931.

Grahame, Kenneth, 1859–1932

FIRST EDITION CLUB. A bibliographical catalogue, p. 74.

Grandgent, Charles Hall, 1862——

A bibliography of Charles Hall Grandgent's writings. Modern language association of America. *Publications,* 47: 911–14, 1932. Arranged chronologically.

Grant, Anne McVicar, 1755–1838

FULLERTON, BRADFORD M. Selective bibliography, pp. 115–16.

Grant, Robert, 1852——

FULLERTON, BRADFORD M. Selective bibliography, p. 116.

Gray, Thomas, 1716–1771

SAWYER and DARTON. English books, v. 1, p. 237; v. 2, pp. 3–12, 16, 381.

Elegy.

CARLTON, W. N. C. Thomas Gray's *Elegy written in a country churchyard:* a bibliographical and critical note. New York, George D. Smith, 1925. 14 pp.

CURRIE, BARTON. Fishers of books. Boston, Little, Brown and co., 1931, pp. 6–7. Facsimile of title-page.

SAWYER and DARTON. English books, v. 2, p. [2]. Facsimile of title-page.

STOKES, FRANCIS G. An elegy written in a country churchyard. The text of the first quarto with the variants of the mss. and of the early editions (1751–71), a bibliographical and historical introduction and appendices on General Wolfe and the "Elegy" and the locality of the churchyard. Oxford, Clarendon press, 1929. 98 pp. Review by Alfred W. Pollard, *Library,* s. 4, 10: 112–13, 1930.

STOKES, FRANCIS G. Gray's *Elegy:* the fourth edition. *Times literary supplement,* December 16, 1926, p. 935.

WINTERICH, JOHN T. Gray's *Elegy. Publishers' weekly,* 116: 2839–44, 1929.

Ode, 1769.

MAGGS BROTHERS. Catalogue no. 550. London, 1931. Facsimile of title-page, opp. p. 280.

Ode on a distant prospect of Eton college, 1747.

SAWYER and DARTON. English books, v. 2, p. [6]. Facsimile of title-page.

Odes, 1757.

SAWYER and DARTON. English books, v. 2, p. [10]. Facsimile of title-page.

Grayson, David, *pseud.*

See Baker, Ray Stannard.

Green, Anna Katharine

See Rohlfs, Anna Katharine (Green).

Green, Samuel Swett, 1837–1918

SHAW, ROBERT K. Samuel Swett Green. Chicago, American library association, 1926. Bibliography, pp. 83–86.

Green, Thomas, 1735–1812

BATES, ALBERT C. The work of Hartford's first printer, with a list of Thomas Green's Hartford imprints, 1764–1768. Bibliographical essays: a tribute to Wilberforce Eames.

Greene, Albert Gorton, 1802–1868

FULLERTON, BRADFORD M. Selective bibliography, pp. 116–17.

Greene, Asa, 1788–1837

FULLERTON, BRADFORD M. Selective bibliography, p. 117.

Greene, Robert, 1558–1592

GREG, WALTER W. Two Elizabethan stage abridgements: *The battle of Alcazar* and *Orlando furioso:* an essay in critical bibliography. Oxford, Clarendon press, 1923. viii+366 pp., 2 facsimiles. Review by E. K. Chambers, *Library,* s. 4, 4: 242–48, 1924.

MUSTARD, WILFRED P. Notes on Robert Greene's plays. *Modern language notes,* 40: 316–17, 1925.

SAWYER and DARTON. English books, v. 1, pp. 67, 74, 83, 96, 120; v. 2, p. 289.

Looking glass for London and England.

BASKERVILLE, CHARLES R. A prompt copy of *A looking glass for London and England. Modern philology,* 30: 29–51, 1932. Facsimiles.

Notable discovery of coosenage.

PRUVOST, R. Greene's *Notable discovery of coosenage. Times literary supplement,* October 6, 1932.

Pandosto, 1588.

SAWYER and DARTON. English books, v. 1, p. [70]. Facsimile of title-page.

See also Harvey, Gabriel.

Greene, Sarah (Pratt, McLean), 1856——

FULLERTON, BRADFORD M. Selective bibliography, pp. 117–18.

Greenlaw, Edwin Almiron, 1874——

THRALL, W. F. Publications of Edwin Greenlaw, 1899–1932. *Studies in philology,* 29: 135–40, 1932.

Gregor, Elmer Russell, 1878——

OVERTON, GRANT. Cargoes for Crusoes. New York, Appleton, [1924], pp. 250–51.

Greville, Fulke, (*Lord Brooke*)

BULLOUGH, GEOFFREY. Fulke Greville's *Workes,* 1633. *Times literary supplement,* October 15, 1931, p. 802.

Griffith, Samuel Walker, (*Sir*), 1845–1920

SERLE, PERCIVAL. Bibliography of Australasian poetry, p. 81.

Gringo, Harry, *pseud.*

See Wise, Henry Augustus.

Griswold, Rufus Wilmot, 1815–1857

FULLERTON, BRADFORD M. Selective bibliography, pp. 118–19.

Guiney, Louise Imogen, 1861–1920

FULLERTON, BRADFORD M. Selective bibliography, p. 119.

JOHNSON, MERLE. American first editions, pp. 78–79 (147–48). The check-list in the 1929 edition was compiled by Frank R. Thomas.

TENISON, EVA M. Louise Imogen Guiney, her life and works. London, Macmillan, 1923. Bibliography, pp. 297–305.

Gunter, Archibald Clavering, 1847–1907

FULLERTON, BRADFORD M. Selective bibliography, pp. 119–20.

Guthrie, Thomas Anstey, 1856——

TURNER, MARTIN J. A bibliography of the works of F. Anstey (Thomas Anstey Guthrie). London, privately printed, 1931. viii+44 pp.

H. H., *pseud.*
See Jackson, Helen (Hunt).

Habberton, John, 1842–1921
FULLERTON, BRADFORD M. Selective bibliography, p. 120.

Haggard, Rider, (*Sir*), 1856——
McKAY, GEORGE L. A bibliography of the writings of Sir Rider Haggard. London, Bookman's journal, 1931. 110 pp. Addenda slip. Review, *Books,* 7 : 19, April 26, 1931.
SHANKS, EDWARD. Sir Rider Haggard and the novel of adventure. *London Mercury,* 11 : 71–79, 1925.

Hakluyt, Richard, 1562(?)–1616
SAWYER and DARTON. English books, v. 1, p. 101.

Hale, Edward Everett, 1822–1909
FULLERTON, BRADFORD M. Selective bibliography, pp. 122–23.

Man without a country.
CURLE, RICHARD. Collecting American first editions, p. 204.

Hale, Katherine, *pseud.*
See Garvin, Amelia Beers (Warnock).

Hale, Lucretia (Peabody), 1820–1900
FULLERTON, BRADFORD M. Selective bibliography, p. 122.

Hale, Sarah Josepha (Buell), 1788–1879
FULLERTON, BRADFORD M. Selective bibliography, pp. 122–23.

Haliburton, Thomas Chandler, 1796–1865
BAKER, RAY P., *ed.* Sam Slick. New York, Doran, 1923. Bibliography, pp. 413–20.
CHITTICK, VICTOR L. O. Thomas Chandler Haliburton. ("Sam Slick") . . . New York, Columbia university press, 1925. Exhaustive bibliography, pp. 655–86.

Hall, David
See Franklin, Benjamin.

Hall, George William Louis Marshall
SERLE, PERCIVAL. Bibliography of Australasian poetry, p. 84.

Hall, Granville Stanley, 1846–1924
OVERTON, GRANT. Cargoes for Crusoes. New York, Appleton, [1924], pp. 165–66.

Hall, James, 1793–1868
FULLERTON, BRADFORD M. Selective bibliography, pp. 123–24.

Halleck, Fitz-Greene, 1795–1867
FULLERTON, BRADFORD M. Selective bibliography, pp. 124–25.

Halloran, Henry
SERLE, PERCIVAL. Bibliography of Australasian poetry, pp. 84–85.

Halpine, Charles Graham, 1829–1868
FULLERTON, BRADFORD M. Selective bibliography, p. 125.

Hamilton, Cosmo, (Cosmo Hamilton Gibbs)
OVERTON, GRANT. Cargoes for Crusoes. New York, Appleton, [1924], pp. 195–96.

Harding, Rebecca, 1831–1910
DOWNEY, FAIRFAX. Portrait of a pioneer. *Colophon,* part 12, 1932. Includes a check-list of the writings of Rebecca Harding.

Hardy, Arthur Sherburne, 1847–1930
FULLERTON, BRADFORD M. Selective bibliography, pp. 125–26.

Hardy, Thomas, 1840–1928

American Art Association. Sales catalogue. First editions of Thomas Hardy, Rudyard Kipling, Robert Louis Stevenson. The renowned collection of George Barr McCutcheon. New York, 1925.

Bliss, H. Thomas Hardy inscriptions. *Times literary supplement,* January 2, 1930, p. 12.

Brennecke, Ernest. Thomas Hardy's universe: a study of a poet's mind. London, Unwin, [1924]. Chronological list of Hardy's writings, pp. 149–50.

Chase, Mary E. Thomas Hardy from serial to novel. Minneapolis, University of Minnesota press, 1927. Bibliography of books and articles on Hardy.

Cutler and Stiles. Modern British authors, pp. 62–65.

Hardy, Florence E. The early life of Thomas Hardy, 1840–1891. Compiled largely from contemporary notes, letters, diaries, and biographical memoranda ... London, Macmillan, 1928.

Hardy, Florence E. The later years of Thomas Hardy, 1892–1928. London, Macmillan, 1930.

Hardy and other first editions. *Times literary supplement,* February 21, 1929, p. 148.

Hickson, Elizabeth C. The versification of Thomas Hardy ... Philadelphia, 1931. (Thesis, University of Pennsylvania.) Bibliography, pp. 128–29.

Hutchins, Margaret. A selected list of references on Thomas Hardy's works. *Bulletin of bibliography,* 12: 25, 51–55, 1924.

Johnson, Lionel. The art of Thomas Hardy ... to which is added a chapter on the poetry by J. E. Barton and a bibliography by John Lane ... New York, Dodd, Mead and co., 1923. "Thomas Hardy: a bibliography of first editions (1865–1922)," pp. 297–346.

Purdy, Richard L. Thomas Hardy, O.M., 1840–1928. Catalogue of a memorial exhibition of first editions, autograph letters, and manuscripts. New Haven, Yale university press, 1928. 41 pp.

TROXELL, GILBERT M. [Exhibition of first editions and manuscripts of Thomas Hardy.] Yale university library. *Gazette,* 2: 72–73, 1928.

WILLIAMS, RANDALL. The Wessex novels of Thomas Hardy: an appreciative study. London, Dent, 1924. Chronological list of Hardy's novels, p. xi.

ZACHRISSON, R. E. Thomas Hardy as man, writer, and philosopher. An appreciation with a Swedish Hardy bibliography. *Studier i modern sprakvetenskap,* 10: 131–56, 1928.

Desperate remedies, 1871.

NEWTON, A. EDWARD. This book-collecting game. Boston, Little, Brown and co., 1928. Facsimile of title-page, p. 203.

Dynasts, 1905.

PURDY, RICHARD L. A 1905 *Dynasts. Times literary supplement,* February 14, 1929, p. 118.

Notes on Stinsford church.

MAGGS BROTHERS. Catalogue no. 555. London, 1931. (Original manuscript described), p. 97.

Harington, John, (*Sir*), 1561–1612

KIRWOOD, ALBERT E. M. *The metamorphosis of Ajax* and its sequels. *Library,* s. 4, 12: [208]–34, 1932.

Harland, Marion, *pseud.*

See Terhune, Mary Virginia (Hawes).

Harper, Edith Alice Mary

See Hepburn, Edith Alice Mary (Harper).

Harper, Johannes

FIRST EDITION CLUB. A bibliographical catalogue, p. 76.

Harpur, Charles, 1817–1868

SERLE, PERCIVAL. Bibliography of Australasian poetry, p. 88.

Harris, Benjamin

MONAGHAN, FRANK. Benjamin Harris, printer, bookseller, and the first American journalist. *Colophon,* part 12, 1932.

Harris, Frank, 1855–1931

TOBIN, A. I., and GERTZ, ELMER. Frank Harris, a study in black and white. Chicago, Madelaine Mendelsohn, 1932. Bibliography, pp. 357–79.

Harris, George Washington, 1814–1869

FULLERTON, BRADFORD M. Selective bibliography, p. 126.

Harris, Joel Chandler, 1848–1908

FULLERTON, BRADFORD M. Selective bibliography, pp. 127–28.

JOHNSON, MERLE. American first editions, pp. 80–82 (149–51). The check-list in the 1929 edition was compiled by J. B. McGee.

MCGEE, J. B. American first editions: Joel Chandler Harris, 1848–1908. *Publishers' weekly,* 103: 1003–4, 1923.

Uncle Remus.

CURLE, RICHARD. Collecting American first editions, p. 204.

WINTERICH, JOHN T. Romantic stories of books. Second series. XVI. *Uncle Remus. Publishers' weekly,* 118: 2279–83, 1930.

Harrison, Susie Frances (Riley)

PIERCE, LORNE. Outline of Canadian literature, pp. 36, 90–91.

Hart, Catherine Julia

FULLERTON, BRADFORD M. Selective bibliography, p. 128.

Hart, Joseph, *d.* 1865

FULLERTON, BRADFORD M. Selective bibliography, pp. 128–29.

Harte, Francis Bret, 1839–1902

AMERICAN ART ASSOCIATION. Sales catalogue. Charles Meeker Kozlay collection. New York, 1926.

FULLERTON, BRADFORD M. Selective bibliography, pp. 129–31.

JOHNSON, MERLE. American first editions, pp. 83–86 (152–55).

STEWART, GEORGE R. Bret Harte: argonaut and exile. Boston, Houghton Mifflin co., 1932. "Chief sources," pp. 337–[340].

Condensed novels, 1867.

VAN PATTEN, NATHAN. Concerning "Condensed novels." Introduction and bibliographical notes. Stanford university, Stanford university press, 1929. xxi pp.

Luck of Roaring camp, 1870.

WINTERICH, JOHN T. Romantic stories of books. Second series. *The luck of Roaring camp. Publishers' weekly,* 117: 2639–43, 1930.

Harvey, Gabriel, 1545(?)–1630

SANDERS, CHAUNCEY. Robert Greene and the Harveys ... Bloomington, Indiana, 1931. (Indiana university. *Studies,* v. 18, *study* no. 93, 1931.) Bibliography, pp. 59–60.

Harvey, John, 1563(?)–1592

See Harvey, Gabriel.

Harvey, Richard, *d.* 1623(?)

See Harvey, Gabriel.

Harvey, William, 1578–1657

KEYNES, GEOFFREY. A bibliography of the writings of William Harvey, M.D., discoverer of the circulation of the blood. Cambridge, Cambridge university press, 1928. xii+68 pp. Review, *Library,* s. 4, 9: 417, 1929.

Hastings, Lansford Warren

Emigrants' guide to Oregon and California, 1845.

HASTINGS, LANSFORD W. *The emigrants' guide to Oregon and California* ... Reproduced in facsimile from the original edition of 1845. With historical note and a bibliography by Charles Henry Carey. Princeton, N. J., Princeton university press, 1932. Bibliography, pp. [xxiii]–xxiv.

Hastings, Warren, 1732–1818

WARD, VERA. Hastings bi-centenary: select list of printed publications. London, Royal empire society, 1932. 11 pp.

Haswell, Anthony, 1756–1816

SPARGO, JOHN. Anthony Haswell, printer, patriot-ballader. A bibliographical study with a selection of his ballads and an annotated bibliographical list of his imprints. Rutland, Vt., Tuttle, 1925. xv+293 pp.

Hawthorne, Nathaniel, 1804–1864

AMERICAN ART ASSOCIATION. Sales catalogue. Stephen H. Wakeman collection. New York, 1924. Items 261–439.

ARVIN, NEWTON. Hawthorne. Boston, Little, Brown and co., 1929. Bibliography, pp. [293]–94.

ARVIN, NEWTON, *ed.* The heart of Hawthorne's journals. Boston, Houghton Mifflin co., 1929. xiv+345 pp.

FULLERTON, BRADFORD M. Selective bibliography, pp. 131–34.

JOHNSON, MERLE. American first editions, pp. 87–89 (156–60).

STEWART, RANDALL, *ed.* The American notebooks by Nathaniel Hawthorne: based upon the original manuscripts in the Pierpont Morgan library. New Haven, Yale university press, 1932. Review by Townsend Scudder, III, *American literature,* 5: 75–79, 1934.

American note-books, 1868.

CURLE, RICHARD. Collecting American first editions, p. 147.

Blithedale romance, 1852.

CURLE, RICHARD. Collecting American first editions, p. 209.

Celestial rail-road, 1843.

AMERICAN ART ASSOCIATION. Sales catalogue. Stephen H. Wakeman collection. New York, 1924. Items 286 and 287. Facsimiles of title-pages.

CURLE, RICHARD. Collecting American first editions, pp. 59, 126–27.

Famous old people, 1841.

CURLE, RICHARD. Collecting American first editions, p. 172.

Fanshawe, 1828.

AMERICAN ART ASSOCIATION. Sales catalogue. Stephen H. Wakeman collection. New York, 1924. Item 264. Facsimile of title-page.

CURLE, RICHARD. Collecting American first editions, p. 181.

CURRIE, BARTON. Fishers of books. Boston, Little, Brown and co., 1931. Facsimile of title-page, p. 115.

STARRETT, VINCENT. Pennywise and book foolish. New York, Covici Friede, 1929. Facsimile of title-page, p. 82.

French and Italian note-books, 1871 and 1872.

CURLE, RICHARD. Collecting American first editions, p. 187.

Grandfather's chair, 1841.

CURLE, RICHARD. Collecting American first editions, p. 172.

House of seven gables, 1851.

CURLE, RICHARD. Collecting American first editions, pp. 17–18.

Liberty tree, 1841.

CURLE, RICHARD. Collecting American first editions, p. 172.

Life of Franklin Pierce, 1852.

CURLE, RICHARD. Collecting American first editions, p. 104.

WINTERICH, JOHN T. Good second-hand condition. (Hawthorne's *Life of Franklin Pierce,* 1852.) *Publishers' weekly,* 121 : 2423–24, 1932.

Hawthorne, Nathaniel (*Continued*)

Marble faun, 1860.

CURLE, RICHARD. Collecting American first editions, p. 149.

REENAN, WILLIAM L. Hawthorne's *Marble faun. Times literary supplement,* October 9, 1930, p. 810.

Mosses from an old manse, 1846.

CURLE, RICHARD. Collecting American first editions, pp. 58, 154–55.

Our old home, 1863.

CURLE, RICHARD. Collecting American first editions, p. 19.

Pansie, 1864.

CURLE, RICHARD. Collecting American first editions, p. 186.

Peter Parley's history, 1837.

CURLE, RICHARD. Collecting American first editions, p. 208.

Scarlet letter, 1850.

CURLE, RICHARD. Collecting American first editions, pp. 14, 45–49, 105, 198. Facsimile of title-page, opp. p. 48.

DARLEY, F. O. C. Forgotten pictures for famous book, *The scarlet letter.* Drawings by F. O. C. Darley. *Century,* 108: 219–24, 1924.

WINTERICH, JOHN T. Books and the man. New York, Greenberg, 1929, pp. 212–29. Facsimile of title-page, p. 225.

Sister years, 1839.

CURLE, RICHARD. Collecting American first editions, p. 172.

Snow image, 1851 and 1852.

CURLE, RICHARD. Collecting American first editions, p. 187.

Spectator.

CHANDLER, E. L. Hawthorne's *Spectator. New England quarterly,* 4: 289–330, 1931.

Tanglewood tales, 1853.

CURLE, RICHARD. Collecting American first editions, pp. 16, 149.

Times' portraiture, 1838 and 1853.

CURLE, RICHARD. Collecting American first editions, pp. 171–72.

Transformation, 1860.

CURLE, RICHARD. Collecting American first editions, pp. 185–86.

True stories, 1851.

CURLE, RICHARD. Collecting American first editions, p. 6.

Twice-told tales, 1837 and 1842.

CURLE, RICHARD. Collecting American first editions, pp. 5, 147, 196.

NEWTON, A. EDWARD. This book-collecting game. Boston, Little, Brown and co., 1928, p. 280.

Wonder book, 1852.

CURLE, RICHARD. Collecting American first editions, p. 149.

Hay, John, 1838–1905

FULLERTON, BRADFORD M. Selective bibliography, pp. 134–35.

JOHNSON, MERLE. American first editions, pp. 90–91 (161–62).

Hayes, Henry, *pseud.*

See Kirk, Ellen Warner (Olney).

Hayne, Paul Hamilton, 1830–1886

FULLERTON, BRADFORD M. Selective bibliography, pp. 135–36.

Hayward, John, (*Sir*), 1564–1627

DOWLING, MARGARET. Sir John Hayward's troubles over his life of Henry IV. *Library,* s. 4, 11 : [212]–24, 1931.

Hazlitt, William, 1778–1830

FIRST EDITION CLUB. A bibliographical catalogue, p. 77.

KEYNES, GEOFFREY. Bibliography of William Hazlitt. London, Nonesuch press, 1931. xix+135 pp., facsimiles.

New and approved grammar of the English tongue, 1810.

KEYNES, GEOFFREY. Hazlitt's *Grammar* abridged. *Library,* s. 4, 13: [97]–98, 1933.

Head, H.

SERLE, PERCIVAL. Bibliography of Australasian poetry, p. 90.

Hearn, Lafcadio, 1850–1904

FULLERTON, BRADFORD M. Selective bibliography, pp. 136–37.

JOHNSON, MERLE. American first editions, pp. 92–95 (163–66).

PERKINS, P. D. (Exhaustive bibliography announced by Mr. P. D. Perkins of Montebello, California.) *See* Johnson, Merle. American first editions, 1929 ed., p. 166.

Heavysege, Charles, 1816–1879

PIERCE, LORNE. Outline of Canadian literature, pp. 63–64.

Hebblethwaite, James, 1857–1921

SERLE, PERCIVAL. Bibliography of Australasian poetry, p. 91.

Hecht, Ben, 1893——

JOHNSON, MERLE. American first editions, pp. 96–97 (167–68). The check-list in the 1929 edition was compiled by Vrest Orton.

Hemingway, Ernest, 1898——

COHN, LOUIS H. A bibliography of the works of Ernest Hemingway. New York, Random house, 1931. 116 pp. Review by Percy H. Muir, *Book-collector's quarterly,* no. 6, April–June, 1932, pp. 83–84.

JOHNSON, MERLE. American first editions, pp. (169–70).

JOHNSON, MERLE. American first editions: Ernest Hemingway, 1898——. *Publishers' weekly,* 121:870, 1932.

ORTON, VREST. Some notes bibliographical and otherwise on the books of Ernest Hemingway. *Publishers' weekly,* 117:884–86, 1930.

Henley, William Ernest, 1849–1903

See entry under Savage, Richard.

Henry, O., *pseud.*

See Porter, William Sidney.

Henryson, Robert, 1430(?)–1506(?)

Testament of Cresseid.

DICKINS, BRUCE, *ed. The testament of Cresseid.* London, Porpoise press, 1925. Bibliographical note.

Henschel, George, (*Sir*), 1850——

FIRST EDITION CLUB. Bibliographical check-list, p. 78.

Hentz, Nicholas Marcellus, 1797–1856

FULLERTON, BRADFORD M. Selective bibliography, p. 137.

Hepburn, Edith Alice Mary (Harper)

SERLE, PERCIVAL. Bibliography of Australasian poetry, p. 87.

Herbert, Henry William, 1807–1858

JOHNSON, MERLE. American first editions, pp. (171–74).

RANDALL, DAVID A. A "Frank Forester" checklist. *Publishers' weekly,* 122:276, 1932. Notes on Seybolt's check-list.

RITTER-HOPSON GALLERIES. Sales catalogue. Sporting books from the library of Harry Worcester Smith, together with his Henry William Herbert (Frank Forester) collection. New York, 1931.

SEYBOLT, PAUL S. First editions of Henry William Herbert, Frank Forester, 1807–1858: a check-list. Medford, Mass., privately printed, 1932. 16 pp.

Hergesheimer, Joseph, 1880——

DRAKE, MARSTON E. American first editions: Joseph Hergesheimer, 1880——. *Publishers' weekly,* 104: 1453, 1923. Corrections to the check-list in same journal, 102: 2221, 1922.

JOHNSON, MERLE. American first editions, pp. 100–101 (175–77). The check-list in the 1929 edition was compiled by Marston E. Drake.

Herrick, Robert, 1591–1674

SAWYER and DARTON. English books, v. 1, pp. 187–89.

Hesperides, 1648.

SAWYER and DARTON. English books, v. 1, p. [198]. Facsimile of title-page.

Hervey, Elizabeth

SADLEIR, MICHAEL. Elizabeth Hervey and some anonymous novels. *Notes and queries,* 153: 350, 1927.

Hewlett, Maurice Henry, 1861–1923

CUTLER and STILES. Modern British authors, pp. 66–68.

MUIR, PERCY H. A bibliography of the first editions of books by Maurice Henry Hewlett (1861–1923). Bibliographies of modern authors. Third series. London, Bookman's journal, 1931, pp. 9–36.

MUIR, PERCY H. Addenda & corrigenda to the bibliography of Maurice Hewlett. 4 pp. (Insert in above work.)

Heywood, Jasper, 1535–1598

GREG, WALTER W. Notes on early plays. Seneca's *Troas* translated by Jasper Heywood. *Library,* s. 4, 11: [162]–72, 1931.

Heywood, John, 1497(?)–1580(?)

SAWYER and DARTON. English books, v. 1, pp. 59, 136–37.

See also Medwall, Henry.

Heywood, Thomas, *d.* 1650(?)

CLARK, ARTHUR M. Thos. Heywood. Oxford bibliographical society. *Proceedings and papers,* 1: 97–155, 1924.

CROMWELL, OTELIA. Thomas Heywood. A study of the Elizabethan dramas of everyday life. New Haven, Yale university press, 1929.

GREG, WALTER W. *The escapes of Jupiter:* an autograph play of Thomas Heywood's. *Anglica,* 2: [211]–43, 1925.

Higginson, Thomas Wentworth, 1823–1911

FULLERTON, BRADFORD M. Selective bibliography, pp. 137–38.

Hildreth, Richard, 1807–1865

FULLERTON, BRADFORD M. Selective bibliography, pp. 138–39.

Hill, George, 1796–1871

FULLERTON, BRADFORD M. Selective bibliography, p. 139.

Hirst, Henry Beck, 1813–1874

FULLERTON, BRADFORD M. Selective bibliography, pp. 139–40.

Hitchcock, Enos, 1744–1803

FULLERTON, BRADFORD M. Selective bibliography, p. 140.

Hodges, George, 1856–1919

HODGES, JULIA S. George Hodges: a biography. New York, Century, [1926]. Bibliography, pp. 239–42.

Hodgson, Ralph

FIRST EDITION CLUB. A bibliographical catalogue, p. 79.

Hoffman, Charles Fenno, 1806–1884

FULLERTON, BRADFORD M. Selective bibliography, pp. 140–41.

Hogg, James, 1770–1835

HOGG, WILLIAM D. The first editions of the writings of James Hogg, The Ettrick shepherd. Edinburgh bibliographical society. *Papers,* 12: 53–68, 1924.

Holland, Josiah Gilbert, 1819–1881
FULLERTON, BRADFORD M. Selective bibliography, pp. 141–42.

Holley, Marietta, 1844–1926
FULLERTON, BRADFORD M. Selective bibliography, pp. 142–43.

Hollyband, Claudius
Italian schoole-maister, 1597.
MAGGS BROTHERS. Catalogue no. 550. London, 1931. Facsimile of title-page, opp. p. 169.

Holmes, Mary Jane (Howe), 1839–1907
FULLERTON, BRADFORD M. Selective bibliography, p. 143.

Holmes, Oliver Wendell, 1809–1894
AMERICAN ART ASSOCIATION. Sales catalogue. Stephen H. Wakeman collection. New York, 1924. Items 440–621.
FULLERTON, BRADFORD M. Selective bibliography, pp. 144–46.
JOHNSON, MERLE. American first editions, pp. 102–3 (178–84).

Astraea, 1850.
CURLE, RICHARD. Collecting American first editions, pp. 58, 139.

Autocrat of the breakfast table, 1858 and 1859.
CURLE, RICHARD. Collecting American first editions, pp. 9–10, 19, 29, 149, 157, 163–66, 174, 178–79.

Bunker Hill memorial, 1875.
CURLE, RICHARD. Collecting American first editions, pp. 67–68.

Contagiousness of puerperal fever, 1843.
CURLE, RICHARD. Collecting American first editions, p. 194.

Currents and counter currents, 1860.
CURLE, RICHARD. Collecting American first editions, p. 171.

Dorothy Q., 1893.

CURLE, RICHARD. Collecting American first editions, p. 192.

Elsie Venner, 1861.

CURLE, RICHARD. Collecting American first editions, p. 11.

Guardian angel, 1867.

CURLE, RICHARD. Collecting American first editions, pp. 209–10.

Harbinger, 1833.

CURLE, RICHARD. Collecting American first editions, p. 182.

Harvard sonnets, 1878.

AMERICAN ART ASSOCIATION. Sales catalogue. Stephen H. Wakeman collection. New York, 1924. Item 549. Facsimile of broadside.

CURLE, RICHARD. Collecting American first editions, p. 172.

Illustrations of Athenaeum gallery, 1830.

CURLE, RICHARD. Collecting American first editions, pp. 181–82.

James Russell Lowell, 1891.

CURLE, RICHARD. Collecting American first editions, p. 172.

John Lothrop Motley, 1879.

CURLE, RICHARD. Collecting American first editions, pp. 75, 134–35.

Mechanism in thought and morals, 1871.

CURLE, RICHARD. Collecting American first editions, p. 171.

Medical essays, 1883.

CURLE, RICHARD. Collecting American first editions, p. 137.

One hoss shay, 1892.

CURLE, RICHARD. Collecting American first editions, p. 192.

Oration, 1863.

AMERICAN ART ASSOCIATION. Sales catalogue. Stephen H. Wakeman collection. New York, 1924. Item 499. Facsimile of title-page.

Holmes, Oliver Wendell (*Continued*)

Over the teacups, 1890 and 1891.
CURLE, RICHARD. Collecting American first editions, pp. 6, 20–21, 60, 187.

Poems, 1836, 1846, and 1849.
CURLE, RICHARD. Collecting American first editions, pp. 88, 102–3, 147, 183, 190–92.

Poet at the breakfast table, 1872.
CURLE, RICHARD. Collecting American first editions, pp. 6, 156–57.

Professor at the breakfast table, 1860.
CURLE, RICHARD. Collecting American first editions, pp. 102–3, 111–12, 157.

Puerperal fever, 1855.
CURLE, RICHARD. Collecting American first editions, p. 194.

Songs in many keys, 1862.
CURLE, RICHARD. Collecting American first editions, p. 17.

Songs of many seasons, 1875.
CURLE, RICHARD. Collecting American first editions, p. 210.

Songs of the class of MDCCCXXIX, 1854.
AMERICAN ART ASSOCIATION. Sales catalogue. Stephen H. Wakeman collection. New York, 1924. Item 471. Facsimile of title-page.
CURLE, RICHARD. Collecting American first editions, p. 208.

Soundings from the Atlantic, 1864.
CURLE, RICHARD. Collecting American first editions, p. 15.

To Christian Gottfried Ehrenberg, 1868.
CURLE, RICHARD. Collecting American first editions, p. 172.

Home, John, 1722–1808
MACMILLAN, DUGALD. The first editions of Home's *Douglas. Studies in philology,* 26: 401–9. 1929.

Honeywood, St. John, 1763–1798

Poems, 1801.

(*Poems,* by St. John Honeywood, New York, 1801.) *Book-collector's packet,* no. 3, p. 16, 1932. Facsimile of title-page.

Hook, Theodore Edward, 1788–1841

BRIGHTFIELD, MYRON F. Theodore Hook and his novels. Cambridge, Harvard university press, 1928. Bibliography, pp. [365]–72.

Hookes, Nathaniel, 1628–1712

SAWYER and DARTON. English books, v. 1, pp. 208–9.

Hookes, Nicholas

See Hookes, Nathaniel.

Hooper, Johnson J., 1815–1863

FULLERTON, BRADFORD M. Selective bibliography, p. 146.

Hopkinson, Francis, 1737–1791

FULLERTON, BRADFORD M. Selective bibliography, p. 147.

HASTINGS, GEORGE E. The life and works of Francis Hopkinson. Chicago, University of Chicago press, [1926]. Bibliography, pp. 481–96.

Hopkinson, Joseph, 1770–1842

FULLERTON, BRADFORD M. Selective bibliography, p. 148.

Horman, William, *d.* 1535

Vulgaria, 1519.

JAMES, MONTAGUE, *ed.* Vulgaria. First printed by Richard Pynson in 1519. Now reprinted with an introduction by . . . London, Roxburghe club, 1926. Appendix, list of works by Horman. Review by Alfred W. Pollard, *Library,* s. 4, 7 : 131–33, 1927.

Hoskyns, Charles Wren

FUSSELL, G. E. Charles Wren Hoskyns. *Notes and queries,* 153 : 42–44, 1927. Bibliography, p. 44.

Hough, Emerson, 1857–1923

OVERTON, GRANT. Cargoes for Crusoes. New York, Appleton, [1924], pp. 245–46.

SMITH, EDWARD L. American first editions: Emerson Hough, 1857–1923. *Publishers' weekly,* 105: 173–74, 1924.

Housman, Laurence, 1865——

FIRST EDITION CLUB. A bibliographical catalogue, p. 80.

RUDOLF, ANNA. Die Dichtung von Laurence Housman. Breslau, 1930. 93 pp. "Anna Rudolf has discovered that he has produced no less than eighty publications . . ."—*Year's work in English studies,* 12: 297, 1931.

Hovey, Richard, 1864–1900

FULLERTON, BRADFORD M. Selective bibliography, pp. 148–49.

JOHNSON, MERLE. American first editions, pp. 105–6 (185–86). The check-list in the 1929 edition was compiled by Vrest Orton.

Howard, Henry, (*Earl of Surrey*), 1517(?)–1547

SAWYER and DARTON. English books, v. 1, pp. 80–81.

Howe, Edgar Watson, 1853——

FULLERTON, BRADFORD M. Selective bibliography, pp. 149–50.

Story of a country town, 1883.

(*Story of a country town,* Atchison, Kansas, 1883.) *The month at Goodspeed's,* 3: 12–14, 1931. Facsimile of title-page.

Howe, Julia Ward, 1819–1910

Later lyrics, 1866.

CURLE, RICHARD. Collecting American first editions, p. 179.

Howell, James, 1594(?)–1666

VANN, WILLIAM H. Notes on the writings of James Howell. Waco, Texas, Baylor university press, 1924. iv+71 pp.

Howells, William Dean, 1837–1920

FIRKINS, OSCAR W. William Dean Howells, a study. Cambridge, Harvard university press, 1924. Bibliography, pp. [337]–46.

FULLERTON, BRADFORD M. Selective bibliography, pp. 151–52.

JOHNSON, MERLE. American first editions, pp. 107–11 (187–91). The check-list in the 1929 edition was compiled by Vrest Orton.

Rise of Silas Lapham, 1885.

CURLE, RICHARD. Collecting American first editions, pp. 12, 204.

Hubbard, Elbert, 1859–1915

FULLERTON, BRADFORD M. Selective bibliography, pp. 152–53.

Message to Garcia, 1899.

VAIL, R. W. G. *A message to Garcia.* A bibliographical puzzle. New York public library. *Bulletin,* 34: 71–78, 1930. Facsimile of title-page.

Hudson, Stephen, *pseud.,* (Sydney Schiff)

GAWSWORTH, JOHN, *pseud.,* (T. Fytton Armstrong). Ten contemporaries: notes toward their definitive bibliography. First series. London, Benn, 1932.

Hudson, William Henry, 1841–1922

AMERICAN ART ASSOCIATION. Sales catalogue. The Edward Garnett collection. Inscribed books and autograph material of Joseph Conrad and W. H. Hudson. New York, 1928.

CUTLER and STILES. Modern British authors, pp. 69–71.

Hughes, Edward Francis

SERLE, PERCIVAL. Bibliography of Australasian poetry, p. 99.

Hughes, Lewis, *fl.* 1620

COLE, GEORGE W. Lewis Hughes, the militant minister of the Bermudas, and his printed works. Worcester, Mass., American antiquarian society, 1928. 67 pp.

Hughes, Thomas, 1822–1896

SAWYER and DARTON. English books, v. 1, pp. 118–19.

Humphreys, David, 1752–1818

FULLERTON, BRADFORD M. Selective bibliography, p. 153.

Huneker, James Gibbons, 1860–1921

DECASSERES, BENJAMIN. James Gibbons Huneker. New York, Lawren, 1925. Bibliography by Joseph Lawren.

HAUNTED BOOKSHOP. American first editions: James Huneker, 1860–1921. *Publishers' weekly,* 104: 173, 1923.

JOHNSON, MERLE. American first editions, pp. 112–13 (192–93).

Hunt, James Henry Leigh, 1784–1859

BREWER, LUTHER A. Leigh Hunt and Charles Dickens: the Skimpole caricatures. Cedar Rapids, Iowa, 1930.

BREWER, LUTHER A. Marginalia. Cedar Rapids, Iowa, 1932. An account of his collection of Leigh Hunt.

BREWER, LUTHER A. My Leigh Hunt library. Cedar Rapids, Iowa, 1932. Relates to the first editions.

BREWER, LUTHER A. Some letters from my Leigh Hunt portfolio, with brief comment. Cedar Rapids, Iowa, 1929. 96 pp.

MILFORD, HUMPHREY S., *ed.* The poetical works of Leigh Hunt. London, Oxford university press, [1923]. A chronological bibliography of the poetry of Leigh Hunt, pp. [736]–65.

MITCHELL, ALEXANDER. A bibliography of Leigh Hunt. *Bookman's journal,* s. 3, 18: 41–72, 1931.

MITCHELL, ALEXANDER. A bibliography of the writings of Leigh Hunt. With critical notes. Bibliographies of modern authors. Third series. London, Bookman's journal, 1931, pp. 9–73.

Huxley, Aldous Leonard, 1894——

CUTLER and STILES. Modern British authors, pp. 72–73.

FIRST EDITION CLUB. A bibliographical catalogue, pp. [81]–88.

MUIR, PERCY H., and VAN THAL, B. Bibliographies of the first editions of the books of Aldous Huxley and T. F. Powys. London, Dulau, 1927. 61 pp.

OVERTON, GRANT. Cargoes for Crusoes. New York, Appleton, [1924], p. 113.

SCHWARTZ, H. WARREN. Check-lists of twentieth-century authors. Second series. Milwaukee, Wis., Casanova booksellers, 1933.

Imlay, Gilbert, *fl.* 1755–1796

EMERSON, OLIVER F. Notes on Gilbert Imlay, early American writer. Modern language association of America. *Publications,* 39: 406–39, 1925. IV. The published works of Gilbert Imlay, pp. 431–39.

Ingraham, Joseph Holt, 1809–1860

FULLERTON, BRADFORD M. Selective bibliography, pp. 153–54.

SEITZ, DON C. A prince of best sellers. *Publishers' weekly,* 119: 940, 1931.

Ireland, Samuel

See Ireland, William Henry.

Ireland, William Henry, 1777–1835

Bodde, D. Shakespeare and the Ireland forgeries. Cambridge, Harvard university press, 1930. 68 pp. Bibliography, pp. 67–68.

Cock, F. William. William H. Ireland. *Notes and queries,* 148: 447, 1925.

French, Joseph L. The book of the rogue: studies of famous scoundrels. New York, Boni and Liveright, 1926. Contains an account of William H. Ireland and his Shakespearian forgeries.

Libbis, G. Hilder. Notes on Samuel and William H. Ireland and the Shakespeare fabrications. *Notes and queries,* 160: 201–4, 219–21, 1931; 162: 236–39, 273–76, 1932.

Libbis, G. Hilder. Samuel Ireland. *Notes and queries,* 148: 408, 1925.

Libbis, G. Hilder. William H. Ireland. *Notes and queries,* 148: 408, 1925.

Libbis, G. Hilder. William Henry Ireland. (Catalogue of works.) *Notes and queries,* 162: 347–50, 1932.

Smith, G. C. M. Bennet Langton and the Ireland forgeries. *Notes and queries,* 162: 367–68, 1932.

Irvine, Gerard Addington D'Arcy

Serle, Percival. Bibliography of Australasian poetry, p. 102.

Irving, John Treat, Jr., 1812–1905

Fullerton, Bradford M. Selective bibliography, p. 154.

Irving, Washington, 1783–1859

Birss, John H. New verses by Washington Irving. *American literature,* 4: 296, 1933.

Catalogue of the Seligman collection of Irvingiana. New York public library. *Bulletin,* 30: 83–109, 1926.

Fullerton, Bradford M. Selective bibliography, pp. 155–58.

GOGGIO, EMILIO. Washington Irving's works in Italy. *Romanic review,* 22: 301–3, 1931.

HELLMAN, GEORGE S. Washington Irving, esq., ambassador from the new world to the old ... New York, Knopf, 1925. Makes use of much new material. The entire work is of considerable bibliographical interest.

JOHNSON, MERLE. American first editions, pp. 114–16 (194–96).

LANGFIELD, WILLIAM R. The poems of Washington Irving brought together from various sources and for the first time. New York public library. *Bulletin,* 34: 763–79, 1930.

LANGFIELD, WILLIAM R. Washington Irving—a bibliography. New York public library. *Bulletin,* 36: 415–22, 487–94, 561–71, 627–36, 683–89, 755–78, 828–41, 1932.

MABBOTT, THOMAS O. An unwritten drama. *American collector,* 1: 64–66, 1926.

VAIL, R. W. G. The Hellman collection of Irvingiana. New York public library. *Bulletin,* 33: 207–19, 1929.

WILLIAMS, STANLEY T. The first version of the writings of Washington Irving in Spanish. *Modern philology,* 28: 185–201, 1931.

WILLIAMS, STANLEY T. The Irving manuscripts. Yale university library. *Gazette,* 1: 35–38, 1927.

Alhambra, 1832.

CURLE, RICHARD. Collecting American first editions, p. 112.

Astoria, 1836.

CURLE, RICHARD. Collecting American first editions, p. 63.

Christopher Columbus, 1828.

CURLE, RICHARD. Collecting American first editions, p. 34.

Conquest of Granada, 1829.

CURLE, RICHARD. Collecting American first editions, p. 112.

Irving, Washington (*Continued*)

Crayon miscellany, 1835.

CURLE, RICHARD. Collecting American first editions, p. 34.

History of New York, 1809.

CURLE, RICHARD. Collecting American first editions, p. 207.

WEBSTER, CLARENCE M. Irving's expurgation of the 1809 *History of New York. American literature,* 4: 293–95, 1933.

James Lawrence.

BLACKBURN, P. C. Irving's biography of James Lawrence. New York public library. *Bulletin,* 36: 742–43, 1932.

Life of Washington, 1855–1859.

CURLE, RICHARD. Collecting American first editions, p. 210.

Salmagundi, 1807–1808.

CURLE, RICHARD. Collecting American first editions, pp. 153, 194.

Sketch book, 1819–1820.

CURLE, RICHARD. Collecting American first editions, pp. 153–54.

WINTERICH, JOHN T. Books and the man. New York, Greenberg, 1929, pp. 291–309. Facsimile of title-page of first edition.

Tales of a traveller, 1824.

CURLE, RICHARD. Collecting American first editions, p. 153.

Wolfert's roost, 1855.

ADKINS, NELSON F. Irving's *Wolfert's roost.* A bibliographical note. *Notes and queries,* 164: 42, 1933. Two additions to Langfield's bibliography.

CURLE, RICHARD. Collecting American first editions, p. 210.

Jackson, Helen Maria (Fiske, Hunt), 1831–1885

FULLERTON, BRADFORD M. Selective bibliography, pp. 158–59.

Jackson, Thomas Jonathan (Stonewall), 1824–1863

TATE, ALLEN. Stonewall Jackson. The good soldier. New York, Minton, Balch and co., 1928. Bibliography, pp. 321–22.

Jacobi, Mary (Putnam), 1842–1906

PUTNAM, RUTH, *ed.* Life and letters, foreword by G. H. Putnam. New York, Putnam, 1925. List of scientific and other writings, pp. 347–54.

James, Henry, 1811–1882

GRATTAN, CLINTON H. The three Jameses: a family of minds, Henry James, sr., William James, Henry James. New York, Longmans, Green and co., 1932. Bibliographical notes, pp. 369–73.

James, Henry, 1843–1916

EDEL, LÉON. A note on translations of Henry James in France. *Revue anglo-américaine,* 7: 539–40, 1930.

FULLERTON, BRADFORD M. Selective bibliography, pp. 159–61.

GOMME, LAURENCE. American first editions: Henry James, 1843–1916. *Publishers' weekly,* 104: 498–99, 1923.

JOHNSON, MERLE. American first editions, pp. 117–20 (197–201). The check-list in the 1929 edition was compiled by Laurence Gomme.

PHILLIPS, LEROY. Bibliography of the writings of Henry James. New York, Coward-McCann, 1930. 285 pp. Review by Percy H. Muir, *Book-collector's quarterly,* no. 1, December, 1930–February, 1931, pp. 41–44.

ROBERTS, MORRIS. Henry James's criticism. Cambridge, Harvard university press, 1930. Bibliography, pp. [121–25].

WALBROOK, H. M. The novels of Henry James. *Fortnightly review,* 127: 680–91, 1930.

See also James, Henry, 1811–1882.

James, Will (William Roderick), 1892——

JOHNSON, MERLE. American first editions, p. (202).

James, William, 1842–1882

See James, Henry, 1811–1882.

Jefferies, Richard, 1848–1887

CARTER, JOHN. Binding variants in English publishing, 1820–1900. London, Constable, 1932.

Jeffers, John Robinson, 1887——

ALBERTS, SYDNEY S. A bibliography of the works of Robinson Jeffers. New York, Random house, 1933. 262 pp., facsimiles.

JEFFERS, ROBINSON. An artist. [Austin, Texas], privately printed by John S. Mayfield, [1928]. Bibliography by R. H. Griffith, p. 14.

JEFFERS, ROBINSON. First book. *Colophon,* part 10, 1932. 8 pp.

JOHNSON, MERLE. American first editions, p. (203).

POWELL, LAWRENCE C. An introduction to Robinson Jeffers . . . Dijon, Imprimerie Bernigaud & Privat, 1932. xvii+248 pp. Bibliography, p. [241].

Jemison, Mary, 1743–1883

Captivities.

[*Captivities.*] *The month at Goodspeed's,* 3 : 186–91, 1932.

STRECKER, FREDERICK. My first years as a Jemisonian. *Colophon,* no. 7, 1931.

Taken by the Indians. *The month at Goodspeed's,* 3 : 163–68, 1932.

Jephson, Robert, 1736–1803

PETERSON, MARTIN S. Robert Jephson (1736–1803). A study of his life and works. Lincoln, Nebraska, 1930. (University of Nebraska. *Studies in language, literature, and criticism,* no. 11.) Bibliography, pp. 44–45.

Jespersen, Otto, 1860——

A grammatical miscellany offered to Otto Jespersen on his seventieth birthday. Copenhagen, Levin and Munksgaard, 1930. Bibliography by Otto Bodelsen, pp. 433–57.

Jewett, Sarah Orne, 1849–1909

FULLERTON, BRADFORD M. Selective bibliography, pp. 161–62.

JOHNSON, MERLE. American first editions, pp. 121–22 (204–5). The check-list in the 1929 edition was compiled by Vrest Orton.

MATTHIESSEN, FRANCIS O. Sarah Orne Jewett. Boston, Houghton Mifflin co., 1929.

Johnson, Andrew, 1808–1875

BEALE, HOWARD K. The critical year: a study of Andrew Johnson and reconstruction. New York, Harcourt, Brace and co., [1930]. Bibliography, pp. 407–35.

STRYCKER, LLOYD P. Andrew Johnson: a study in courage. New York, Macmillan, 1929. "Authorities," pp. 838–44.

Johnson, Charles, 1649–1748

GOSSE, PHILIP. A bibliography of the works of Capt. Charles Johnson. London, Dulau, 1927. 80 pp.

Johnson, E. Pauline, 1862–1913

PIERCE, LORNE. Outline of Canadian literature, pp. 78–81.

Johnson, Lionel Pigot, 1867–1902

FIRST EDITION CLUB. A bibliographical catalogue, pp. 89–90.

JOHNSON, LIONEL. [Poems]. London, Benn, [1932]. Bibliography, page at end.

Johnson, Richard Malcolm, 1822–1898

FULLERTON, BRADFORD M. Selective bibliography, pp. 162–63.

Johnson, Samuel, 1709–1784

ADAM, ROBERT B. The R. B. Adam library relating to Dr. Samuel Johnson and his era. New York, Oxford university press, 1929. 3 v. *Contents:* I. Letters of Samuel Johnson, James Boswell, Edmund Burke, Joshua Reynolds, and David Garrick. II. Catalogue of books. III. Miscellaneous autograph letters.

CHAPMAN, ROBERT W. Johnsonian bibliography. *Colophon,* part 12, 1932.

CHAPMAN, ROBERT W. Proposals for a new edition of Johnson's letters. *Essays and studies by members of the English association.* Oxford, 1926, v. 12, pp. 47–62.

CHAPMAN, ROBERT W., *ed. Proposals for the publisher,* 1744. Now printed in facsimile and for the first time ascribed to Samuel Johnson. London, Oxford university press, 1930. 6 pp.

COURTNEY, WILLIAM P., and SMITH, DAVID N. A bibliography of Samuel Johnson. Oxford, Clarendon press, 1925. viii+186 pp. A re-issue of the edition of 1915. Review, *Library,* s. 4, 6 : 201–2, 1926.

ELKIN MATHEWS, LTD. A catalogue of books by or relating to Dr. Johnson & members of his circle offered for sale by Elkin Mathews, ltd. With an introduction by John Drinkwater. London, 1925. vi+110 pp. (Compiled by A. W. Evans.)

GRAY, W. FORBES. Dr. Johnson's publisher. *Fortnightly review,* 135 : 245–50, 1931.

HEYMAN, HARALD. Samuel Johnsons till Svenska, med bibliografi, inlendning, anmärkningar, och register. Första delen: 1709–1753. Stockholm, Albert Bonneirs Förlag, 1926. Review by Frederick A. Pottle, *Saturday review of literature,* 3 : 826, 1927.

Johnson and Burns. *Times literary supplement,* June 13, 1929, p. 480.

Johnsoniana. *Times literary supplement,* January 29, 1931. p. 84.

LANSDOWNE, HENRY WILLIAM, (*Sixth Marquis*), *ed.* Johnson and Queeney: letters from Dr. Johnson to Queeney Thrale, from the Bowood papers . . . London, Cassell, 1932. xxxiv+64 pp.

NEWTON, A. EDWARD. Mr. Strahan's dinner party, a comedy. San Francisco, Book club of California, 1930. 64 pp.

SAWYER and DARTON. English books, v. 1, p. 366.

STRUBLE, MILDRED C. Johnson handbook. New York, Crofts, 1933. xi+353 pp.

TYSON, MOSES, and GUPPY, HENRY, *eds.* French journals of Mrs. Thrale and Dr. Johnson: edited from the original mss. in the John Rylands library and the British museum. Manchester, Manchester university press, 1932. xi+274 pp.

TYSON, MOSES. Unpublished manuscripts, papers, and letters of Dr. Johnson, Mrs. Thrale, and their friends, in the John Rylands library. John Rylands library. *Bulletin,* 15: 467–88, 1931.

WILLIAMS, IOLO A. The elusive Mr. Johnson. *Book-collector's quarterly,* no. 7, July–September, 1932, pp. 53–59.

WRIGHT, J. D., *ed.* Some unpublished letters to and from Samuel Johnson. Manchester, Manchester university press, 1932. 55 pp.

English dictionary, 1755.

SAWYER and DARTON. English books, v. 1, p. [348]. Facsimile of title-page.

WINTERICH, JOHN T. Books and the man. New York, Greenberg, 1929, pp. 230–50. Facsimile of title-page.

Johnson, Samuel (*Continued*)

Journey to the western islands, 1775.

CHAPMAN, ROBERT W. Johnson's *Journey,* 1775. Bibliographical notes concerning three editions of 1775 with identical title-pages.

MCKINLAY, ROBERT. Some notes on Dr. Johnson's *Journey to the western islands.* Glasgow bibliographical society. *Records,* 7(pt. 2): 144–50, 1930.

Life of Savage, 1744.

SAWYER and DARTON. English books, v. 1, p. 293. Facsimile of title-page.

Lives of the English poets, 1781.

MAGGS BROTHERS. Catalogue no. 550. London, 1931. Facsimile of the rare leaf of printed labels, opp. p. 360.

London, 1738.

MAGGS BROTHERS. Catalogue no. 550. London, 1931. Facsimile of title-page, opp. p. 361.

SAWYER and DARTON. English books, v. 1, p. 286. Facsimile of title-page.

Preface to his edition of Shakespeare's plays, 1765.

MAGGS BROTHERS. Catalogue no. 550. London, 1931. Facsimile of title-page, opp. p. 376.

Proposals for his edition of Shakespeare, 1765.

SAWYER and DARTON. English books, v. 1, p. [344]. Facsimile of title-page.

Rasselas, 1759.

CHAPMAN, ROBERT W., *ed.* The history of Rasselas, Prince of Abissinia. A tale. Oxford, Clarendon press, 1927. Introduction contains bibliographical notes.

SAWYER and DARTON. English books, v. 1, p. 359. Facsimile of title-page.

TINKER, CHAUNCEY B. *Rasselas* in the new world. New Haven, Yale university press, 1925. 31 pp. Reprinted from *Yale review,* 14: 95–107, 1925.

Taxation no tyranny, 1775.

SAWYER and DARTON. English books, v. 1, p. [357]. Facsimile of title-page.

Vanity of human wishes, 1749.

SAWYER and DARTON. English books, v. 1, p. [341]. Facsimile of title-page.

Johnston, Mary, 1870——

CAPPON, JAMES L. Bibliography of Virginia history since 1865. University, Va., Institute for research in the social sciences, 1930.

JOHNSON, MERLE. American first editions, pp. (206–7).

JOHNSON, MERLE. American first editions: Mary Johnston, 1870——. *Publishers' weekly,* 118: 276–77, 1930.

OVERTON, GRANT. Cargoes for Crusoes. New York, Appleton, [1924], pp. 387–88.

Jones, James Athearn, 1791–1854

FULLERTON, BRADFORD M. Selective bibliography, pp. 163–64.

Jonson, Benjamin, 1573(?)–1637

FORD, HERBERT L. Collation of the Ben Jonson folios, 1616–1631, 1640. Oxford, Oxford university press, 1932. 30 pp.

GREG, WALTER W. The riddle of Jonson's chronology. *Library,* s. 4, 6: [340]–47, 1926.

GREG, WALTER W. Some notes on Ben Jonson's works. *Review of English studies,* 2: 129–45, 1926.

GREG, WALTER W. Thomas Walkley and the Ben Jonson "Works" of 1640. *Library,* s. 4, 11: [461]–65, 1931.

HERFORD, CHARLES H., and SIMPSON, PERCY. Ben Jonson. The man and his work. Oxford, Clarendon press, 1925.

SAWYER and DARTON. English books, v. 1, pp. 120–33.

Celia.

MACNAGHTEN, HUGH. Ben Jonson's *Celia. National review,* 84: 721–24, 1925. Cf. *ibid.,* p. 956.

Jonson, Benjamin (*Continued*)

Fortunate isles, 1624.

SAWYER and DARTON. English books, v. 1, p. [128]. Facsimile of title-page.

Masque of queenes, 1609.

SAWYER and DARTON. English books, v. 1, p. [127]. Facsimile of title-page.

Phoenix and the turtle, 1601.

GOLLANCZ, ISRAEL, (*Sir*). Ben Jonson's *Ode to the phoenix and the turtle. Times literary supplement,* October 8, 1925. Cf. Percy Simpson, *ibid.,* October 15, 1925.

Staple of news, 1631.

ENDERS, JOHN F. A note on Jonson's *Staple of news. Modern language notes,* 40: 419–21, 1925.

POTTLE, FREDERICK A. Two notes on Ben Jonson's *Staple of news. Modern language notes,* 40: 223–26, 1925.

Workes, 1616–1640.

MAGGS BROTHERS. Catalogue no. 550. London, 1931. Facsimile of title-page, opp. p. 377.

See also Chapman, George, and Walkley, Thomas.

Jourdain, Silvester, *d.* 1650

SAWYER and DARTON. English books, v. 1, p. 194.

Joyce, James, 1882——

GORMAN, HERBERT S. James Joyce: his first 40 years. New York, Huebsch, 1924. Bibliography, pp. 233–38.

SCHWARTZ, H. WARREN. Check-lists of twentieth-century authors. Second series. Milwaukee, Wis., Casanova booksellers, 1933.

WILSON, EDMUND. James Joyce. *New republic,* 61: 84–93, 1929.

Ulysses, 1922.

GILBERT, STUART. Joyce's *Ulysses.* A study. London, Faber, 1930.

MUIR, EDWIN. A note on *Ulysses. New republic,* 41: supplement, 4–6, 1924.

Judd, Sylvester, 1813–1853
FULLERTON, BRADFORD M. Selective bibliography, pp. 165–66.

Judson, Edward L. C., 1822–1886
FULLERTON, BRADFORD M. Selective bibliography, p. 166.

Judson, Emily Chubbock, 1817–1854
FULLERTON, BRADFORD M. Selective bibliography, p. 166.

Kaler, James Otis, 1848–1912
FULLERTON, BRADFORD M. Selective bibliography, pp. 166–67.

Kay-Shuttleworth, James Phillips, (*Sir*), 1804–1877
SMITH, FRANK. Life and work of Sir James Kay-Shuttleworth. London, Murray, 1923. Selective bibliography, pp. 347–48.

Keats, John, 1795–1821
LOWELL, AMY. John Keats. Boston, Houghton Mifflin co., [1925]. 2 v. Chronological list of Keats's poems, v. 2, pp. 531–34.

RUSK, RALPH L. Keats in the Wordsworth country. *North American review,* 219: 392–97, 1925. Reprints a chapter of Keats's journal from an obscure Kentucky magazine of 1836.

Endymion, 1818.
SAWYER and DARTON. English books, v. 2, p. [62]. Facsimile of title-page.

La belle dame sans merci.
MABBOTT, THOMAS O. *Arcturus* and Keats. An early American publication of Keats's *La belle dame sans merci. American literature,* 2: 430–32, 1931

Keats, John (*Continued*)

Lamia, Isabella, etc., 1820.

SAWYER and DARTON. English books, v. 2, p. [66]. Facsimile of title-page.

Poems, 1817.

SAWYER and DARTON. English books, v. 2, p. [36]. Facsimile of title-page.

Keenan, Henry Francis, 1850——

Money makers, 1885.

BENDER, CLIFFORD A. Another forgotten novel (*The money makers*). *Modern language notes,* 41 : 319–22, 1926.

Kellogg, Elijah, 1813–1901

FULLERTON, BRADFORD M. Selective bibliography, p. 167.

Kemble, John Mitchell, 1807–1857

Solomon and Saturn, 1848.

LARSEN, HENNING. Kemble's *Solomon and Saturn. Modern philology,* 26 : 445–50, 1929. A bibliographical study of the Aelfric society edition of 1848 and of an earlier but little known edition.

Kendall, Henry Clarence, 1841–1882

SERLE, PERCIVAL. Bibliography of Australasian poetry, pp. 108–9.

Kennedy, John Pendleton, 1795–1870

FULLERTON, BRADFORD M. Selective bibliography, pp. 168–69.

JOHNSON, MERLE. American first editions, p. (208).

JOHNSON, MERLE. American first editions: John Pendleton Kennedy, 1795–1870. *Publishers' weekly,* 122 : 589, 1932.

UHLER, J. E. Kennedy's novels and his posthumous works. *American literature,* 3 : 469–77, 1932.

Kent, Rockwell, 1882——

Arens, Egmont. Rockwell Kent, illustrator. *Book-collector's quarterly,* no. 9, December–February, pp. 45–47, 1932.

Armitage, Merle. Rockwell Kent. New York, Knopf, 1932. Bibliography, pp. 67–72.

Kerr, Barry, *pseud.*

See Tully, Michael Joseph.

Kerr, Joan (Torrance)

Serle, Percival. Bibliography of Australasian poetry, p. 202.

Kettell, Samuel, 1800–1855

Fullerton, Bradford M. Selective bibliography, p. 169.

Key, Francis Scott, 1780–1843

Fullerton, Bradford M. Selective bibliography, pp. 169–70.

Kilmer, Alfred Joyce, 1886–1918

Johnson, Merle. American first editions, p. (212).

King, Charles, 1844–1933

Fullerton, Bradford M. Selective bibliography, p. 170.

King, Grace Elizabeth, 1852–1932

Fullerton, Bradford M. Selective bibliography, p. 171.

King, William, 1685–1763

Williams, Harold. The old trumpeter of Liberty Hall. *Book-collector's quarterly,* no. 4, October–December, 1931, pp. 29–56. Bibliographical list, pp. 44–56.

Kingsley, Charles, 1819–1875

Rhys, Ernest, *ed.* The poems of Charles Kingsley. New York, Dutton, 1927. Bibliographical notes by Mary Morton.

Kingsley, Henry, 1830–1876

Ellis, Steward M. Henry Kingsley, 1830–1876: towards a vindication. London, Richards, 1931. Bibliography, pp. 269–78.

Kingsley, Mary Henrietta, 1862–1900

Gwynn, Stephen L. The life of Mary Kingsley. London, Macmillan, 1932. Bibliography, p. 268.

Kipling, Rudyard, 1865——

American Art Association. Sales catalogue. An English collection of first editions of Rudyard Kipling, manuscripts, autograph presentation copies, autograph letters, and proof-sheets. New York, 1928.

American Art Association. Sales catalogue. First editions including the fine collection of Rudyard Kipling formed by Paul Hyde Bonner . . . New York, 1926.

American Art Association. Sales catalogue. First editions, inscribed copies, and autograph letters of Joseph Conrad, property of Mrs. Ford Madox Hueffer; an important Kipling collection; the fine Poe collection of Mr. Joseph Jackson. New York, 1928.

American Art Association. Sales catalogue. First editions of Thomas Hardy, Rudyard Kipling, Robert Louis Stevenson. The renowned collection of George Barr McCutcheon. New York, 1925.

Anderson Galleries. Sales catalogue. A Kipling collection formed by Messrs. E. P. Dutton & co. New York, 1925.

Chandler, Lloyd H. A Kipling problem, Three and an extra. *Colophon,* part 4, 1930.

Cutler and Stiles. Modern British authors, pp. 74–98.

First Edition Club. A bibliographical catalogue, pp. 91–93.

Four hitherto unknown Kipling items. *Bookman's journal,* 10: 210–11, 1924.

GROLIER CLUB. Catalogue of the works of Rudyard Kipling exhibited at the Grolier club . . . New York, 1930. Review, *Books,* 7 : 23, October 12, 1930.

LIVINGSTON, FLORA V. Bibliography of the works of Rudyard Kipling. New York, E. H. Wells, 1927. xviii+523 pp. Review, *Bookman* (New York), 64 : xxiii, February, 1927.

LIVINGSTON, FLORA V. A footnote on bibliography. *Colophon,* part 7, 1931.

PURE, SIMON, *pseud.* Some Kipling rarities. *Bookman* (New York), 65 : 549, 1927.

SAWYER and DARTON. English books, v. 2, pp. 351–57.

Departmental ditties, 1886.

STARRETT, VINCENT. Pennywise and book foolish. New York, Covici Friede, 1929. Facsimile of front cover, p. 72.

Light that failed, 1890.

VAN PATTEN, NATHAN. Kipling and his pirates. *Bookman's journal,* 11 : 42–44, 1925.

Phantom rickshaw, 1888.

SAWYER and DARTON. English books, v. 2, p. [330]. Facsimile of title-page.

Schoolboy lyrics, 1881.

NEWTON, A. EDWARD. This book-collecting game. Boston, Little, Brown and co., 1928. Facsimile of title-page, p. 14.

Kirby, William, 1817–1906

PIERCE, LORNE. Outline of Canadian literature, pp. 27–29.

Kirk, Ellen Warner (Olney), 1842——

FULLERTON, BRADFORD M. Selective bibliography, p. 171.

Kirkland, Caroline Matilda (Stansbury), 1801–1864

FULLERTON, BRADFORD M. Selective bibliography, pp. 171–72.

Kirkland, Joseph, 1830–1894
FULLERTON, BRADFORD M. Selective bibliography, pp. 172–73.

Kitz, Henry Walter
SERLE, PERCIVAL. Bibliography of Australasian poetry, p. 112.

Klaeber, Frederick, 1863——
EINARSSON, STEFÁN. A bibliography of the works of Frederick Klaeber. Studies in English philology: a miscellany in honor of Frederick Klaeber, 1929, pp. 477–85.

Knapp, Charles, 1868——
KNAPP, CHARLES. Bibliography of Charles Knapp, 1893–1923. Geneva, N.Y., W. F. Humphrey, 1923. 77 pp.

Knickerbocker, Dietrich, *pseud.*
See Irving, Washington.

Knowles, Marion (Miller)
SERLE, PERCIVAL. Bibliography of Australasian poetry, p. 137.

Korzeniowski, Joseph Teodor Konrad
See Conrad, Joseph.

Kyd, Thomas, 1558–1594
BALDWIN, THOMAS W. On the chronology of Thomas Kyd's plays. *Modern language notes,* 40: 343–49, 1925.
MUSTARD, WILFRED P. Notes on Thomas Kyd's works. *Philological quarterly,* 5: 85–86, 1926.

Spanish tragedy.
FORSYTHE, ROBERT S. Notes on the *Spanish tragedy. Philological quarterly,* 5: 78–84, 1926.
GREG, WALTER W. *The Spanish tragedy*—a leading case. *Library,* s. 4, 6: [47]–56, 1926.

Lamar, Mirabeau Buonaparte, 1798–1859
FULLERTON, BRADFORD M. Selective bibliography, p. 173.

Lamb, Charles, 1775–1834

BLUNDEN, EDMUND C. Charles Lamb and his contemporaries. Cambridge, Cambridge university press, 1933.

FIRST EDITION CLUB. A bibliographical catalogue, p. 94.

Lamb, Keats, and Shelley mss. *Times literary supplement,* March 7, 1929, p. 192.

SAWYER and DARTON. English books, v. 2, pp. 47–48, 90–96, 122–30.

Album verses, 1830.

PAYEN-PAYNE, DE V. An unrecorded issue of Lamb's *Album verses. Times literary supplement,* March 27, 1930, p. 274.

TURNBULL, JOHN M. An unrecorded issue of Lamb's *Album verses. Times literary supplement,* March 20, 1930, p. 247.

Book of the ranks and dignities of British society.

SHORTER, CLEMENT. Charles Lamb and titles of honor. *Now & then,* no. 14, 15–17, 1924. Cf. *London Mercury,* 11 : 86, 1925.

Essays of Elia, 1823.

SAWYER and DARTON. English books, v. 2, p. 91. Facsimile of title-page.

Last essays of Elia, 1833.

TURNBULL, JOHN M. Cancels in *Last essays of Elia. Times literary supplement,* June 23, 1932, p. 464. Refers to second edition (1835).

Mrs. Leicester's school, 1809.

SAWYER and DARTON. English books, v. 2, p. [126]. Facsimile of title-page.

Tales from Shakespeare, 1807.

AMERICAN ART ASSOCIATION. Sales catalogue. The library of Frank Irving Fletcher. Facsimile of title-page, p. [113].

SAWYER and DARTON. English books, v. 2, p. [125]. Facsimile of title-page.

Lamb, Mary Ann, 1764–1847
See Lamb, Charles.

Lampman, Archibald, 1861–1899
Pierce, Lorne. Outline of Canadian literature, pp. 81–84.

Landor, Walter Savage, 1775–1864
Ashley-Montagu, M. F. Another unpublished *Imaginary conversation* by Walter Savage Landor. *Nineteenth century,* 110: 353–58, 1931.
Wise, Thomas J. A Landor library. A catalogue of printed books, manuscripts, and autograph letters by Walter Savage Landor ... London, privately printed, 1928. xxiv+102 pp., facsimiles. Contents: 1, the writings of Walter Savage Landor; 2, Landoriana.

Lanier, Sidney, 1842–1881
Fullerton, Bradford M. Selective bibliography, pp. 173–75.
Hubbell, Jay B. A commencement address by Sidney Lanier. *American literature,* 2: 385–404, 1931.
Annual address before the Furlow masonic female college, June 30th, 1869, printed in *Catalogue ... of Furlow masonic female college, Americus, Ga., 1868–1869,* Macon, Ga., 1869.
Johnson, Merle. American first editions, pp. 123 (213–15).
Starke, Aubrey. Sidney Lanier, a biographical and critical study ... Chapel Hill, N.C., University of North Carolina press, 1933. Bibliography, pp. [455]–73.

Lansdowne, Henry Charles, (*Fifth Marquis*), 1845–1927
Newton, Thomas W. L. Lord Lansdowne: a biography. London, Macmillan, 1929.

"Lanthe," *pseud.*
See Embury, Emma Catharine (Manley).

Larcom, Lucy, 1824–1893
Fullerton, Bradford M. Selective bibliography, p. 175.

Lardner, Ringold Walter, 1885——

JOHNSON, MERLE. American first editions, pp. 124 (216–17). The check-list in the 1929 edition was compiled by Vrest Orton.

Laut, Agnes Christina, 1871——

PIERCE, LORNE. Outline of Canadian literature, pp. 37–38.

Lawrence, David Henry, 1885–1932

CUTLER and STILES. Modern British authors, pp. 99–102.

FABES, GILBERT H. First editions and their values. Number two. D. H. Lawrence, his first editions: points and values. London, Foyle, [1933]. 112 pp.

MCDONALD, EDWARD D. A bibliography of the writings of D. H. Lawrence. Foreword by D. H. Lawrence. Philadelphia, Centaur bookshop, 1926. 146 pp.

MCDONALD, EDWARD D. D. H. Lawrence: a bibliographical supplement. Philadelphia, Centaur bookshop, 1931. Review, *Book-collector's quarterly,* no. 5, January–March, pp. 32–34, 1932.

POTTER, STEPHEN. D. H. Lawrence. London, Cape, [1930]. List of principal publications, pp. 157–59.

SAWYER and DARTON. English books, v. 2, p. 332.

SELIGMAN, HERBERT J. D. H. Lawrence: an American interpretation. New York, Seltzer, 1924. Bibliography, p. 77.

SNYDER, HAROLD J. A catalogue of English and American first editions, 1911–1932, of D. H. Lawrence. Check-list no. 1. New York, Harold J. Snyder, 1932. 20 pp.

Lawrence, Herbert

Life and adventures of common-sense, 1762.

MAGGS BROTHERS. Catalogue no. 493. Shakespeare and Shakespeareana. London, 1927. Facsimile of title-page of second edition, opp. p. 88; facsimile of title-page of first French edition, Avignon, 1777, opp. p. 89; facsimile of title-page of first Swiss edition, Yverdon, 1777, opp. p. 104.

MAGGS BROTHERS. Catalogue no. 550. London, 1931. Facsimile of title-page, opp. p. 600.

Lawrence, Thomas Edward, 1888——
GERMAN-REED, T. Bibliographical notes on T. E. Lawrence's *Seven pillars of wisdom* and *Revolt in the desert.* London, Foyle, 1928. 16 pp.

Lawson, Henry Archibald, 1867–1922
SERLE, PERCIVAL. Bibliography of Australasian poetry, pp. 114–15.

Lawson, James, 1799–1880
FULLERTON, BRADFORD M. Selective bibliography, pp. 175–76.

Lawson, William, 1876——
SERLE, PERCIVAL. Bibliography of Australasian poetry, p. 116.

Lazarus, Emma, 1849–1887
FULLERTON, BRADFORD M. Selective bibliography, p. 176.

Lea, Henry Charles, 1825–1909
BRADLEY, EDWARD S. Henry Charles Lea: a biography ... Philadelphia, University of Pennsylvania press, 1931. Bibliography, pp. [365]–84. "The excellent bibliography of Lea's writings ... provides an excellent guide for students and is at the same time the record of one of the finest scholarly achievements known to the republic of letters."—Ernest W. Nelson, *American literature,* 4: 339, 1933.

Leech, John, 1817–1864
COOLIDGE, BERTHA. John Leech on my shelves. Privately printed for William B. Osgood Field at the Bremer presse, Munich, 1930. 313 pp.

Le Fanu, Joseph Sheridan, 1814–1873
ELLIS, STEWART M. Wilkie Collins, Le Fanu, and others. London, Constable, 1931. Bibliographies at the end of chapters.

Le Gallienne, Richard, 1866——

CUTLER and STILES. Modern British authors, pp. 103–6.

LINGEL, R. J. C. A bibliographical checklist of the writings of Richard Le Gallienne. Introduction by Temple Scott. Metuchen, N.J., Heartman, 1926. 95 pp.

Leggett, William, 1802–1839

FULLERTON, BRADFORD M. Selective bibliography, pp. 176–77.

Leland, Charles Godfrey, 1824–1903

FULLERTON, BRADFORD M. Selective bibliography, pp. 177–78.

(The Hans Breitmann books.) *The month at Goodspeed's,* 3 : 306–9, 1932.

JACKSON, JOSEPH. A bibliography of the works of Charles Godfrey Leland. Philadelphia, 1927. 129 pp., facsimiles. Reprinted from the *Pennsylvania magazine of history and biography,* v. 49–51, 1925–1927.

Lenton, Francis, *fl.* 1630–1640

WILLIS, LEOTA (SNIDER). Francis Lenton, queen's poet . . . Philadelphia, 1931. (Thesis, University of Pennsylvania.) Bibliography, pp. 94–98.

Leprohon, Rosanna Eleanor (Mullins), 1832–1879

PIERCE, LORNE. Outline of Canadian literature, p. 29.

Leslie, Eliza, 1787–1858

FULLERTON, BRADFORD M. Selective bibliography, p. 178.

Lewes, Marian Evans

See Eliot, George.

Lewis, Alfred Henry, 1858–1914

FULLERTON, BRADFORD M. Selective bibliography, p. 179.

Lewis, Charles Bertrand, 1842–1927

FULLERTON, BRADFORD M. Selective bibliography, pp. 179–80.

Lewis, Harry Sinclair, 1885——

JOHNSON, MERLE. American first editions, pp. 125 (218–19). The check-list in the 1929 edition was compiled by A. C. Mears.

VAN DOREN, CARL. Sinclair Lewis, a biographical sketch . . . with a bibliography by Harvey Taylor. Garden City, Doubleday, 1933. Bibliography of the writings of Sinclair Lewis, pp. 77–205. Contents: books, contributions to periodicals, selected biographical and critical notices in books, selected biographical and critical notices in periodicals.

WALDMAN, MILTON. Contemporary American authors. III. Sinclair Lewis. *London Mercury,* 13: 273–81, 1926.

Elmer Gantry, 1927.

BIRKHEAD, L. M. Is *Elmer Gantry* true? Girard, Kansas, 1928. (*Little blue books,* no. 1265.) Bibliography of material used in writing *Elmer Gantry,* pp. 14–16.

Lewis, Wyndham, 1886——

GAWSWORTH, JOHN, *pseud.,* (T. Fytton Armstrong). Apes, japes, and Hitlerism. London, Unicorn press, 1932. Contains a bibliography of Wyndham Lewis's works.

Lichfield, Leonard, *d.* 1657.

See Taylor, John.

Lighthall, William Douw, 1857——

PIERCE, LORNE. Outline of Canadian literature, pp. 32–33, 89–90.

Lincoln, Abraham, 1809–1865

ANDERSON GALLERIES. Sales catalogue. The Lincoln collection of Emanuel Hentz. Part I, autographs; part II, books, broadsides, and medals. New York, 1927.

CUSHMAN, ESTHER C. The McLellan Lincoln collection at Brown university. *American collector,* 4: 199–205, 1927.

GRIFFITH, ALBERT H. Lincoln literature, Lincoln collections, and Lincoln collectors. *Wisconsin magazine of history,* 15: 148–67, 1931.

OAKLEAF, JOSEPH B. Lincoln bibliography: a list of books and pamphlets relating to Abraham Lincoln. Cedar Rapids, Iowa, Torch press, 1925. iv+424 pp. Excludes titles in Fish's bibliography (1906).

STARR, JOHN W. Bibliography of Lincolniana not included in the compilations of Daniel Fish and Benjamin Oakleaf. Millersburg, Pa., privately printed, 1926. 69 pp.

Gettysburg address, 1863.

(*Gettysburg address,* New York, 1863.) *The month at Goodspeed's,* 2: 196–97, 1931. Facsimile of title-page.

Lincoln, Joseph Crosby, 1870——

OVERTON, GRANT. American nights entertainment. New York, Appleton, 1923, pp. 343–44.

OVERTON, GRANT. Authors of the day. New York, Doran, [1924], pp. 187–88.

Lindsay, David, (*Sir*), 1490–1555

HAMER, DOUGLAS. The bibliography of Sir David Lindsay (1490–1555). *Library,* s. 4, 10: [1]–42, 1930.

Lindsay, Nicholas Vachel, 1879–1931

JOHNSON, MERLE. American first editions, pp. 126–27 (220–21). The check-list in the 1929 edition was compiled by Frederic G. Melcher.

Ling, Nicholas

HEBEL, J. WILLIAM. Nicholas Ling and *Englands Helicon. Library,* s. 4, 5: [153]–160, 1925.

Lingham, Henry Charles

SERLE, PERCIVAL. Bibliography of Australasian poetry, p. 119.

Linn, John Blair, 1777–1804

FULLERTON, BRADFORD M. Selective bibliography, p. 180.

Lippard, George, 1822–1854

JACKSON, JOSEPH. Bibliography of the works of George Lippard. *Pennsylvania magazine of history and biography,* 54: 131–54, 1930.

Little, William

SERLE, PERCIVAL. Bibliography of Australasian poetry, pp. 119–20.

Livesay, Florence (Randal)

PIERCE, LORNE. Outline of Canadian literature, p. 99.

Locke, David Ross, 1833–1888

FULLERTON, BRADFORD M. Selective bibliography, pp. 180–81.

Locke, John, 1632–1704

CHRISTOPHERSON, H. O. Bibliographical introduction to the study of John Locke. *Skrifter utgitt av det Norske videnskaps-akademi i Oslo, 2, hist. filos. klasse,* no. 8, 1930.

Locker-Lampson, Frederick, 1821–1895

LIVINGSTON, FLORA V. A bibliography of the works of F. Locker-Lampson. *Bookman's journal,* 10: 46–47, 145–46, 175–77, 211–12, 1924. Comment by A. M. Cohn, *ibid.,* p. 106.

Lockwood, Ralph Ingersoll, 1798–1855

FULLERTON, BRADFORD M. Selective bibliography, p. 181.

Lodge, Thomas, 1558(?)–1625

PARADISE, N. BURTON. Thomas Lodge: the history of an Elizabethan. New Haven, Yale university press, 1931. The last two of the five chapters are largely bibliographical and critical. There is a chronological list of Lodge's writings.

SAWYER and DARTON. English books, v. 1, p. 103.

Logan, John Daniel, 1869–1929

PIERCE, LORNE. Outline of Canadian literature, pp. 86–97.

London, John Griffiths, (Jack), 1876–1916

JOHNSON, MERLE. American first editions, pp. 128–30 (222–25). The check-list in the 1929 edition was compiled by Charles Romm.

ROMM, CHARLES. American first editions: Jack London, 1876–1916. *Publishers' weekly,* 103: 1463–64, 1923.

TAYLOR, HARVEY. (Bibliography in preparation.) *American literature,* 4: 214, 1933.

Longfellow, Henry Wadsworth, 1807–1882

AMERICAN ART ASSOCIATION. Sales catalogue. Stephen H. Wakeman collection. New York, 1924. Items 622–800.

FULLERTON, BRADFORD M. Selective bibliography, pp. 181–84.

HATFIELD, JAMES T. An unknown prose tale by Longfellow. *American literature,* 3: 136–49, 1932. "The wondrous tale of a little man in Gosling green," in *New Yorker,* November 1, 1834.

JOHNSON, MERLE. American first editions, pp. 131–34 (226–31). The check-list in the 1929 edition was compiled by Vrest Orton.

THOMPSON, RALPH. Additions to Longfellow bibliography, including a new prose tale. *American literature,* 3: 303–8, 1932.

Aftermath, 1873.

CURLE, RICHARD. Collecting American first editions, pp. 60, 90, 175.

Ballads, 1842.

CURLE, RICHARD. Collecting American first editions, pp. 58, 100–101, 182–83.

Bayard Taylor, 1879.

CURLE, RICHARD. Collecting American first editions, p. 172.

Belfry of Bruges, 1846.

CURLE, RICHARD. Collecting American first editions, p. 157.

Longfellow, Henry Wadsworth (*Continued*)

Christus, 1872.

CURLE, RICHARD. Collecting American first editions, pp. 130–31, 137.

Divine tragedy, 1871.

CURLE, RICHARD. Collecting American first editions, pp. 111, 130, 175.

Don Jorge Manrique, 1833.

CURLE, RICHARD. Collecting American first editions, p. 136.

Early poems, 1879.

CURLE, RICHARD. Collecting American first editions, p. 186.

Estray, 1847.

CURLE, RICHARD. Collecting American first editions, p. 158.

Evangeline, 1847.

CURLE, RICHARD. Collecting American first editions, pp. 11, 35, 41–43, 58, 150.

French grammar, second edition, 1831.

CURLE, RICHARD. Collecting American first editions, pp. 26, 195.

Golden legend, 1851.

CURLE, RICHARD. Collecting American first editions, pp. 130, 183.

Hanging of the crane, 1875.

CURLE, RICHARD. Collecting American first editions, pp. 131–33, 145–46, 176.

Hiawatha, 1855.

CURLE, RICHARD. Collecting American first editions, pp. 80–83, 87–88, 183. Facsimile of title-page, opp. p. 80.

Hyperion, 1839.

CURLE, RICHARD. Collecting American first editions, p. 103.

In the harbor, 1882.

CURLE, RICHARD. Collecting American first editions, p. 210.

Kavanagh, 1849.

CURLE, RICHARD. Collecting American first editions, pp. 17, 51, 91–94, 140.

Masque of Pandora, 1875.

CURLE, RICHARD. Collecting American first editions, pp. 107–10.

Michael Angelo, 1884.

CURLE, RICHARD. Collecting American first editions, p. 137.

Miles Standish, 1858.

CURLE, RICHARD. Collecting American first editions, pp. 17, 80–83, 189–90. Facsimile of title-page, p. 80.

Ministre de Wakefield, 1831.

CURLE, RICHARD. Collecting American first editions, pp. 26–27.

My lost youth.

HATFIELD, JAMES T. Longfellow's "Lapland song." Modern language association of America. *Publications,* 45: 1188–92, 1930. Refers to Longfellow's use of the "Lapland song" as a refrain in "My lost youth." Facsimile of manuscript, 6 pages, between pp. 1192 and 1193.

New England tragedies, 1868.

AMERICAN ART ASSOCIATION. Sales catalogue. Stephen H. Wakeman collection. New York, 1924. Facsimile of title-page.

CURLE, RICHARD. Collecting American first editions, pp. 130, 172, 175.

Noël, 1864.

AMERICAN ART ASSOCIATION. Sales catalogue. Stephen H. Wakeman collection. New York, 1924. Item 725. Facsimile of title-page.

CURLE, RICHARD. Collecting American first editions, p. 208.

Longfellow, Henry Wadsworth (*Continued*)

Outre-mer, 1833, 1834, 1835, 1846.

CURLE, RICHARD. Collecting American first editions, pp. 140, 155, 196.

Poems on slavery, 1842.

CURLE, RICHARD. Collecting American first editions, pp. 49–50, 58–59.

Seaside and fireside, 1850.

CURLE, RICHARD. Collecting American first editions, pp. 69, 115, 140–41.

Spanish student, 1843.

CURLE, RICHARD. Collecting American first editions, p. 58.

Three books of song, 1872.

CURLE, RICHARD. Collecting American first editions, p. 175.

Ultima thule, 1880.

CURLE, RICHARD. Collecting American first editions, p. 210.

Voices of the night, 1839.

CURLE, RICHARD. Collecting American first editions, pp. 135–36, 182.

Waif, 1845.

CURLE, RICHARD. Collecting American first editions, p. 158.

Wayside inn, 1863.

CURLE, RICHARD. Collecting American first editions, pp. 15–16.

Longstreet, Augustus Baldwin, 1790–1870

FULLERTON, BRADFORD M. Selective bibliography, p. 184.

WADE, JOHN D. Augustus Baldwin Longstreet: a study of the development of culture in the South. New York, Macmillan, 1924. Bibliography, pp. 373–83.

Loos, Anita, (Mrs. John Emerson), 1893——

Gentlemen prefer blondes, 1925.

CURRIE, BARTON. Fishers of books. Boston, Little, Brown and co., 1931. Facsimile of title-page, opp. p. 128.

Lothrop, Harriet Mulford (Stone), 1844–1924

FULLERTON, BRADFORD M. Selective bibliography, p. 185.

Lowell, Amy, 1874–1925

CESTRE, CHARLES. Poetry of Amy Lowell . . . with a bibliography and critical appreciation. Boston, Houghton Mifflin co., 1927.

JOHNSON, MERLE. American first editions, pp. 135–36 (232–33). The check-list in the 1929 edition was compiled by Mildred C. Smith.

SMITH, MILDRED C. American first editions: Amy Lowell, 1874——. *Publishers' weekly,* 103: 1515, 1923.

Lowell, James Russell, 1819–1891

AMERICAN ART ASSOCIATION. Sales catalogue. Stephen H. Wakeman collection. New York, 1924. Items 801–930.

CAMPBELL, KILLIS. Bibliographical notes on Lowell. University of Texas, *Studies in English,* 4: 115–19, 1924.

FUESS, CLAUDE. Some forgotten political essays by Lowell. Massachusetts historical society. *Proceedings,* 62: 3–13, 1930.

FULLERTON, BRADFORD M. Selective bibliography, pp. 185–88.

GOODSPEED, GEORGE T. A unique Lowell item. *American collector,* 3: 241–43, 1927.

JOHNSON, MERLE. American first editions, pp. 137–39 (234–37).

PLAZA ART GALLERIES. Sales catalogue. A collection of first editions including association copies of James Russell Lowell from the library of Carlotta Russell Lowell. New York, 1931.

Lowell, James Russell (*Continued*)

Among my books, 1870.

CURLE, RICHARD. Collecting American first editions, p. 210.

Among my books, second series, 1876.

CURLE, RICHARD. Collecting American first editions, pp. 80, 127–28. Facsimile of title-page, opp. p. 126.

Biglow papers, 1848.

AMERICAN ART ASSOCIATION. Sales catalogue. Stephen H. Wakeman collection. New York, 1924. Item 843. Facsimile of title-page.

CURLE, RICHARD. Collecting American first editions, pp. 102–3, 193.

WINTERICH, JOHN T. Romantic stories of books. Second series. *The Biglow papers. Publishers' weekly,* 119: 1605–10, 1931.

Biglow papers, second series, 1862, 1864, 1865, 1867.

CURLE, RICHARD. Collecting American first editions, pp. 145, 175, 188.

Conversations on some old poets, 1845.

CURLE, RICHARD. Collecting American first editions, pp. 157–58.

Fable for critics, 1848.

CURLE, RICHARD. Collecting American first editions, pp. 96–100. Facsimile of title-page, opp. p. 98.

Heartsease and rue, 1888.

CURLE, RICHARD. Collecting American first editions, pp. 155–56.

Last poems, 1895.

CURLE, RICHARD. Collecting American first editions, p. 174.

Mason and Slidell, 1862.

CURLE, RICHARD. Collecting American first editions, p. 209.

My study windows, 1871.
CURLE, RICHARD. Collecting American first editions, p. 149.

Ode recited at the commemoration, 1865.
AMERICAN ART ASSOCIATION. Sales catalogue. Stephen H. Wakeman collection. New York, 1924. Item 862. Facsimile of title-page.
CURLE, RICHARD. Collecting American first editions, p. 208.

On democracy, 1884.
CURLE, RICHARD. Collecting American first editions, p. 186.

Poems, 1844.
CURLE, RICHARD. Collecting American first editions, p. 111.

Poems, second series, 1848.
CURLE, RICHARD. Collecting American first editions, pp. 89, 139–40, 147.

Sir Launfal, 1848.
CURLE, RICHARD. Collecting American first editions, p. 58.

Three books of song, 1872.
CURLE, RICHARD. Collecting American first editions, p. 175.

Three memorial poems, 1877.
CURLE, RICHARD. Collecting American first editions, pp. 90, 176.

Under the willows, 1869.
CURLE, RICHARD. Collecting American first editions, pp. 6, 69, 175.

Year's life, 1841.
CURLE, RICHARD. Collecting American first editions, pp. 6, 64.

Lowell, Maria (White), 1821–1853

Poems, 1855.
AMERICAN ART ASSOCIATION. Sales catalogue. Stephen H. Wakeman collection. New York, 1924. Item 843. Facsimile of title-page.

Lowell, Robert Traill Spence, 1816–1891

FULLERTON, BRADFORD M. Selective bibliography, p. 188.

Lucas, Edward Verrall, 1868–1933

OVERTON, GRANT. Cargoes for Crusoes. New York, Appleton, [1924], pp. 229–31.

Lydgate, John, 1370(?)–1451(?)

Fall of princes.

BERGEN, HENRY, *ed.* Lydgate's *Fall of princes. Part 4.* Washington, Carnegie institution, 1927. (Carnegie institution of Washington. *Publications,* no. 262.) Bibliographical introduction, notes, and glossary. *Ibid.,* Early English text society. Extra series, no. 124. London, Milford, 1927.

Lyly, John, 1554(?)–1606

MUSTARD, WILFRED P. Notes on John Lyly's plays. *Studies in philology,* 22: 267–71, 1925.

SAWYER and DARTON. English books, v. 1, pp. 102–3.

Euphues, 1579.

MUSTARD, WILFRED P. Notes on Lyly's *Euphues. Modern language notes,* 40: 120–21, 1925.

Midas, 1592.

MUSTARD, WILFRED P. Notes on John Lyly's *Midas. Modern language notes,* 41: 193, 1926.

Lyndsay, David, (*Sir*), 1490–1555

Ane satyre of the thrie estaits, 1602.

MAGGS BROTHERS. Catalogue no. 550. London, 1931. Facsimile of title-page, opp. p. 409.

Lytton, Edward George Earle Bulwer-Lytton, (*First baron*), 1803–1873

[Autograph letters of . . .] *Bodleian quarterly record,* 7: 71, 1932.

SADLEIR, MICHAEL. Bulwer: a panorama. Edward and Rosina, 1803–1836. London, Constable, 1931. xviii+451 pp. In large part based upon exhaustive bibliographical research.

Mabie, Hamilton Wright, 1849–1916

FULLERTON, BRADFORD M. Selective bibliography, p. 189.

Macartney, Frederick Thomas Bennett, 1887——

SERLE, PERCIVAL. Bibliography of Australasian poetry, p. 123.

Macaulay, Thomas Babington, (*First Baron*), 1800–1859

SAWYER and DARTON. English books, v. 2, p. 324.

McCrae, George Gordon, 1833——

SERLE, PERCIVAL. Bibliography of Australasian poetry, p. 124.

McCrae, Hugh Raymond, 1876——

SERLE, PERCIVAL. Bibliography of Australasian poetry, pp. 124–25.

McCrae, John, 1872–1918

PIERCE, LORNE. Outline of Canadian literature, p. 99.

Macdonald, George, 1824–1905

BULLOCK, JOHN M. A centennial bibliography of George Macdonald. Aberdeen, University press, 1925. 72 pp. Reprinted with additions and corrections from Aberdeen university library's *Bulletin,* 5:679–747, 1925.

MACDONALD, GREVILLE. George Macdonald and his wife, with an introduction by G. K. Chesterton. London, Allen & Unwin, [1924]. Bibliography, pp. 563–65.

SAWYER and DARTON. English books, v. 2, p. 142.

MacDonald, Wilson, 1880——

PIERCE, LORNE. Outline of Canadian literature, pp. 101–2.

McFee, William, 1881——

BABB, JAMES T. A bibliography of the writings of William McFee. Garden City, Doubleday, Doran and co., 1932. 149 pp. Review, *Book-collector's quarterly,* no. 8, October–December, 1932, p. 60.

JOHNSON, MERLE. American first editions, pp. 145–46 (238–40). The check-list in the 1929 edition was compiled by Frank Shay.

MAULE, HARRY E. William McFee . . . Garden City, Doubleday, Doran and co., [1928]. 42 pp. Complete chronological bibliography.

Machar, Agnes Maule, 1834–1927

PIERCE, LORNE. Outline of Canadian literature, p. 32.

Machen, Arthur, 1863——

CUTLER and STILES. Modern British authors, pp. 107–9.

DANIELSON, HENRY. Arthur Machen: a bibliography. With notes, biographical and critical, by Arthur Machen; with an introduction by Henry Savage. London, 1923. 70 pp.

SAWYER and DARTON. English books, v. 1, p. 277; v. 2, pp. 361, 366.

VAN PATTEN, NATHAN. Arthur Machen—a bibliographical note. *Queen's quarterly,* 33: 351–54, 1926.

VAN PATTEN, NATHAN. An unacknowledged work of Arthur Machen? Bibliographical society of America. *Papers,* 20: 95–97, 1926.

McHenry, James, 1785–1845

FULLERTON, BRADFORD M. Selective bibliography, p. 189.

Machlinia, William de, *fl.* 1482–1490

SAWYER and DARTON. English books, v. 1, p. 54.

SMITH, GEORGE D. William de Machlinia: the Primer on vellum printed by him in London about 1484, newly found and described . . . with facsimiles of the woodcuts. London, Ellis, 1929. 26 pp., 9 facsimiles. Review by Alfred W. Pollard, *Library,* s. 4, 10: 231–32, 1930.

MacInnes, Tom, 1867——

PIERCE, LORNE. Outline of Canadian literature, pp. 95–96.

Mackay, Isabel Ecclestone, 1875——

PIERCE, LORNE. Outline of Canadian literature, p. 96.

Mackay, Jessie, 1864——

SERLE, PERCIVAL. Bibliography of Australasian poetry, pp. 127–28.

MacKaye, Percy Wallace, 1875——

GROVER, EDWIN O. Annals of an era: Percy MacKaye and the MacKaye family, 1826–1932 . . . Washington, D.C., Pioneer press, 1932. "The MacKaye collection: a supplemental bibliography, 1761–1931, of material preserved in the Dartmouth college library . . . ," pp. [299]–534.

GROVER, EDWIN O. Percy MacKaye: a biographical bibliography of Percy MacKaye, 1890–1930. Winter Park, Fla., Angel alley press, 1931.

JOHNSON, MERLE. American first editions, pp. 140–42 (241–44). The check-list in the 1929 edition was compiled by Vrest Orton.

MacKaye, Steele, 1842–1894

MACKAYE, PERCY. Epoch. The life of Steele MacKaye . . . New York, Boni & Liveright, [1927]. 2 v. A chronological list of the dramatic works of Steele MacKaye, v. 2, pp. [xvi–xvii].

McKenna, Stephen, 1888——

OVERTON, GRANT. Authors of the day. New York, Doran, [1924], pp. 389–90.

Mackenzie, Compton, 1883——

KAYE-SMITH, SHEILA. Compton Mackenzie and his work. *Bookman* (New York), 62: 391–95, 1925.

Mackenzie, Edward, (*Sir*)

Serle, Percival. Bibliography of Australasian poetry, p. 128.

Mackenzie, Henry, 1745–1831

Sawyer and Darton. English books, v. 1, p. 54.

Mackenzie, James, (*Sir*), 1853–1925

Monteith, W. R. B. Bibliography with synopsis of the original papers of the writings of Sir James Mackenzie. London, Oxford university press, 1930. 97 pp.

McMurtrie, Douglas C., 1888——

Books and pamphlets on the history of printing, by Douglas C. McMurtrie. Chicago, Calhoun club, 1932. 14 pp. Lists 86 items.

Macpherson, James, 1736–1796

Black, George F. Macpherson's Ossian. New York public library. *Bulletin,* 30: 413–15, 1926.

Black, George F. Macpherson's Ossian and the Ossianic controversy. A contribution towards a bibliography. New York public library. *Bulletin,* 30: 424–39, 508–24, 1926.

Bowman, Mary R. The reception of Ossian in America ... Chicago, 1926. (Thesis, University of Chicago.) Typewritten. Bibliography, leaves 54–56.

Carpenter, Frederic I. The vogue of Ossian in America: a study in taste. *American literature,* 2: 405–17, 1931.

Fraser, G. M. The truth about Macpherson's Ossian. *Quarterly review,* 245: 331–45, 1925.

MacDonald, Gordon G. The Ossian manuscripts. A note. New York public library. *Bulletin,* 34: 79–81, 1930.

Sawyer and Darton. English books, v. 1, p. 291.

Mair, Charles, 1840–1927

Pierce, Lorne. Outline of Canadian literature, pp. 66–67.

Major, Charles, 1856–1913

FULLERTON, BRADFORD M. Selective bibliography, p. 190.

Malone, Edmund, 1741–1812

SAWYER and DARTON. English books, v. 1, pp. 5, 8, 26–29, 169, 291, 302.

Malory, Thomas, (*Sir*), *fl.* 1460–1470

SAWYER and DARTON. English books, v. 1, p. 48.

VINAVER, EUGÈNE. Malory . . . Oxford, Clarendon press, 1929. 208 pp., facsimiles. Bibliography, pp. [189]–98. A comprehensive treatment biographical, bibliographical, and critical.

Malthus, Thomas Robert, 1766–1834

Essay on the principles of population.

AMERICAN ART ASSOCIATION. Sales catalogue. Library of Frank Irving Fletcher. New York, 1932. Facsimile of title-page, p. 123.

Mandeville, Bernard, 1670(?)–1733

KAYE, FREDERICK B., *ed.* The fable of the bees. Oxford, Clarendon press, 1924. Description of editions, pp. 386–400; criticisms, pp. 401–17; chronological list of references to Mandeville, pp. 418–54.

SAWYER and DARTON. English books, v. 1, pp. 248, 267.

Manly, John Matthews, 1865——

Manly anniversary studies in language and literature. Chicago, University of Chicago press, 1923. Bibliography, pp. 426–28.

Mansfield, Katherine

See Murry, Katherine Middleton.

Maquarie, Arthur, *pseud.*

See Mullens, Arthur Frank Macquarie.

Mare, Walter de la

See De la Mare, Walter.

Markham, Edwin, 1852——

FULLERTON, BRADFORD M. Selective bibliography, pp. 190–91.

Markham, Gervase, 1568(?)–1637

MAGGS BROTHERS. Catalogue no. 550. London, 1931. His edition of Juliana Berners' *Treatise of hawking,* London, 1595. Facsimile of title-page, opp. p. 632.

Marlowe, Christopher, 1564–1593

SAWYER and DARTON. English books, v. 1, pp. 25–26, 134–35.

Tragedie of Dido, 1594.

SAWYER and DARTON. English books, v. 1, p. [22]. Facsimile of title-page.

Marquis, Thomas Guthrie, 1864——

PIERCE, LORNE. Outline of Canadian literature, p. 37.

Marryat, Frederick, 1792–1848

Naval light literature. *Times literary supplement,* August 6, 1925, pp. [513]–14.

SAWYER and DARTON. English books, v. 2, p. 314.

Marsh, John, 1799–1856

LYMAN, GEORGE. John Marsh ... New York, Scribner, 1930. Bibliography, pp. 343–84.

Marshall, Bernard

OVERTON, GRANT. Cargoes for Crusoes. New York, Appleton, [1924].

Marshall, William

SAWYER and DARTON. English books, v. 1, pp. 137, 188, 197, 199, 212; v. 2, pp. 155, 157.

Marshall, William Emerson, 1859——

PIERCE, LORNE. Outline of Canadian literature, p. 89.

Marston, John, 1575(?)–1634

Brettle, Robert E. Bibliographical notes on some Marston quartos and early collected editions. *Library,* s. 4, 7: [336]–48, 1927.

Brettle, Robert E. More bibliographical notes on Marston. *Library,* s. 4, 12: [235]–42, 1932.

Sawyer and Darton. English books, v. 1, pp. 133–34.

Histrio-mastix, or The player whipt, 1610.

Maggs Brothers. Catalogue no. 550. London, 1931. Facsimile of title-page, opp. p. 440.

See also Chapman, George.

Martin, Arthur Patchett, 1851–1902

Serle, Percival. Bibliography of Australasian poetry, p. 132.

Marvel, Ik, *pseud.*

See Mitchell, Donald Grant.

Marvell, Andrew, 1621–1678

Sawyer and Darton. English books, v. 1, pp. 193–94.

Masefield, John, 1878——

Cutler and Stiles. Modern British authors, pp. 111–14.

First Edition Club. A bibliographical catalogue, pp. 95–96.

Nevinson, Henry W. John Masefield. An appreciation. London, Heinemann, 1931. 17 pp. Bibliography.

Simmons, Charles H. A bibliography of John Masefield. London, Oxford university press; New York, Columbia university press, 1930. xi+171 pp. Reviews, by Alfred W. Pollard, *Library,* s. 4, 11: 509–10, 1931; *Books,* 7: 19, April 19, 1931; by Viscount Esher, *Book-collector's quarterly,* no. 3, June–August, 1931 (includes a list of doubtful points).

Thomas, Gilbert O. John Masefield. London, Butterworth, [1932]. Bibliography, pp. 257–61.

Massinger, Phillip, 1583–1640

Eight plays of Massinger. *Times literary supplement,* May 9, 1929, p. 388.

McIlwraith, A. K. Some bibliographical notes on Massinger. *Library,* s. 4, 11 : [78]–92, 1931.

Cruickshank, Alfred H. Massinger corrections. *Library,* s. 4, 5 : [175]–79, 1925.

Greg, Walter W. More Massinger corrections. *Library,* s. 4, 5 : [59]–91, 1925.

Duke of Milan, 1673.

Greg, Walter W. Massinger's autograph corrections in *The Duke of Milan,* 1673. *Library,* s. 4, 4 : 207, 1924.

Masters, Edgar Lee, 1869——

Johnson, Merle. American first editions, pp. 143–44 (245–46). The check-list in the 1929 edition was compiled by E. Jacoby Van de Water.

Mather, Cotton, 1662–1728

Greenough, Chester N. A letter relating to the publication of Cotton Mather's *Magnalia,* with remarks. Colonial society of Massachusetts. *Publications. Transactions,* pp. 388–401 (1924–1926), 1927.

Greenough, Chester N. The publication of Cotton Mather's *Magnalia.* Colonial society of Massachusetts. *Publications,* 26 : 296–312, 1928.

Holmes, Thomas J. Cotton Mather and his writings on witchcraft. Bibliographical society of America. *Papers,* 18 : 31–59, 1924.

Holmes, Thomas J. The surreptitious printing of one of Cotton Mather's mss. Bibliographical essays, a tribute to Wilberforce Eames.

Wonders of the invisible world, 1693.

Holmes, Thomas J. *More wonders of the invisible world.* Bibliographical essays, a tribute to Wilberforce Eames.

WALDMAN, MILTON. Americana. New York, Holt, 1925. Facsimile of title-page, opp. p. 170.

See also Mather, Increase.

Mather, Increase, 1639–1723

HOLMES, THOMAS J. Increase Mather: a bibliography ... with an introduction by George Parker Winship and supplementary material by Kenneth Ballard Murdock and George Francis Dow ... Cleveland, 1931. 2 v.

HOLMES, THOMAS J. Increase Mather. His works, being a short-title catalogue of the published writings that can be ascribed to him. Cleveland, privately printed, 1930. 59 pp.

HOLMES, THOMAS J. The Mather literature. Cleveland, privately printed, 1927. viii+64 pp.

MURDOCK, KENNETH B. Increase Mather. The foremost American puritan. Cambridge, Harvard university press, 1925. "List of books referred to," pp. [407]–15; "Check list of Mather's writings," pp. [416]–22.

MURDOCK, KENNETH B. Notes on Increase and Cotton Mather. Unitarian historical society. *Proceedings,* 1: 22–44, 1925.

Mathews, Cornelius, 1817–1889

FULLERTON, BRADFORD M. Selective bibliography, p. 191.

Maugham, William Somerset, 1874——

BASON, FREDERICK T. A bibliography of the writings of William Somerset Maugham. London, Unicorn press, 1931. 78 pp. Review, *Book-collector's quarterly,* January–March, no. 5, pp. 34–36, 1932. Contains many corrections of errors in the bibliography. Review, Library association. *Record,* n.s., 2: 72, 1932.

OVERTON, GRANT. Authors of the day. New York, Doran, [1924], pp. 363–65.

Maurice, Furnley, *pseud.*

See Wilmot, Frank Leslie Thompson.

May, Sophie, *pseud.*
See Clarke, Rebecca Sophia.

May, Thomas, 1595–1650
CHESTER, ALLAN G. Thomas May: man of letters, 1595–1650 ... Philadelphia, 1932. (Thesis, University of Pennsylvania.) Bibliography, pp. 189–96.

Mayo, William Starbuck, 1812–1895
FULLERTON, BRADFORD M. Selective bibliography, pp. 191–92.

Medwall, Henry, *fl.* 1486–1500
REED, A. W. Early Tudor drama: Medwall, the Rastells, Heywood, and the More circle. London, Methuen, 1931.

Meek, Alexander Beaufort, 1814–1865
FULLERTON, BRADFORD M. Selective bibliography, p. 192.

Melville, Herman, 1819–1891
BIRSS, JOHN H. An obscure Melville letter. *Notes and queries,* 163:275, 1932.
FREEMAN, JOHN. Herman Melville. New York, Macmillan, 1926. Bibliographical note, pp. 197–98.
FULLERTON, BRADFORD M. Selective bibliography, pp. 192–94.
JOHNSON, MERLE. American first editions, pp. 147–48 (247–48). The check-list in the 1929 edition was compiled by Meade Minnigerode.
MARSHALL, H. P. Herman Melville. *London Mercury,* 11: 56–70, 1925. The story of the writing of Melville's books.
MINNIGERODE, MEADE, *ed.* Some personal letters of Herman Melville and a bibliography. New York, Brick row bookshop, 1922.

Clarel, 1876.
CURLE, RICHARD. Collecting American first editions, p. 208.

Confidence man, 1857.

CURLE, RICHARD. Collecting American first editions, p. 105.

Israel Potter, 1855.

CURLE, RICHARD. Collecting American first editions, p. 9.

John Marr, 1888.

CURLE, RICHARD. Collecting American first editions, p. 208.

Mardi, 1849.

CURLE, RICHARD. Collecting American first editions, pp. 105, 129–30.

Moby-Dick, 1851.

AMENT, WILLIAM S. Bowdler and the whale. Some notes on the first English and the first American editions of *Moby-Dick. American literature,* 4: 39–46, 1933.

CURLE, RICHARD. Collecting American first editions, pp. 62, 104–5, 164, 174, 183–84. Facsimile of title-page, opp. p. 164.

GARNETT, R. S. Moby-Dick and Mocha-Dick. A literary find. *Blackwood's magazine,* 226: 841–58, 1929.

WINTERICH, JOHN T. Romantic stories of books. Second series. IV: *Moby-Dick. Publishers' weekly,* 116: 2391–94, 1929.

Omoo, 1847.

CURLE, RICHARD. Collecting American first editions, pp. 105, 129, 142–43.

Piazza tales, 1856.

CURLE, RICHARD. Collecting American first editions, p. 210.

Pierre, 1852.

CURLE, RICHARD. Collecting American first editions, p. 105.

Redburn, 1849.

CURLE, RICHARD. Collecting American first editions, p. 210.

Timoleon, 1891.

CURLE, RICHARD. Collecting American first editions, p. 208.

Melville, Herman (*Continued*)

Typee, 1846.

ADKINS, N. F. A note on Herman Melville's *Typee. New England quarterly,* 5: 348–51, 1932.

CURLE, RICHARD. Collecting American first editions, pp. 58, 129, 194.

Whale, 1851.

CURLE, RICHARD. Collecting American first editions, pp. 183–84.

White-jacket, 1850.

CURLE, RICHARD. Collecting American first editions, p. 105.

Mencken, Henry Louis, 1880——

BOYD, ERNEST A. H. L. Mencken. New York, McBride, 1925. Bibliography, pp. 87–89.

FREY, CARROLL. A bibliography of the writings of H. L. Mencken. Philadelphia, Centaur book shop, 1924. 70 pp.

JOHNSON, MERLE. American first editions, pp. 149–50 (249–52). The check-list in the 1929 edition was compiled by David Moss.

MOSS, DAVID. American first editions: H. L. Mencken, 1880——. *Publishers' weekly,* 103: 1327–28, 1923.

Mercer, Thomas

SERLE, PERCIVAL. Bibliography of Australasian poetry, p. 135.

Meredith, George, 1828–1909

CARTER, JOHN. Binding variants in English publishing, 1820–1900. London, Constable, 1932.

COOLIDGE, BERTHA. A catalogue of the Altschul collection of George Meredith in the Yale university library ... with an introduction by Chauncey Brewster Tinker. New York, privately printed, 1931. xvii+196 pp. Reviews, *Books,* 7: 19, June 14, 1931; *Book-collector's quarterly,* no. 3, June–August, 1931, pp. 94–99.

FIRST EDITION CLUB. A bibliographical catalogue, pp. 97–98.

FORMAN, MAURICE B. Meredithiana: being a supplement to the bibliography of George Meredith. Edinburgh, Dunedin press, 1925. (Bibliographical society, small quarto series.)

SAWYER and DARTON. English books, v. 2, pp. 344–45, 350.

Meredith, Louisa Anne

See Twamley, Louisa Anne (Meredith).

Meres, Francis, 1565–1647

Palladis tamia, 1598.

A copy of F. Meres' *Palladis tamia* (1598) sold (to Dr. A. S. Rosenbach). *Times literary supplement,* June 2, 1932, p. 412.

Meynell, Alice Christina (Thompson), 1850–1922

STONEHILL, C. A., and STONEHILL, H. W. Bibliographies of modern authors. Second series. London, Castle, [1925].

TUELL, ANNE K. Mrs. Meynell and her literary generation. New York, Dutton, [1925]. Bibliographical notes, pp. 259–71.

Middleton, Thomas, 1570(?)–1627

Game at chesse.

BALD, R. C., *ed.* "Assembled texts," *Library,* s. 4, 12: [243]–48, 1932.

BALD, R. C., *ed.* A game at chesse, by Thomas Middleton. Cambridge, Cambridge university press, 1929. Contains notes of bibliographical interest.

Millay, Edna St. Vincent, 1892——

JOHNSON, MERLE. American first editions, pp. (253–54).

YOST, KARL. (Bibliography nearing completion.) *Publishers' weekly,* 122: 2201, 1932.

Miller, Joaquin Cincinnatus Heine, 1841–1913

Bland, Henry M. Joaquin Milleriana. *American collector,* 4: 154–58, 1927.

Fullerton, Bradford M. Selective bibliography, pp. 195–96.

Johnson, Merle. American first editions, pp. 153–55 (255–57).

Keough, M. J. American first editions: Joaquin Miller, 1841–1913. *Publishers' weekly,* 103: 1146–47, 1923.

Pacific poems, 1871.

American Art Association. Sales catalogue. Library of Frank Irving Fletcher. Facsimile of title-page, p. 128.

Miller, John Henry, 1702–1782

Dapp, Charles F. Evolution of an American patriot; being an intimate study of the patriotic activities of John Henry Miller, German printer, publisher, and editor of the American revolution. Philadelphia, 1924. (Thesis, University of Pennsylvania.) Bibliographical footnotes; bibliography, pp. 66–68. Facsimile of "Staatsbote," published in Philadelphia, 1762–1776.

Miller, Marion

See Knowles, Marion (Miller).

Milne, Allan Alexander, 1882——

Cutler and Stiles. Modern British authors, pp. 115–17.

Milton, John, 1608–1674

Agar, Herbert. Milton and Plato ... Princeton, N.J., Princeton university press, 1928. (Thesis, Princeton university.) Bibliography, pp. [73]–76.

Fletcher, Harris F. Contributions to a Milton bibliography, 1800–1930, being a list addenda to Stevens's *Reference guide to Milton.* Urbana, Ill., University of Illinois press, 1931. (University of Illinois. *Studies in language and literature,* v. 16, no. 1.) 166 pp.

FLETCHER, HARRIS F. Milton's Semitic studies. Chicago, University of Chicago press, 1927. Long classified bibliography.

HANFORD, JAMES H. Milton handbook. London, Bell; New York, Columbia university press, 1927. vii+304 pp. Review, *Modern language review,* 23 : 111–12, 1928.

MOORE, C. A. Miltoniana (1679–1741). *Modern philology,* 24 : 321–39, 1927.

ORAS, ANTS. Milton's editors and commentators from Patrick Hume to Henry John Todd (1695–1801). A study in critical views and methods. Dorpat, Estonia, University of Tartu; London, Milford, 1931. 281 pp.

SAWYER and DARTON. English books, v. 1, pp. 184–88.

STEVENS, DAVID H. Reference guide to Milton from 1800 to the present day. Chicago, University of Chicago press, 1930. "It includes every document relating to Milton and Miltonic scholarship between 1800 and 1928."—Review by Edith C. Batho and Elinor J. Vaughan, *Modern language review,* 26 : 203–4, 1931.

WITHERSPOON, ALEXANDER M. Exhibition of first and rare editions of Milton. Yale university library. *Gazette,* 7 : 10–14, 1932.

Comus, 1637.

CARLTON, W. N. C. The first edition of Milton's *Comus.* *American collector,* 5 : 107–13, 1928.

Decree ordering the burning of Milton's Eikonoklastes and Defensio populi, 1683.

MAGGS BROTHERS. Catalogue no. 550. London, 1931. Facsimile of title-page, opp. p. 505.

Lycidas, 1638.

TROXELL, GILBERT M. Milton's *Lycidas.* Yale university library. *Gazette,* 3 : 60, 1929.

Maske, 1637.

NEWTON, A. EDWARD. This book-collecting game. Boston, Little, Brown and co., 1928. Facsimile of title-page, p. 40.

Milton, John (*Continued*)

Paradise lost, 1667.

DARBISHIRE, HELEN, *ed.* The manuscript of Milton's *Paradise lost,* book I. London, Oxford university press, 1931. xlvii+38+74 pp.

MAGGS BROTHERS. Catalogue no. 550. London, 1931. Facsimile of title-page, opp. p. 489.

SAWYER and DARTON. English books, v. 1, pp. 16, 184–86. Facsimiles of first and second title-pages.

Mitchell, Donald Grant, 1822–1908

FULLERTON, BRADFORD M. Selective bibliography, pp. 195–96.

Reveries of a bachelor, 1850.

CURLE, RICHARD. Collecting American first editions, p. 204.

Mitchell, Isaac, *d.* 1812.

FULLERTON, BRADFORD M. Selective bibliography, pp. 196–97.

Mitchell, Silas Weir, 1829–1914

BURR, ANNA R. Weir Mitchell: his life and letters. New York, Duffield, 1929. Bibliography, pp. 397–413.

FULLERTON, BRADFORD M. Selective bibliography, pp. 197–98.

JOHNSON, MERLE. American first editions, pp. 197–98 (258–60). The check-list in the 1929 edition was compiled by Alfred P. Lee.

LEE, ALFRED P. American first editions, S. Weir Mitchell, 1829–1914. *Publishers' weekly,* 103: 415–16, 1923.

Montague, Charles Edward, 1867–1928

MONTAGUE, CHARLES E. A writer's notes on his trade. Introduction by H. M. Tomlinson. London, Chatto & Windus, 1930.

Montefiore, Moses Haim, (*Sir*), 1784–1885

GOODMAN, PAUL. Moses Montefiore. Philadelphia, Jewish publication society of America, 1925. Bibliography, pp. [231]–50.

Moody, William Vaughn, 1869–1910

JOHNSON, MERLE. American first editions, pp. 159 (261).

Moore, Clement Clarke, 1779–1863

FULLERTON, BRADFORD M. Selective bibliography, pp. 198–99.

Moore, Edward, 1712–1757

CASKEY, JOHN H. The life and works of Edward Moore. New Haven, Yale university press, 1927. (Thesis, Yale university.)

Moore, George, 1852——

CUTLER and STILES. Modern British authors, pp. 118–21.

FIRST EDITION CLUB. A bibliographical catalogue, pp. 99–100.

Moore, Julia A. (Davis), 1847–1920

The sweet singer. *The month at Goodspeed's,* 1:163–65, 1930. Facsimile of the cover of *The sentimental song book,* Cleveland, 1877.

Moore, Thomas, 1779–1852

MACMANUS, M. J. A bibliography of Thomas Moore. *Dublin magazine,* 1933.

More, Thomas, (*Sir*), 1478–1535

The English works of Sir Thomas More. Reproduced in black-letter facsimile from the only previous edition, edited by William Rastell in 1557. Now re-edited with a version in modern spelling by W. E. Campbell. With historical introduction and with philological notes, collations, and appendices by A. W. Reed and R. W. Chambers, together with an essay and collations by W. A. S. Doyle-Davidson. London, Eyre & Spottiswoode, 1931– (To be completed in seven volumes).

More, Thomas (*Continued*)

Doyle-Davidson, W. A. S. Essay and collation in the English works of Sir Thomas More. London, Eyre and Spottiswoode, 1931.

Utopia.

Gee, John A. The second edition of the *Utopia,* Paris, 1517. Yale university library. *Gazette,* 7 : 87–88, 1933.

Tannenbaum, Samuel. The booke of Sir Thomas More. (A bibliotic study.) New York, privately printed, [1927]. 155 pp., 22 facsimiles. Review by Walter W. Greg, *Library,* s. 4, 9 : 202–11, 1929.

Workes, 1557.

Maggs Brothers. Catalogue no. 555. London, 1931. Facsimile of title-page, p. 504.

See also Medwall, Henry.

Morley, Christopher, 1890——

Johnson, Merle. American first editions, pp. 160–63 (262–67). The check-list in the 1929 edition was compiled by Aaron Mendoza.

Mendoza, Aaron. American first editions: Christopher Morley, 1890——. *Publishers' weekly,* 103 : 1705–6, 1768–70; 104 : 109, 1923.

Overton, Grant. American nights entertainment. New York, Appleton, 1923, pp. 378–79.

Overton, Grant. Authors of the day. New York, Doran, [1924], pp. 218–19.

Schwartz, H. Warren. Check-lists of twentieth-century authors. Milwaukee, Wis., Casanova booksellers, 1933.

Stone, Harry. Christopher Morley. His books in first editions. Introduction by Burton Emmett. New York, Harry Stone, 1930. xxiii pp.

Morley, John, (*Viscount*), 1838–1923

Harvey, F. Brompton. Two anonymous books by Lord Morley. *Contemporary review,* 132 : [750]–56, 1927.

Morris, George Pope, 1802–1864
FULLERTON, BRADFORD M. Selective bibliography, p. 199.

Morris, Gouverneur, 1752–1816
WALTHER, DANIEL. Gouverneur Morris, témoin de deux révolutions ... Lausanne, Imprimerie Mérinat-Brive, 1932. (Thesis, Université de Genève.) Bibliography, pp. [291]–307.

Morris, William, 1834–1896
SPARLING, H. HALLIDAY. The Kelmscott press and William Morris. London, Macmillan, 1924. 187 pp.

Morton, Nathaniel, 1613–1685
LORD, ARTHUR. Remarks on the editions of Nathaniel Morton's *New England's memorial.* Colonial society of America. *Publications,* 26: 158–62, 1927.

Morton, Sarah Wentworth, 1759–1846
FULLERTON, BRADFORD M. Selective bibliography, p. 200.
See also Brown, William Hill.

Motley, John Lothrop, 1814–1877
FULLERTON, BRADFORD M. Selective bibliography, pp. 200–201.

Moulton, Ellen Louise (Chandler), 1835–1908
FULLERTON, BRADFORD M. Selective bibliography, p. 201.

Mullens, Arthur Frank Macquarie
SERLE, PERCIVAL. Bibliography of Australasian poetry, p. 143.

Munday, Anthony, 1553–1633
HAYES, GERALD R. Anthony Munday's romances, a postscript. *Library,* s. 4, 7: [31]–38, 1927.
HAYES, GERALD R. Anthony Munday's romances of chivalry. *Library,* s. 4, 7: [57]–81, 1927.
SAWYER and DARTON. English books, v. 1, pp. 72–74.

Munday, Anthony (*Continued*)

TURNER, CELESTE. Anthony Munday, an Elizabethan man of letters. Berkeley, Cal., 1928. Bibliography, pp. 199–223.

Paradoxes, 1602.

BENNETT, R. E. Munday's *Paradoxes. Times literary supplement,* August 20, 1931, p. 633. Relates to a fragment of the 1602 edition in the Bodleian library.

Sir Thomas More.

SAWYER and DARTON. English books, v. 1, p. [143]. Facsimile of a page of the manuscript said to be in the handwriting of Shakespeare.

Munroe, Kirk, 1850——

FULLERTON, BRADFORD M. Selective bibliography, p. 202.

Murphy, Paddy, *pseud.*

See Bracken, Thomas.

Murry, Katherine Middleton, 1888–1923

CUTLER and STILES. Modern British authors, p. 110.

MANTZ, RUTH E. The critical bibliography of Katherine Mansfield. London, Constable, 1931. xx+204 pp. Review by Percy H. Muir, *Book-collector's quarterly,* no. 5, pp. 89–91, January–March, 1931.

STONEHILL, C. A., and STONEHILL, H. W. Bibliographies of modern authors. Second series. London, Castle, [1925].

Myers, Peter Hamilton, 1812–1878

FULLERTON, BRADFORD M. Selective bibliography, p. 203.

Nasby, Petroleum V., *pseud.*

See Locke, David Ross.

Nash, Thomas, 1567–1601

KANE, ROBERT J. Anthony Chute, Thomas Nashe, and the first English work on tobacco. *Review of English studies,* 7: 151–59, 1931.

SAWYER and DARTON. English books, v. 1, pp. 103, 137–39.

Return of the renowned cavaliero Pasquill of England, 1589.

SAWYER and DARTON. English books, v. 1, p. [138]. Facsimile of title-page.

Nathan, George Jean, 1882——

GOTHAM BOOK MART. American first editions: George Jean Nathan, 1882——. *Publishers' weekly,* 104: 380, 1923.

JOHNSON, MERLE. American first editions, pp. 165–66 (270–71). The check-list in the 1929 edition was compiled by David Moss.

Nathan, Robert Gruntal, 1894——

JOHNSON, MERLE. American first editions, p. (272).

Neal, John, 1793–1876

FULLERTON, BRADFORD M. Selective bibliography, pp. 203–5.

Neal, Joseph Clay, 1807–1847

FULLERTON, BRADFORD M. Selective bibliography, p. 205.

Neihardt, John Gneisenau, 1881——

JOHNSON, MERLE. American first editions, pp. 167–68 (273–74).

Newell, Robert Henry, 1836–1891

FULLERTON, BRADFORD M. Selective bibliography, pp. 205–6.

Newman, John Henry, (*Cardinal*), 1801–1890

Apologia pro vita sua, 1864.

AMERICAN ART ASSOCIATION. Sales catalogue. The library of Frank Irving Fletcher. Facsimile of title-page, p. 165.

Newman's *Apologia pro vita sua.* The two versions of 1864 and 1865 . . . Introduction by Wilfred Ward. London, Oxford university press, 1932.

Newton, A. Edward, 1863——

HEARTMAN, CHARLES F. Sales catalogue. The library of the late George H. Sargent. Part II. The eminent A. Edward Newton collection. Metuchen, N.J., 1931.

SARGENT, GEORGE H. The writings of A. Edward Newton: a bibliography . . . with cogitations by Christopher Morley . . . Philadelphia, Rosenbach, 1927. xx+52 pp.

Norden, John, 1548–1625(?)

POLLARD, ALFRED W. The unity of John Norden: surveyor and religious writer. *Library,* s. 4, 7: [233]–52, 1927.

Norris, Frank (Benjamin Franklin), 1870–1902

EDGAR, RANDOLPH. American first editions: Frank Norris. *Publishers' weekly,* 103: 637, 1923.

FULLERTON, BRADFORD M. Selective bibliography, p. 206.

JOHNSON, MERLE. American first editions, pp. 169–70 (275–77). The check-list in the 1929 edition was compiled by Randolph Edgar.

TAYLOR, HARVEY. Frank Norris, two poems and "Kim" reviewed. With a bibliography by . . . San Francisco, Frank Taylor, 1930. 42 pp. Review, *American Mercury,* 21: xlvi (December), 1930.

WALKER, F. Frank Norris at the University of California. University of California. *Chronicle,* 33: 320–49, 1930. Bibliography covering 1890–1894.

Octopus, 1901.

MARTIN, WILLARD E., JR. The establishment of the order of printings in books printed from plates. Illustrated in Frank Norris' *The octopus,* with full collations. *American literature,* 5: 17–28, 1934.

Nott, Henry Junius, 1799–1837

FULLERTON, BRADFORD M. Selective bibliography, p. 207.

Nye, Bill, *pseud.*
See Nye, Edgar Watson.

Nye, Edgar Watson, 1850–1896
FULLERTON, BRADFORD M. Selective bibliography, p. 207.

Oakman, John, 1748(?)–1793
CARVER, P. L. A continuation of *John Gilpin. Review of English studies,* 8:205–10, 1932.

O'Brien, Fitz-James, 1828–1862
FULLERTON, BRADFORD M. Selective bibliography, p. 208.

Odell, Jonathan, 1737–1818
FULLERTON, BRADFORD M. Selective bibliography, pp. 254–55.

O'Dowd, Bernard Patrick, 1866——
SERLE, PERCIVAL. Bibliography of Australasian poetry, pp. 149–50.

O'Flaherty, Liam, 1897——
GAWSWORTH, JOHN, *pseud.,* (T. Fytton Armstrong). Ten contemporaries: notes toward their definitive bibliography. Second series. London, Joiner & Steele, 1932.

Ogilby, John, 1600–1676
CLAPP, SAMUEL L. C. The subscription enterprises of John Ogilby and Richard Blome. *Modern philology,* 30:365, 1933.
FORDHAM, HERBERT G., (*Sir*). John Ogilby (1600–1676). His *Britannia* and the British itineraries of the eighteenth century. *Library,* s. 4, 6: [157]–78, 1926.

Ogilvie, William Henry, 1869——
SERLE, PERCIVAL. Bibliography of Australasian poetry, pp. 150–51.

O'Hara, John Bernard, 1862——
SERLE, PERCIVAL. Bibliography of Australasian poetry, p. 151.

Oliver, George, 1873——

GAWSWORTH, JOHN, *pseud.,* (T. Fytton Armstrong). Ten contemporaries: notes toward their definitive bibliography. First series. London, Benn, 1932.

O'Neill, Eugene, 1888——

CLARK, BARRETT H. Eugene O'Neill. New York, McBride, 1926. Bibliography, pp. 101–10.

JOHNSON, MERLE. American first editions, pp. 171–72 (278–79). The check-list in the 1929 edition was compiled by Frank Shay.

MACKAIL, L. L. Notes for bibliophiles: Eugene O'Neill's bibliography. (A review.) *Books,* 7: 15, August 9, 1931.

SANBORN, RALPH, and CLARK, BARRETT H. A bibliography of the works of Eugene O'Neill. New York, Random house, 1931. xiv+171 pp.

SHAY, FRANK. American first editions: Eugene O'Neill, 1888——. *Publishers' weekly,* 103: 1216, 1923.

Onions, Oliver, *pseud.*

See Oliver, George.

Oppenheim, Edward Phillips, 1866——

OVERTON, GRANT. Cargoes for Crusoes. New York, Appleton, [1924], pp. 138–42.

Optic, Oliver, *pseud.*

See Adams, William Taylor.

O'Reilly, John Boyle, 1844–1890

FULLERTON, BRADFORD M. Selective bibliography, p. 209.

Orrery, Roger Boyle, (*Earl*), 1621–1679

CLARK, WILLIAM S. Notes on two Orrery manuscripts. *Modern language notes,* 44: 1–6, 1929.

Osborn, Sarah Byng, 1693–1775
McClelland, John, *ed.* Letters of Sarah Byng Osborn, 1721–1773. Stanford university, Stanford university press, 1931. Brief bibliography.

Ossian, *pseud.*
See Macpherson, James.

Ossoli, Sarah Margaret (Fuller) d', 1810–1850
Fullerton, Bradford M. Selective bibliography, pp. 210–11.

Otis, James, *pseud.*
See Kaler, James Otis.

Otway, Thomas, 1652–1685
Ghosh, J. C., *ed.* The works of Thomas Otway: plays, poems, and love letters. Oxford, Clarendon press, 1932. 2 v. Bibliography, v. 1, pp. [64]–84.
Sawyer and Darton. English books, v. 1, p. 210.

Owens, Robert, 1771–1858
National Library of Wales. A bibliography of Robert Owens, the socialist, 1771–1858. Cardiff, 1925. viii+90 pp. (Second edition.)

Oxford, Edward de Vere, (*17th Earl*)
See De Vere, Edward.

Packard, Frank Lucius, 1877——
Overton, Grant. Cargoes for Crusoes. New York, Appleton, [1924], pp. 346–47.

Page, Thomas Nelson, 1853–1922
Cappon, Lester J. Bibliography of Virginia history since 1865. University, Va., Institute for research in the social sciences, 1930.
Fullerton, Bradford M. Selective bibliography, p. 211.
Johnson, Merle. American first editions, pp. 173–74 (280–82).

Paine, Robert Treat, Jr., 1773–1811

Fullerton, Bradford M. Selective bibliography, p. 212.

Paine, Thomas, 1737–1809

Smith, Frank. New light on Thomas Paine's first year in America, 1775. *American literature,* 1 : 347–71, 1930. List of contributions to periodicals.

Painter, William, 1540(?)–1594

Palace of pleasure, 1566.

Sawyer and Darton. English books, v. 1, p. 104. Facsimile of title-page.

Palmer, Herbert Edward, 1880——

Gawsworth, John, *pseud.,* (T. Fytton Armstrong). Ten contemporaries: notes toward their definitive bibliography. First series. London, Benn, 1932.

Parker, Gilbert, (*Sir*), 1862–1932

Pierce, Lorne. Outline of Canadian literature, pp. 29–32, 93–94.

Parker, Matthew, 1504–1575

Pearce, E. C. Matthew Parker. *Library,* s. 4, 6 : [209]–28, 1926.

Parkes, Henry, (*Sir*), 1815–1896

Serle, Percival. Bibliography of Australasian poetry, p. 155.

Parks, William, *d.* 1750

Wroth, Lawrence. William Parks, printer and journalist of England and Colonial America. With a list of the issues of his several presses and a facsimile of the earliest Virginia imprint known to be in existence. Richmond, Va., 1926. (The William Parks club. *Publications,* no. 3.)

Parley, Peter, *pseud.*

See Goodrich, Samuel Griswold, *and* Hawthorne, Nathaniel.

Parsons, Thomas William, 1819–1892

FULLERTON, BRADFORD M. Selective bibliography, pp. 212–13.

Partington, Mrs., *pseud.*

See Shillaber, Benjamin Penhallow.

Parton, James, 1822–1891

FULLERTON, BRADFORD M. Selective bibliography, p. 213.

Parton, Sarah Willis, 1811–1872

FULLERTON, BRADFORD M. Selective bibliography, p. 214.

Partridge, John, 1644–1715

EDDY, W. A. The wits vs. John Partridge, astrologer. *Studies in philology,* 29: 29–40, 1932. Includes a bibliography.

Pater, Erra

Prognostications, ca. 1604.

MAGGS BROTHERS. Catalogue no. 550. London, 1931. Facsimile of title-page.

Pater, Walter Horatio, 1839–1894

CARTER, JOHN. Binding variants in English publishing, 1820–1900. London, Constable, 1932.

CUTLER and STILES. Modern British authors, p. 122.

FARMER, ARTHUR J. Walter Pater as a critic of English literature. Grenoble, Didier et Richard, 1931. Bibliography, pp. [108]–9.

STONEHILL, C. A., and STONEHILL, H. W. Bibliographies of modern authors. Second series. London, Castle, [1925].

Paterson, Andrew Barton, 1864——

SERLE, PERCIVAL. Bibliography of Australasian poetry, p. 156.

Paterson, Daniel, 1738–1825

FORDHAM, HERBERT G., (*Sir*). *Paterson's roads.* Daniel Paterson, his maps and itineraries, 1738–1825. *Library,* s. 4, 5: [332]–56, 1925. Facsimiles.

Patten, William, *fl.* 1548–1580

Expedicion into Scotlande, 1548.

MAGGS BROTHERS. Catalogue no. 550. London, 1931. Facsimile of title-page, opp. p. 584.

Paulding, James Kirke, 1778–1860

FULLERTON, BRADFORD M. Selective bibliography, pp. 214–16.

HEROLD, AMOS L. James Kirke Paulding. New York, Columbia university press, 1926. (Columbia university. *Studies in English and comparative literature.*) Published also as thesis, Columbia university. Bibliography, pp. 148–60.

JOHNSON, MERLE. American first editions, pp. (283–85).

Westward ho! 1832.

ADKINS, NELSON F. A study of James K. Paulding's *Westward ho! American collector,* 3: 221–29, 1927.

Payne, John Howard, 1792–1852

FULLERTON, BRADFORD M. Selective bibliography, p. 216.

Peacock, Thomas Love, 1785–1866

BRETT-SMITH, H. F. B., and JONES, C. E., *eds.* The collected works of Thomas Love Peacock. London, Constable, 1931. Each volume has a series of bibliographical notes.

Peck, George Wilbur, 1840–1916

FULLERTON, BRADFORD M. Selective bibliography, pp. 216–17.

Peck, Samuel Minturn, 1854——

FULLERTON, BRADFORD M. Selective bibliography, p. 217.

Peele, George, 1588(?)–1597(?)

GREG, WALTER W. A Collier mystification. *Review of English studies,* 1: 452–54, 1925.

LARSEN, THORLEIF. The growth of the Peele canon. *Library,* s. 4, 11: [300]–311, 1931.

See also Shakespeare, William.

Pennell, Joseph, 1860–1926

PENNELL, JOSEPH. The adventures of an illustrator ... Little, Brown and co., 1925. "Books illustrated and written by Joseph Pennell," pp. 363–64.

Pepys, Samuel, 1633–1703

Diary, 1825.

TANNER, FRANK R. Mr. Pepys: an introduction to the diary, together with a sketch of his later life. London, Bell, 1925. Bibliographical note, pp. 229–30.

WINTERICH, JOHN T. Books and the man. New York, Greenberg, 1929. Facsimile of title-page, p. 321.

Percival, James Gates, 1795–1856

FULLERTON, BRADFORD M. Selective bibliography, pp. 217–18.

Percy, Florence, *pseud.*

See Allen, Elizabeth Ann (Akers).

Percy, Thomas, 1729–1811

Reliques, 1765.

POWELL, L. F. Percy's *Reliques. Library,* s. 4, 9: [113]–37, 1929. Facsimile of title-page.

Phelps, Elizabeth (Stuart), 1815–1852

FULLERTON, BRADFORD M. Selective bibliography, pp. 218-19.

Phillpotts, Eden, 1862——

Hinton, Percival. Eden Philpotts: a bibliography of first editions. Birmingham, Greville Worthington, 1931. xvi+164 pp. Review, *Book-collector's quarterly,* no. 5, January–March, 1932.

"Phiz," *pseud.*

See Browne, Hablot Knight.

Phoenix, John, *pseud.*

See Derby, George Horatio.

Piatt, John James, 1835–1917

Fullerton, Bradford M. Selective bibliography, p. 219.

Pickering, William, 1796–1854

Keynes, Geoffrey. William Pickering, publisher. A memoir & a hand-list of his editions. London, The Flueron, 1924. 110 pp., facsimiles. List of authorities, p. 85.

Pickthall, Marjorie Lowery Christie, 1883–1922

Pierce, Lorne. Outline of Canadian literature, pp. 103–5.

Pierpont, John, 1785–1866

Fullerton, Bradford M. Selective bibliography, pp. 219–20.

Pike, Albert, 1809–1891

Fullerton, Bradford M. Selective bibliography, pp. 220–21.

Pike, Zebulon Montgomery, 1779–1813

Hart, Stephen H., and Hulbert, Archer B. Arkansaw journal . . . with bibliographical résumé. Denver, Colo., Stewart commission of Colorado college, 1932.

Pinckney, Edward Coote, 1802–1828

Fullerton, Bradford M. Selective bibliography, pp. 221–22.

Piozzi, Hester Lynch

See Thrale, Hester (Lynch), *and* Johnson, Samuel.

Poe, Edgar Allan, 1809–1849

ALLEN, HARVEY. Israfel. New York, Doran, 1926.

AMERICAN ART ASSOCIATION. Sales catalogue. First editions, inscribed copies, and autograph letters of Joseph Conrad, property of Mrs. Ford Madox Hueffer; an important Kipling collection; the fine Poe collection of Mr. Joseph Jackson. New York, 1928.

AMERICAN ART ASSOCIATION. Sales catalogue. Stephen H. Wakeman collection. New York, 1924. Items 931–71.

BLOMBERG, HUSE. A bibliography of Edgar Allan Poe. New York, Random house, 1932. 140 pp., 10 facsimiles.

CAMPBELL, KILLIS. Recent books about Poe. *Studies in philology,* 24: 474–79, 1927.

ENGLEKIRK, J. E. *The song of Hollands,* an inedited tale ascribed to Poe. *New Mexico quarterly,* 1: 247–70, 1931.

FULLERTON, BRADFORD M. Selective bibliography, pp. 222–24.

HEARTMAN, CHARLES F., and REDE, KENNETH. Census of first editions and source materials by Edgar Allan Poe in American collections . . . Metuchen, N.J., 1932. Contents, v. 1, Bibliographical check-list of first editions of Edgar Allan Poe; v. 2, Edgar Allan Poe's contributions to annuals and periodicals: a check-list.

Helen, Israfel, and other masterpieces. *The month at Goodspeed's,* 2: 59–64, 1930. Facsimile of title-page of *Poems,* second edition, New York, 1831.

HUNGERFORD, EDWARD. Poe and phrenology. *American literature,* 2: 209–31, 1930–1931.

HUTCHERSON, DUDLEY. The Philadelphia *Saturday museum* text of Poe's poems. *American literature,* 5: 36–48, 1934.

Poe, Edgar Allan (*Continued*)

JOHNSON, MERLE. American first editions, pp. 175–76 (286–88).

LEMONNIER, LÉON. Les traducteurs d'Edgar Poe en France de 1845 à 1875: Charles Baudelaire. Paris, Presses universitaires, 1928. 214 pp.

MABBOTT, THOMAS O. Newly-identified reviews by Edgar Poe. *Notes and queries,* 163: 441, 1932.

PHILLIPS, MARY E. Edgar Allan Poe, the man. Philadelphia, Winston, 1926. 2 v.

REDE, KENNETH. New Poe manuscript. *American collector,* 3: 100–102, 1927.

REDE, KENNETH. Poe notes from an investigator's note book. *American literature,* 5: 49–54, 1934. Material acquired in connection with the collection of materials for a bibliographical census of Poe.

REDE, KENNETH. Poe's *Annie.* Leaves from the lonesome later years. *American collector,* 4: 21–28, 1927.

RICHARDS, IRVING T. A new Poe poem. *Modern language notes,* 42: 158–62, 1927.

SCHULTE, AMANDA P. Facts about Poe . . . with a sketch of the life of Poe by James S. Wilson. Charlotteville, Va., University of Virginia, 1926. Selected bibliography, pp. 23–25.

SEYLAZ, LOUIS. Edgar Poe et les premiers symbolistes français. Lausanne, La Concorde, 1923. Bibliography, pp. [179]–83.

SPARKE, ARCHIBALD. Edgar Allen Poe: bibliography. *Notes and queries,* 159: 465, 1930. Brief list of sources for a Poe bibliography.

WALLACE, ALFRED R. Edgar Allan Poe: a series of seventeen letters concerning Poe's scientific erudition in *Eureka* and his authorship of *Leonainie.* New York, Union square bookshop, 1930. 18 pp.

WEGELIN, OSCAR. Poe's first printer. *American collector,* 3: 31, 1927.

WING, DONALD G. Poe exhibition. Yale university library. *Gazette,* 4: 51–52, 1930.

Al Aaraaf, 1820 [i.e., 1829].

AMERICAN ART ASSOCIATION. Sales catalogue. Stephen H. Wakeman collection. New York, 1924. Item 936. Facsimile of title-page.

CURLE, RICHARD. Collecting American first editions, p. 119.

MABBOTT, THOMAS O. Al Aaraaf: reproduced from the edition of 1829; with a bibliographical note by . . . New York, Columbia university press, 1933. (Facsimile text society, series 1, language and literature, v. 9.) *Ibid.,* London, Oxford university press, 1933.

Arthur Gordon Pym, 1838.

CURLE, RICHARD. Collecting American first editions, pp. 184–85.

Conchologist's first book, 1839.

CURLE, RICHARD. Collecting American first editions, pp. 31–32.

Doings of Gotham.

Doings of Gotham, by Edgar Allan Poe. As described in a series of letters to the editors of the *Columbia Spy* together with various editorial comments and criticisms by Poe. Also a poem entitled "New years address of the carriers of the Columbia Spy." Now first collected by Jacob E. Spannuth with a preface, introduction, and comments by Thomas Ollive Mabbott. Pottsville, Pa., Spannuth, 1929. Bibliographical notes. Review by Lewis Chase, *American literature,* 2: 200–201, 1931.

English notes, 1842.

CARLTON, W. N. C. The authorship of *English notes,* by Quarles Quickens. *American collector,* 1: 186–90, 1926.

Eureka, 1848.

CURLE, RICHARD. Collecting American first editions, pp. 106–7.

Poe, Edgar Allan (*Continued*)

Journal of Julius Rodman.

CRAWFORD, POLLY P. Lewis and Clark's expedition as a source of Poe's *Journal of Julius Rodman.* University of Texas. *Studies in English,* 12: 158–70, 1932.

Mesmerism, 1846.

CURLE, RICHARD. Collecting American first editions, p. 186.

Murders in the Rue Morgue, 1843.

CURLE, RICHARD. Collecting American first editions, p. 169.

Poems, 1831.

AMERICAN ART ASSOCIATION. Sales catalogue. Stephen H. Wakeman collection. New York, 1924. Item 935. Facsimile of title-page of second edition, 1831.

CURLE, RICHARD. Collecting American first editions, p. 119. Facsimile of title-page of second edition (New York, 1831), opp. p. 118.

Raven, 1845.

CURLE, RICHARD. Collecting American first editions, pp. 184–85, 197–98. Facsimile of title-page, frontispiece.

Tales, 1845 and 1846.

CURLE, RICHARD. Collecting American first editions, pp. 184–86.

WINTERICH, JOHN T. Books and the man. New York, Greenberg, 1929, pp. 251–65. Facsimile of title-page of first edition.

Tales of the grotesque, 1840.

AMERICAN ART ASSOCIATION. Sales catalogue. Library of Frank Irving Fletcher. New York, 1932. Facsimile of title-page, p. 140.

CURLE, RICHARD. Collecting American first editions, p. 208.

Tamerlane, 1827.

CURLE, RICHARD. Collecting American first editions, p. 169.

STARRETT, VINCENT. Pennywise and book foolish. New York, Covici Friede, 1929. Facsimile of title-page, p. 24.

WINTERICH, JOHN T. Books and the man. New York, Greenberg, 1929. Facsimile of title-page, p. 252.

Polmon, John

Famous battels, ca. 1586.

MAGGS BROTHERS. Catalogue no. 550. London, 1931. Facsimile of title-page, opp. p. 488.

Pope, Alexander, 1688–1744

AUDRA, E. L'influence française dans l'œuvre de Pope. Paris, Champion, 1931. Includes an exhaustive bibliography.

AUDRA, E. Les traductions françaises de Pope (1717–1825). Étude de bibliographie. Paris, Champion, 1931. xviii+136 pp. "Starting with the translations to be found at the Bibliothèque nationale, he followed these up by references to other Parisian libraries, to those in the French provinces, in Holland and Belgium, to the Preussische Staatsbibliothek, the British museum and the Bodleian."—*Year's work in English studies,* 12: 243–44, 1931. Bibliographical details are given and copies located.

CASE, ARTHUR E. Notes on the bibliography of Pope. *Modern philology,* 24: 297–313, 1927.

SAWYER and DARTON. English books, v. 1, pp. 250–56.

WISE, THOMAS J. A Pope library, a catalogue of plays, poems, and prose writings by Alexander Pope . . . London, privately printed, 1931. xxiv+113 pp., facsimiles. Contents, part 1, the writings of Alexander Pope; part 2, Popeiana.

Dunciad, 1728.

CHANDLER, W. K. The first edition of the *Dunciad. Modern philology,* 29: 59–72, 1932.

Pope, Alexander (*Continued*)

Essay on criticism, 1711.

SAWYER and DARTON. English books, v. 1, p. ⌊236⌋. Facsimile of title-page.

Iliad.

GRIFFITH, REGINALD H. A piracy of Pope's *Iliad. Studies in philology,* 28: 737–41, 1931. Refers to T. Johnson's Dutch edition, 1718–1721.

Porter, William Sidney, 1862–1910

O. Henry papers: containing some sketches of his life, together with an alphabetical index to his complete works. Garden City, Doubleday, ⌊1923⌋. Revised edition. Bibliography, pp. ⌊42–44⌋.

JOHNSON, MERLE. American first editions, pp. 98–99 (289–90). The check-list in the 1929 edition was compiled by Henry C. Quinby.

Post, Melville Davisson, 1871——

OVERTON, GRANT. Cargoes for Crusoes. New York, Appleton, ⌊1924⌋.

Postl, Karl, 1793–1864

DJORDJEWITSCH, MILOSCH. Charles Sealsfields Auffassung des Amerikanertums und seine literarhistorische Stellung. Weimar, Duncker, 1931. "Literatur," pp. ⌊128⌋–35.

Pound, Ezra Louis, 1865——

JOHNSON, MERLE. American first editions, pp. 177–78 (291–93). The check-list in the 1929 edition was compiled by Vrest Orton.

Power, D'Arcy, (*Sir*), 1855——

Selected writings, 1877–1930. Oxford, Clarendon press, 1931. Short-title bibliography of 609 entries. Review by Alfred W. Pollard, *Library,* s. 4, 11: 515–16, 1931.

Powys, Theodore Francis, 1875——

CUTLER and STILES. Modern British authors, pp. 123–24.

MUIR, PERCY H., and VAN THAL, B. Bibliographies of the first editions of books by Aldous Huxley and T. F. Powys. London, Dulau, 1927. 61 pp.

Pratt, E. J., 1883——

PIERCE, LORNE. Outline of Canadian literature, pp. 102–3.

Prentice, George Denison, 1802–1870

FULLERTON, BRADFORD M. Selective bibliography, pp. 224–25.

Preston, Margaret (Junkin), 1825–1897

FULLERTON, BRADFORD M. Selective bibliography, p. 225.

Preston, Thomas, 1537–1598

SAWYER and DARTON. English books, v. 1, p. 119.

Priestley, John Boynton, 1894——

JONES, L. ALYN. The first editions of J. B. Priestley. *Bookman* (London), 80: 46, 1931.

Pringle, Thomas, 1789–1834

ROBINSON, GEORGE W. A bibliography of Thomas Pringle's *Afar in the desert.* Bibliographical society of America. *Papers,* 17: 21–54, 1923.

Prior, Matthew, 1664–1721

Letters of Matthew Prior. *Times literary supplement,* April 25, 1929, p. 344.

Prynne, William, 1600–1669

KIRBY, ETHYN W. William Prynne: a study in puritanism. Cambridge, Harvard university press, 1931. "There is a full bibliography of Prynne's own works and a good list of selected books, contemporary and subsequent, which have to do with his activities."—*Year's work in English studies,* 12: 201, 1931.

Purney, Thomas

WHITE, H. O., *ed.* The works of Thomas Purney . . . Oxford, Blackwell, 1933. Bibliography, pp. 91–93. Facsimiles of title-pages of *Ordinary of Newgate,* 1723; *Pastorals,* 1717; *Pastorals, viz The bashful swain,* 1717.

Pyle, Howard, 1853–1911

FULLERTON, BRADFORD M. Selective bibliography, p. 226.

JOHNSON, MERLE. American first editions, pp. 179–81 (294–96).

Quad, M., *pseud.*

See Lewis, Charles Bertrand.

Quarles, Francis, 1592–1644

USTICK, W. L. Later editions of Quarles's *Enchiridion. Library,* s. 4, 9: [184]–86, 1929.

Quickens, Quarles, *pseud.*

See Poe, Edgar Allan.

Rae, John

SERLE, PERCIVAL. Bibliography of Australasian poetry, p. 164.

Rae, John ("Australian sparrow")

SERLE, PERCIVAL. Bibliography of Australasian poetry, pp. 164–65.

Raleigh, Walter, (*Sir*), 1552(?)–1618

SAWYER and DARTON. English books, v. 1, p. 140.

WALDMAN, MILTON. Sir Walter Raleigh. New York, Harper, 1928. *Ibid.,* London, Lane, [1928]. Bibliography, pp. 239–44.

Raleigh, Walter Alexander, (*Sir*), 1861–1922

RALEIGH, LUCIE G., (*Lady*), *ed.* The letters of Sir Walter Raleigh, (1879–1922). New York, Macmillan, 1926. *Ibid.,* London, Methuen, [1926]. 2 v.

Ramsay, Allan, 1686–1758

MARTIN, BURNS. Allan Ramsay, a study of his life and works. Cambridge, Harvard university press, 1931.

MARTIN, BURNS. Bibliography of Allan Ramsay. Glasgow, Jackson, Wylie and co., 1931. 114 pp. Reprinted from the Glasgow bibliographical society. *Records,* v. 10, 1932.

Christ's kirk on the green, 1718.

MAGGS BROTHERS. Catalogue no. 550. London, 1931. Facsimile of title-page, opp. p. 536.

Rand, Theodore Harding, 1835–1900

PIERCE, LORNE. Outline of Canadian literature, p. 89.

Randall, James Ryder, 1839–1903

FULLERTON, BRADFORD M. Selective bibliography, pp. 226–27.

Randolph, Thomas, 1605–1635

DAY, CYRUS L. New poems by Randolph. *Review of English studies,* 8: 29–36, 1932.

MOORE-SMITH, G. C. New poems by Randolph. *Review of English studies,* 8: 202–3, 1932. Refers to the article by Cyrus L. Day.

MOORE-SMITH, G. C. Some unpublished poems of Thomas Randolph. *Anglica,* 2: [244]–57, 1925.

Drinking academy.

MOORE-SMITH, G. C. "The drinking academy" and its attribution to Thomas Randolph. Modern language association of America. *Publications,* 44: 631–34, 1929.

Rastell, John, *ca.* 1475–1536

GREG, WALTER W. Notes on some early plays. *Library,* s. 4, 12: [44]–56, 1932. Refers to Rastell's *Nature of the four elements.*

Read, Alexander, 1580(?)–1641

MENZIES, WALTER. Alexander Read, physician and surgeon, 1580–1640; his life, works, and library. *Library,* s. 4, 12: [46]–74, 1932.

Read, Opie, 1852——

FULLERTON, BRADFORD M. Selective bibliography, p. 227.

Read, Thomas Buchanan, 1822–1872

FULLERTON, BRADFORD M. Selective bibliography, pp. 227–28.

Reade, Charles, 1814–1884

CARTER, JOHN. Binding variants in English publishing, 1820–1900. London, Constable, 1932.

ELWIN, MALCOLM. Charles Reade, a biography. London, Cape, [1931]. Bibliography, pp. 365–72; "List of London theatrical productions and revivals," pp. 373–74.

SAWYER and DARTON. English books, v. 2, p. 314.

Cloister and the hearth, 1861.

(*Cloister and the hearth.*) *Times literary supplement,* August 15, 1929, p. 640.

Remington, Frederic Sackrider, 1867–1909

FULLERTON, BRADFORD M. Selective bibliography, p. 228.

JOHNSON, MERLE. American first editions, pp. 182–83 (297–98).

Rentoul, Annie Rattray

SERLE, PERCIVAL. Bibliography of Australasian poetry, p. 167.

Repplier, Agnes, 1855——

FULLERTON, BRADFORD M. Selective bibliography, p. 229.

Reynolds, John Hamilton, *pseud.,* 1796–1852

MARSH, G. L. The writings of Keats's friend Reynolds. (Bibliography.) *Studies in philology,* 25: 491–510, 1928.

Richards, Laura Elizabeth (Howe), 1850——
FULLERTON, BRADFORD M. Selective bibliography, p. 229.

Richardson, Dorothy M.
GAWSWORTH, JOHN, *pseud.,* (T. Fytton Armstrong). Ten contemporaries: notes toward their definitive bibliography. Second series. London, Joiner & Steele, 1932.

Richardson, John, (*Sir*), 1787–1865
PIERCE, LORNE. Outline of Canadian literature, pp. 25–27.

Riggs, Lynn, 1899——
STANLEY, W. S. CAMPBELL. Lynn Riggs: poet and dramatist. *Southwest review,* 15: 64–70, 1929.

Riley, James Whitcomb, 1849–1916
FULLERTON, BRADFORD M. Selective bibliography, pp. 229–30.
JOHNSON, MERLE. American first editions, pp. 184–85 (299–301). The check-list in the 1929 edition was compiled by Frederic Melcher.

Rinehart, Mary (Roberts), 1876——
OVERTON, GRANT. Authors of the day. New York, Doran, [1924], pp. 274–76.
RINEHART, MARY ROBERTS. My story. New York, Farrar and Rinehart, [1931].

Ritchie, Anne Isabella (Thackeray), (*Lady*), 1838–1918
RITCHIE, HESTER THACKERAY, *ed.* Thackeray and his daughter: the letters and journals of Anne Thackeray, with many letters of William Makepeace Thackeray ... New York, Harper, 1924. Chronological list of Lady Ritchie's books, p. 331.

Roberts, Charles George Douglas, 1860——
JOHNSON, MERLE. American first editions, pp. 186–88. Check-list compiled by O. L. Griffith.
PIERCE, LORNE. Outline of Canadian literature, pp. 33–35, 71–73.

Roberts, Theodore Goodridge, 1877——

Pierce, Lorne. Outline of Canadian literature, pp. 40–42.

Robertson, Morgan, 1861–1915

Johnson, Merle. American first editions, pp. (302–3).

Robinson, Edwin Arlington, 1869——

Beebe, Lucius, and Bulkley, Robert J., jr. A bibliography of the writings of Edwin Arlington Robinson. Cambridge, Dunster house bookshop, 1931. 59 pp.

Fullerton, Bradford M. Selective bibliography, p. 231.

Johnson, Merle. American first editions, pp. 189–90 (304–7). The check-list in the 1929 edition was compiled by Harold S. Latham.

Latham, Harold S. American first editions: Edwin Arlington Robinson. *Publishers' weekly,* 103: 945, 1923.

Morris, Lloyd R. The poetry of Edwin Arlington Robinson ... New York, Doran, 1923. Bibliography by W. Van R. Whitall, pp. [81]–112.

Redman, Ben R. Edwin Arlington Robinson. New York, McBride, 1926. Books by E. A. Robinson, 1 leaf at end.

Robinson, Edwin A. The first seven years. *Colophon,* part 4, 1930.

Robinson, Michael Massey

Serle, Percival. Bibliography of Australasian poetry, pp. 170–71.

Robinson, Richard, *fl.* 1574

McKerrow, Ronald B. Richard Robinson's *Eupolemia* and the licensers. *Library,* s. 4, 11: [173]–78, 1931.

Robinson, Rowland Evans, 1833–1900

Fullerton, Bradford M. Selective bibliography, p. 231.

Roby, John, 1793–1850
Duke of Mantua, 1823.
ELKIN MATHEWS, LTD. Byron and Byroniana. London, E. Mathews, 1930. Facsimile of title-page, p. 91.

Rochester, John Wilmot, (*Second Earl*), 1647–1680
See Wilmot, John.

Roe, Edward Payson, 1838–1888
FULLERTON, BRADFORD M. Selective bibliography, pp. 231–32.

Rogers, Bruce, 1870——
B. R.iana. *Book-collector's packet,* no. 7, pp. 35–37, 1932.
BABINGTON, PERCY L. The first book decorated by Mr. Bruce Rogers. *Library,* s. 4, 5 : [171], 1925. Refers to *Homeward songs by the way,* Portland, Me., 1895.
ROLLINS, CARL P. B. R., America's typographic playboy. New York, Georgian press, 1927.
WARDE, FREDERIC. Bruce Rogers, designer of books. With a list of books printed under Mr. Rogers's supervision. Cambridge, Harvard university press, 1925. v+77+15 pp.

Rohlfs, Anna Katharine (Green), 1846——
FULLERTON, BRADFORD M. Selective bibliography, p. 233.

Rolfe, Frederick William, *d.* 1913
SYMONS, A. J. A. Frederick, Baron Corvo. London, Sette of odd volumes, 1926.

Roosevelt, Theodore, 1858–1919
COTTON, EDWARD H. Teodoro Roosevelt, l'Americano . . . con una introduzione della signora Corinne Roosevelt Robinson. Boston, Beacon press, [1926]. "Il Roosevelt literazione," p. 189; "bibliografia," pp. 190–92.
FULLERTON, BRADFORD M. Selective bibliography, p. 233.
JOHNSON, MERLE. American first editions, pp. 191–95 (308–12).

Root, George Frederick, 1820–1895

FULLERTON, BRADFORD M. Selective bibliography, pp. 233–34.

Ross, David Macdonald, 1865——

SERLE, PERCIVAL. Bibliography of Australasian poetry, p. 173.

Ross, Ronald, (*Sir*), 1857——

GAWSWORTH, JOHN, *pseud.,* (T. Fytton Armstrong). Ten contemporaries: notes toward their definitive bibliography. First series. London, Benn, 1932.

MÉGROZ, RODOLPHE L. Ronald Ross, discoverer and creator . . . London, Allen & Unwin, [1931]. Bibliography, pp. 263–73.

Rossetti, Christina Georgina, 1830–1894

CARTER, JOHN. Binding variants in English publishing, 1820–1900. London, Constable, 1932.

FIRST EDITION CLUB. A bibliographical catalogue, p. 101.

MAGGS BROTHERS. Catalogue no. 555. London, 1931, p. 183. Describes the complete autograph manuscript of her poems as prepared for the edition published in 1893.

Rossetti, Dante Gabriel, 1828–1882

BAUM, PAULL F., *ed.* Dante Gabriel Rossetti, an analytical list of manuscripts in the Duke university library with hitherto unpublished verse and prose. Durham, N.C., Duke university press, 1931. vii+122 pp.

DEVANE, WILLIAM C. The harlot and the thoughtful young man: a study of the relation between Rossetti's *Jenny* and Browning's *Fifine at the fair. Studies in philology,* 29: 463–84, 1932.

MÉGROZ, RODOLPHE L. Dante Gabriel Rossetti, painter poet of heaven in earth. London, Faber & Gwyer, [1928]. Bibliographical list of sources of information, pp. 319–21.

SMITH, SIMON N. Bibliographical note on *The ballad of Jan Van Hunks. Times literary supplement,* September 10, 1931, p. 683.

SYMONS, ARTHUR. Notes on two manuscripts. *English review,* 54: 514–20, 1932. Refers to the original manuscript of *Eden Bower.*

Rowe, Nicholas, 1674–1718

SUTHERLAND, J. R. Three plays by Nicholas Rowe, edited by ... with introduction, notes, and a bibliography. London, Scholartis press, 1929.

WAGENKNECHT, EDWARD. The first editor of Shakespeare. *Colophon,* part 8, 1931.

Rowlands, Samuel, 1570(?)–1630(?)

SAWYER and DARTON. English books, v. 1, pp. 96–97.

Rowson, Susanna (Haswell), 1763–1824

FULLERTON, BRADFORD M. Selective bibliography, pp. 234–35.

JOHNSON, MERLE. American first editions, p. (313).

VAIL, R. W. G. Susanna Haswell Rowson, author of *Charlotte Temple,* a bibliographical study. Worcester, Mass., American antiquarian society, 1933. 116 pp. (Reprinted from *Proceedings,* April, 1932.)

Royce, Josiah, 1855–1916

AARONSON, MOSES J. La philosophie morale de Josiah Royce. Paris, Felix Alcan, 1928. Extensive bibliography.

Rush, Rebecca

FULLERTON, BRADFORD M. Selective bibliography, p. 235.

Ruskin, John, 1819–1900

The contents of Brentwood. *The month at Goodspeed's,* 3: 131–36, 1932.

FRENCH, ROBERT D. The R. B. Adam collection of Ruskin. Yale university library. *Gazette,* 4: 1–7, 1929.

Ruskin manuscripts and books. *Times literary supplement,* July 31, 1930, p. 632.

WEIHE, KENNETH G. A collection of Ruskin manuscripts. Yale university library. *Gazette,* 5: 47–49, 1931.

Russell, Bertrand Arthur William, (*Third Earl*), 1872——
JACOB, GERTRUDE. Bertrand Russell. An essay toward a bibliography. *Bulletin of bibliography,* 13: 198–99, 1929.

Russell, George William, 1867——
Bibliography of "A. E.," George Russell. *Dublin magazine,* 5: 44–52, 1930.
MCANALLY, HENRY, (*Sir*). An "A. E." curiosity. *Book-collector's quarterly,* no. 3, June–August, 1931, pp. 67–69. Refers to a copy, possibly unique, of *Standish James O'Grady* ... by Hugh Art O'Grady, Dublin, 1929, which through "an error of a copyist" contains nine poems by Russell. The edition was destroyed.

Russell, Irwin, 1853–1879
FULLERTON, BRADFORD M. Selective bibliography, pp. 235–36.

Rutherford, Mark, *pseud.*
See White, William Hale.

Ryan, Abram Joseph, 1839–1896
FULLERTON, BRADFORD M. Selective bibliography, p. 236.

Sackville-West, Victoria Mary, 1892——
OVERTON, GRANT. American nights entertainment. New York, Appleton, 1923, p. 118.
OVERTON, GRANT. Authors of the day. New York, Doran, [1924], p. 80.

St. German, Christopher, 1460(?)–1540
THORNE, S. E. St. German's *Doctor and student. Library,* s. 4, 10: [421]–26, 1930.

Saltus, Edgar Evertson, 1858–1921
FULLERTON, BRADFORD M. Selective bibliography, p. 237.
GOTHAM BOOK MART. American first editions: Edgar Saltus, 1858–1921. *Publishers' weekly,* 104: 1880, 1923.

JOHNSON, MERLE. American first editions, pp. 196–98 (314–16). The check-list in the 1929 edition was compiled by David Moss.

SALTUS, EDGAR E. Uplands of dream. Chicago, Covici, 1925. Bibliography by Charles Honce.

Sandburg, Carl, 1878——

JOHNSON, MERLE. American first editions, pp. 199 (317–18). The check-list in the 1929 edition was compiled by Frederic Melcher.

MELCHER, FREDERIC. American first editions: Carl Sandburg, 1878——. *Publishers' weekly,* 103: 149, 1923.

Sands, Robert Charles, 1799–1832

FULLERTON, BRADFORD M. Selective bibliography, pp. 237–38.

Sanford, James, *fl.* 1567

Henrie Cornelius Agrippa, 1569

MAGGS BROTHERS. Catalogue no. 550. London, 1931. Facsimile of title-page, opp. p. 552.

Sangster, Charles, 1822–1893

PIERCE, LORNE. Outline of Canadian literature, pp. 65–66.

Santayana, George, 1863——

FULLERTON, BRADFORD M. Selective bibliography, p. 238.

Sargent, Epes, 1813–1880

FULLERTON, BRADFORD M. Selective bibliography, p. 239.

Savage, Richard, *d.* 1743

OSBORNE, LUCY E. Richard Savage. The sorry story of an early Georgian poet and a late Victorian play. *Colophon,* part 6, 1931. 12 pp. Inserted are facsimiles of the title-page of J. M. Barrie's *Richard Savage,* privately printed, 1891, of a four-page folder containing the prologue written by W. E. Henley, and the program for the play's production at the Criterion theatre, London, April 16th, 1891.

Say, Thomas, 1787–1834
WEISS, HARRY B., and ZEIGLER, GRACE M. Thomas Say, early American naturalist. Springfield, Ill., Thomas, 1931. Bibliography, pp. 243–52.

Sayle, Charles Edward, 1864——
GRAY, GEORGE J. The writings of Charles Sayle. *Library,* s. 4, 6: [82]–89, 1926.
POLLARD, ALFRED W. Charles Sayle. *Library,* s. 4, 5: [267]–70, 1925.

Scollard, Clinton, 1866——
FULLERTON, BRADFORD M. Selective bibliography, p. 240.

Scot, Michael, 1175(?)–1234(?)
FERGUSON, JOHN. Bibliographical notes on the works of Michael Scot. Glasgow bibliographical society. *Records,* v. 9, 1931. Review, *Year's work in English studies,* 12: 316, 1931.

Scott, Duncan Campbell, 1867——
PIERCE, LORNE. Outline of Canadian literature, pp. 84–86.

Scott, Fred Newton, 1860——
Fred Newton Scott anniversary papers . . . Chicago, University of Chicago press, [1929]. Bibliography, pp. 313–19.

Scott, Frederick George, 1861——
PIERCE, LORNE. Outline of Canadian literature, pp. 86–87.

Scott, Walter, (*Sir*), 1771–1832
BROTHERTON LIBRARY. Catalogue of the Sir Walter Scott centenary exhibition . . . Leeds, 1932. Facsimiles.
COLUMBIA UNIVERSITY. LIBRARY. Sir Walter Scott . . . list of the autograph manuscripts and the editions of his works in a commemorative exhibition, 1832–1932 . . . [New York, 1932]. 19 pp.

CAPLAN, ALBERT. The bibliography of Sir Walter Scott. Philadelphia, 1927. 52 pp.

CARSWELL, DONALD. The dates of the Waverley novels. *Times literary supplement,* May 5, 1932, p. 331.

HOLLOWAY, O. E. Sir Walter Scott and Douce. *Bodleian quarterly record,* 7 : 99–102, 1932.

LANDRUM, GRACE W. Sir Walter Scott and his literary rivals in the Old South. *American literature,* 2 : 256–76, 1931. Bibliography of sources, pp. 274–76.

PARTINGTON, WILFRED, *ed.* The private letter books of Sir Walter Scott. Selections from the Abbotsford manuscripts now first published with an introduction by Hugh Walpole. London, Hodder and Stoughton, 1930.

POTTLE, FREDERICK A. The Scott-Croker correspondence in the Yale university library. Yale university library. *Gazette,* 2 : 33–45, 1928.

RUFF, WILLIAM. Yale's collection of Walter Scott. Yale university library. *Gazette,* 6 : 31–32, 1932.

SAWYER and DARTON. English books, v. 2, pp. 85–90.

SCOTLAND. NATIONAL GALLERY. Catalogue of the Sir Walter Scott exhibition in the National gallery of Scotland. Edinburgh, 1932.

Scott first editions. *Times literary supplement,* July 24, 1930, p. 616.

VAN ANTWERP, WILLIAM C. A collector's comment on his first editions of the works of Sir Walter Scott. San Francisco, Gelber, Lilienthal, 1932. viii+156 pp. Review by Greville Worthington, *Book-collector's quarterly,* no. 8, October–December, 1932, pp. 53–55.

VAN ANTWERP, WILLIAM C. Short-title catalogue of first editions of Sir Walter Scott in the library of William C. Van Antwerp. [San Francisco], privately printed, 1933. 26 pp.

Scott, Walter (*Continued*)

WORTHINGTON, GREVILLE, (*Sir*). A bibliography of the Waverley novels. London, Constable, 1931. xvi+144 pp., 21 facsimiles. Reviews by Alfred W. Pollard, *Library,* s. 4, 11 : 508–9, 1931 ; J. C. Butterwick, *Book-collector's quarterly,* no. 2, March–May, 1931, pp. 40–44.

Redgauntlet, 1824.

MACRITCHIE, DAVID. The proof-sheets of *Redgauntlet. Times literary supplement,* September 11, 1924, p. 556.

Siege of Malta.

LAFERLA, ALB. V. Scott's "The siege of Malta." *Times literary supplement,* February 11, 1926, p. 99.

Vision of Don Roderick, 1811.

[*Vision of Don Roderick.*] *The month at Goodspeed's,* 2: 48–52, 1931.

Waverley novels.

POPE-HENNESSY, UNA. The dates of the *Waverley novels. Times literary supplement,* April 28, 1932, p. 311.

Waverley, 1814.

SAWYER and DARTON. English books, v. 2, p. [84]. Facsimile of title-page.

Waverley poetry.

RENDALL, VERNON. *Waverley poetry:* a rare item. *Notes and queries,* 148 : 7, 1925.

Sealsfield, Charles, *pseud.*

See Postl, Karl.

Sedgwick, Catharine Maria, 1789–1867

FULLERTON, BRADFORD M. Selective bibliography, pp. 240–41.

Sedley, Charles, (*Sir*), 1639(?)–1701

PINTO, VIVIAN DE SOLA. Sir Charles Sedley, 1639–1701: a study in the life and literature of the restoration. New York, Boni, 1927. Bibliography, pp. 363–88. *Ibid.,* London, Constable, 1927.

Sergeant, John, 1622–1707

BRADISH, NORMAN C. John Sergeant, a forgotten critic of Descartes and Locke. *Monist,* 39: [571]–628, 1929. Bibliography of John Sergeant's published writings.

Seton-Thompson, Ernest, 1860——

FULLERTON, BRADFORD M. Selective bibliography, p. 243.

JOHNSON, MERLE. American first editions, pp. 200–201 (319–21).

Sewall, Jonathan Mitchell, 1748–1808

FULLERTON, BRADFORD M. Selective bibliography, p. 243.

Sewall, Mary (Wright), 1844——

NUGENT, MAY. Grandmother to *Black beauty. London Mercury,* 26: 52–60, 1932. Mary Sewall and her works.

Shadwell, Thomas, 1642(?)–1692

BORGMAN, ALBERT S. Thomas Shadwell: his life and comedies. New York, New York university press, 1928.

Shakespeare, William, 1564–1616

Aberdeen university library's first folio. Aberdeen university library. *Bulletin,* 6: 411–18, 1927.

ADAMS, JOSEPH Q., JR. A life of William Shakespeare. Boston, Houghton Mifflin co., 1923. Bibliographical notes.

ALBRIGHT, EVELYN M. Dramatic publication in England, 1580–1640. New York, Heath, 1927.

ALDEN, RAYMOND M. The punctuation of Shakespeare's printers. Modern language association of America. *Publications,* 39: 557–80, 1924.

Shakespeare, William (*Continued*)

ALVOR, PETER. Die Shakespeare Frage und das Ben Jonson Problem. Würzburg, 1931.

ALVOR, PETER. Eine neue Shakespeare-Bibliographie. Würzburg, 1930.

BABCOCK, R. W. A preliminary bibliography of eighteenth century criticism of Shakespeare. *Studies in philology,* v. 26, extra series, no. 1, pp. 58–76, 1929.

BABCOCK, R. W. A secondary bibliography of Shakespeare criticism in the eighteenth century. *Studies in philology,* v. 26, extra series, no. 1, pp. 77–87, 1929.

BALD, R. C. Some Elizabethan dramatic manuscripts. Sydney, Australasian medical publishing co., 1927. 33 pp. (Australasian English association. *Leaflets,* no. 7.)

BALDWIN, THOMAS W. The revels books of 1604–5 and 1611–12. *Library,* s. 4, 10: [327]–38, 1930.

BARNARD, ETWELL A. B. New links with Shakespeare. Cambridge, Harvard university press, 1930. xix+135 pp.

BECKMANN, B. Zeitschriftenschau. *Shakespeare Jahrbuch,* 63: 219–32, 1927.

BECKMANN, B. Zeitschriftenschau. *Shakespeare Jahrbuch,* 64: 203–20, 1928.

BOAS, F. S. Shakespeare's library. *Golden book,* 8: 537–39, 1928.

BODDE, DERK. Shakespeare and the Ireland forgeries. Cambridge, Harvard university press, 1930. 68 pp. (*Harvard honors theses,* 2.) Bibliography, pp. 67–68.

BODLEIAN LIBRARY. Specimens of Shakespeariana in the Bodleian library at Oxford. London, Oxford university press, 1927. 68 pp.

BRADBY, G. F. About Shakespeare and his plays. London, Oxford university press, 1926.

BREWER, WILMON. Shakespeare's influence on Sir Walter Scott. Boston, Cornhill publishing co., [1925]. Bibliography, pp. 489–91.

BUTLER, PEIRCE. Materials for the life of Shakespeare. Chapel hill, N.C., University of North Carolina press, 1930. Selected bibliography, pp. [191]–94.

CHAMBERS, EDMUND K. The first illustration to "Shakespeare." *Library,* s. 4, 5 : [326]–30, 1925. Refers to a drawing by Henry Peacham.

CHAMBERS, EDMUND K. William Shakespeare, a study of facts and problems. Oxford, Clarendon press, 1930. 2 v. Bibliographical footnotes and in v. 2 a list of books "mainly intended to elucidate the footnote references." Reviews by Alfred W. Pollard, *Library,* s. 4, 11 : 378–83, 1931; J. Dover Wilson, *Modern language review,* 26 : 189–98, 1931.

CLARK, EVA T. Shakespeare's plays in the order of their writing. London, Palmer, 1930.

[Collections of Shakespeariana.] *Saturday review of literature,* 4 : 1024, 1928.

CRAIG, HARDIN. Recent Shakespearian scholarship. Shakespeare association. *Bulletin,* 5 : 39–54, 1931.

DEGROOT, H. Een nieuwe methode in het Shakespeareonderzoek. *De gids,* 88 : 76–87, 1924. Refers to the bibliographical methods of Alfred W. Pollard.

DUBEUX, A. Les traductions françaises de Shakespeare. Paris, 1925. 81 pp.

EBISCH, WALTHER, and SCHÜCKING, LEVIN L. A Shakespeare bibliography. Oxford, Clarendon press, 1931. xviii+294 pp. Reviews by Alfred W. Pollard, *Library,* s. 4, 11 : 510–11, 1931; H. M. Flasdieck, *Englische Studien,* 67 : 121–23, 1932.

GARLAND, HERBERT. Do we possess a Shakespeare manuscript? *Book notes,* 2 : 93–94, 1924.

Shakespeare, William (*Continued*)

Goldsworthy, W. Lansdowne. Ben Jonson and the first folio. London, Palmer, 1931. 64 pp.

Gray, Henry D. Chronology of Shakespeare's plays. *Modern language notes,* 46: 147–50, 1931.

Haines, C. M. Shakespeare in France. Criticism. Voltaire to Victor Hugo. London, Oxford university press, 1925. viii+170 pp. Review, *Library,* s. 4, 6: 194–95, 1926.

Hartl, Edward. Shakespeare Bibliographie. *Shakespeare Jahrbuch,* 62: 200–254, 1926.

Hartl, Edward. Shakespeare Bibliographie. *Shakespeare Jahrbuch,* 63: 270–92, 1927.

Hartl, Edward. Shakespeare Bibliographie. *Shakespeare Jahrbuch,* 65: 258–92, 1929.

Hartl, Edward. Shakespeare Bibliographie. *Shakespeare Jahrbuch,* 66: 252–77, 1930.

Henry Clay Folger and the Shakespeare library. *Amherst graduates quarterly,* 20: 1–16, 1931.

Holland, L. B. The Folger Shakespeare library. *American magazine of art,* 24: 183–90, 1932.

Jackson, Alfred. Rowe's edition of Shakespeare. *Library,* s. 4, 10: [455]–73, 1930.

Jaggard, William. Shakespeare music and song. *Times literary supplement,* June 30, 1932, p. 480.

Jantzen, H. Neue Shakespeare Literatur. *Neuphilologische Monatschrift,* 1: 567–71, 1930.

Johnson, Edward D. First folio of Shakespeare. London, Palmer, 1932. 91 pp.

Keller, W. Bücherschau. *Shakespeare Jahrbuch,* 63: 194–215, 1927.

Keller, W. Bücherschau. *Shakespeare Jahrbuch,* 64: 188–202, 1928.

KELLNER, L. Restoring Shakespeare, a critical analysis of the misreadings in Shakespeare's works, with facsimiles and numerous plates. Leipzig, Tauchnitz; London, Allen and Unwin, 1925. Review by Walter W. Greg, *Review of English studies,* 1: 463–78, 1925.

KEYNES, GEOFFREY. A note on Shakespearian end-papers. *Library,* s. 4, 6: [280]–81, 1926.

LAWRENCE, WILLIAM J. The secret of the bad quartos. *Criterion,* 10: 447–61, 1931.

LAWRENCE, W. J. Shakespeare's workshop. Oxford, Blackwell; Boston, Houghton Mifflin co., 1928.

LEE, SIDNEY, (*Sir*), and CHAMBERS, EDMUND, (*Sir*). A Shakespeare reference library. London, Oxford university press, 1925. (English association. *Pamphlets,* no. 61.)

MADAN, FALCONER. A catalogue of Shakespeariana. With some notes and a preface by ... London, Michelmore, 1927. 290 pp.

MAGGS BROTHERS. Catalogue no. 493. Shakespeare and Shakespeareana. London, 1927. 1383 items. Facsimiles of title-pages, portraits, and manuscripts. Includes facsimiles of title-pages of fourth folio, opp. p. 9; *ibid.,* with "Joseph Knight" imprint, opp. p. 8; third folio, opp. p. 5.

MAGGS BROTHERS. Shakespeare and Shakespeareana. London, 1927. 450 pp., 69 illustrations.

MOLIN, NILS. Shakespeare och Sverige intill 1800—talets mitt–översikt av hans inflytande. Göteborg, Elanders, 1930.

NOBLE, RICHMOND. The facsimile folio texts. *Times literary supplement,* August 8, 1929, p. 624.

PAR, ALFONSO. Contribución a la bibliografía española de Shakespeare. Barcelona, Imprenta de la Casa provincial de caridad, 1930. 79 pp.

Shakespeare, William (*Continued*)

Pollard, Alfred W. The foundation of Shakespeare's text. London, British academy, 1923.

Popovíc, Vladeta. Shakespeare in Serbia. London, Oxford university press, 1928. Bibliography, pp. [125]–28.

Ralli, Augustus. A history of Shakespearian criticism . . . London, Oxford university press, 1932. 2 v.

Rhodes, R. Crompton. Shakespeare's first folio, a study. Oxford, Blackwell, 1923. 147 pp.

Sargent, George H. Shakespeare treasure-trove in the H. C. Folger library. *American collector,* 6: 57–62, 1928.

Sawyer and Darton. English books, v. 1, pp. 5, 10, 65, 67, 73, 83, 85–86, 92, 102–3, 131–32, 135, 137, 143–72, 192, 210, 295–96, 345; v. 2, pp. 174–76, 343, 369, 378.

Schücking, Levin L. Neue Shakespeare Literatur. *Deutsche Vierteljahrschrift,* 6: 179–98, 1928.

The Shakespeare allusion book: a collection of allusions to Shakespeare from 1591 to 1700. Originally compiled by C. M. Ingleby, Miss L. T. Smith, and F. J. Furnivall . . . re-edited, revised, and rearranged, with an introduction by J. Munro, [1909], and now reissued with a preface by Sir Edmund Chambers. London, Oxford university press, 1932. 2 v. Review, *Times literary supplement,* June 30, 1932, pp. 469–70.

Shakespeare and Garrick. *Times literary supplement,* June 28, 1928, p. 492.

Shakespeare Association. *Bulletin,* v. 1–7, 1926–1932.

Shakespeare folios. *Times literary supplement,* August 2, 1928, p. 572.

Shakespeare folios. *Times literary supplement,* November 29, 1928, p. 944.

Shakespeare Jahrbuch, v. 59–68, 1923–1932.

Shakespeare prices. *Times literary supplement,* November 27, 1930, p. 1020.

The Shakespeare quartos presented by W. A. White to Harvard library. *Harvard library notes,* no. 21, pp. 185–95, 1928.

SIMPSON, PERCY. The bibliographical study of Shakespeare. Oxford bibliographical society. *Proceedings and papers,* 1: 19–49, 1923.

SISSON, CHARLES J. Shakespeare in India. Popular adaptations on the Bombay stage. London, Milford, 1926. 26 pp. (English association. *Pamphlets,* no. 94.)

SMITH, ROBERT M. A banner year for Shakespeare folios. *Books,* February 10, 1929, p. 27; February 17, 1929, p. 27.

SMITH, ROBERT M. The formation of Shakespeare libraries in America. Shakespeare association. *Bulletin,* 4: 65–74, 1929.

SMITH, ROBERT M. Notes on Shakespeare. Shakespeare association. *Bulletin,* 5: 140–41, 1929.

SMITH, ROBERT M. Notes on Shakespeare. Shakespeare association. *Bulletin,* 6: 678–79, 1931.

SMITH, ROBERT M. Notes on Shakespeare first folios. *Books,* October 9, 1927, p. 43.

SMITH, ROBERT M. Owners and values of the folios. Shakespeare association. *Bulletin,* 4: 121–25, 1929.

SMITH, ROBERT M. Shakespeare folios in America. *Saturday review,* August 13, 1927, p. 41.

SMITH, ROBERT M. The various issues of Shakespeare's second folio and Milton's first published English poems, a bibliographical problem. Bethlehem, Pa., Lehigh university, 1928. 62 pp., 13 facsimiles.

Shakespeare, William (*Continued*)

SMITH, ROBERT M., and LEACH, HOWARD S. The Shakespeare folios and the forgeries of Shakespeare's handwriting in the Lucy Packer Linderman memorial library of Lehigh university. With a list of original folios in American libraries. Bethlehem, Pa., Lehigh university, 1927. 47 pp.

SPENCER, HAZELTON. Improving Shakespeare: some bibliographical notes on the restoration adaptations. Modern language association of America. *Papers,* 41:727–46, 1926.

SPENCER, HAZELTON. Shakespeare improved: the restoration revisions in quarto and on the stage. Cambridge, Harvard university press, 1927. 418 pp.

SPIELMAN, MARION H. The title-page of the first folio of Shakespeare's plays. London, Oxford university press, 1931.

SPIELMAN, MARION H.; WILSON, J. DOVER; LEE, SIDNEY (*Sir*); GREG, WALTER W.; and ALLARDYCE, NICOLL. 1623–1923. Studies in the first folio . . . with an introduction by Sir Israel Gollancz. London, Oxford university press, 1924. xxxiv+180 pp. Review by Alfred W. Pollard, *Library,* n.s. 4, 6:182–85, 1926.

STAMP, A. E. The disputed revels accounts. London, Oxford university press, 1930. Reviews, C. J. Sisson, *Review of English studies,* 8:103–5, 1932; W. J. Lawrence, *Modern language review,* 27:87–88, 1932.

STERNAUX, L. Bibliophile Shakespeare Ausgaben. *Philobiblon,* 1:125–28, 1928.

STOCKWELL, LATOURETTE. A handlist of the editions of Shakespeare printed in Ireland during the eighteenth century. *Dublin magazine,* 4:33–45, 1929.

STOCKWELL, LATOURETTE. Shakespeare and the Dublin pirates. *Dublin magazine,* 4:21–32, 1929.

TANNENBAUM, SAMUEL A. Another Shakespeare forgery. *Modern language notes,* 44: 13–15, 1929. Refers to Collier's alleged entry in the Stationers' Registers concerning *A ballad of Macbeth.*

TANNENBAUM, SAMUEL A. Classified bibliography of Shakespeariana published in 1927. Shakespeare association. *Bulletin,* 3: 1–21, 1928.

TANNENBAUM, SAMUEL A. Classified bibliography of Shakespeariana published in 1928. Shakespeare association. *Bulletin,* 4: 1–30, 1929.

TANNENBAUM, SAMUEL A. Classified bibliography of Shakespeariana published in 1929. Shakespeare association. *Bulletin,* 5: 1–35, 84–92, 1930.

TANNENBAUM, SAMUEL A. Classified bibliography of Shakespeariana published in 1930. Shakespeare association. *Bulletin,* 6: 1–36, 1931.

TANNENBAUM, SAMUEL A. Classified bibliography of Shakespeariana published in 1931. Shakespeare association. *Bulletin,* 7: 3–46, 1932.

TANNENBAUM, SAMUEL A. Classified bibliography of Shakespeariana published in 1932. Shakespeare association. *Bulletin,* 8: 3–46, 51–88, 1933.

TANNENBAUM, SAMUEL A. Classified index of Shakespeariana in the periodicals of 1926. Shakespeare association. *Bulletin,* 2: 7–14, 1927.

TAYLOR, GEORGE C. The date of Edward Capell's *Notes and various readings to Shakespeare,* volume II. *Review of English studies,* 5: 317–19, 1929.

Third folio sold at Sotheby's. *Times literary supplement,* April 4, 1929, p. 279.

TILLEY, M. P. Shakespeare's "purge" of Jonson. *Times literary supplement,* October 11, 1928, p. 736.

WALCH, G. T. Shakespeare: a handbook of information. London, Medici society, 1924. 34 pp.

Wantage-Crawford first folio. *Times literary supplement,* February 2, 1928, p. 84.

Shakespeare, William (*Continued*)

WELLSTOOD, FREDERICK. Catalogue of the books, manuscripts, works of art, antiquities, and relics exhibited in Shakespeare's birthplace. With a preface by Sir Sidney Lee. Stratford on Avon, 1925. 176 pp.

WHICHER, G. The Folger Shakespeare library. *Theatre arts monthly,* 16: 108–16, 1932.

WILLOUGHBY, EDWIN E. The heading, actus primus, scaena prima, in the first folio. *Review of English studies,* 4: 323–26, 1928.

WILLOUGHBY, EDWIN E. An interruption in the printing of the first folio. *Library,* s. 4, 9: [262]–66, 1929.

WILLOUGHBY, EDWIN E. A note on the pagination of the first folio. *Modern language notes,* 44: 373–74, 1929.

WILLOUGHBY, EDWIN E. A note on the typography of the running titles of the first folio. *Library,* s. 4, 9: [385]–87, 1929.

WILLOUGHBY, EDWIN E. The typography of the act-headings of the first folio. *Review of English studies,* 5: 198–200, 1929.

WILSON, F. P. The Jaggards and the first folio of Shakespeare. *Times literary supplement,* November 5, 1925, p. 737.

WILSON, J. DOVER. Act and scene divisions in the plays of Shakespeare. *Review of English studies,* 3: 385–97, 1927.

Antony and Cleopatra.

WILSON, J. DOVER, *ed.* Antony and Cleopatra, (a facsimile of the first folio text). Introduction and list of modern readings. London, Faber & Gwyer, 1929.

As you like it.

WILSON, J. DOVER, *ed.* As you like it, (a facsimile of the first folio text). Introduction and list of modern readings. London, Faber & Gwyer, 1929.

Coriolanus.

SCHULTZ, W. Shakespeares *Coriolanus* in der deutschen Shakespeare-Literatur des 19 und 20 Jahrhunderts. *Zeitschrift für Deutschkunde,* no. 2, 120–29, 1931.

WILSON, J. DOVER, *ed.* Coriolanus, (a facsimile of the first folio text). Introduction and list of modern readings. London, Faber & Gwyer, 1928.

Hamlet.

GRAY, HENRY D. Thomas Kyd and the first quarto of *Hamlet.* Modern language association of America. *Publications,* 42 : 723–35, 1927.

LAWRENCE, WILLIAM J. The mystery of the *Hamlet* first quarto. *Criterion,* 5 : 191–201, 1926.

LAWRENCE, WILLIAM J. The pirates of *Hamlet. Criterion,* 8 : 642–46, 1929.

MAGGS BROTHERS. Catalogue no. 493. Shakespeare and Shakespeareana. London, 1927. Facsimile of title-page of the first Russian edition, St. Petersburg, 1748, opp. p. 41.

Shakespeare's *Hamlet.* The first quarto 1603. Reproduced in facsimile from the copy in the Henry E. Huntington library. Cambridge, Harvard university press, 1931. (Huntington library. *Publications.*) Review by Ronald B. McKerrow, *Review of English studies,* 8 : 369–70, 1932.

WIDMANN, WILHELM. Hamlets Buhnenlaufbahn (1601–1877) Aus dem Nachlass herausgeben von Joseph Schick und Werner Deetjen. Leipzig, Tauchnitz, 1931. List of *Hamlet* parodies, pp. 174–77.

WILLOUGHBY, EDWIN E. A note on the relationship of the first and second quartos of *Hamlet. Anglia,* 52 : [288], 1928.

WILSON, J. DOVER. Spellings and misprints in the second quarto of *Hamlet.* London, Milford, 1924. (English association. *Essays and studies by members,* v. 10, no. 2.)

Shakespeare, William (*Continued*)

Henry V.

CRAIG, HARDIN. Relation of the first quarto versions to the first folio version of *Henry V*. *Philological quarterly,* 6: 225–34, 1927.

POEL, W. The five act division in *Henry V*. *Times literary supplement,* October 6, 1927, p. 694.

WILSON, J. DOVER, *ed.* Henry V, (a facsimile of the first folio text). Introduction and list of modern readings. London, Faber & Faber, 1931.

Henry VI.

BROOKE, T. Elizabethan proof corrections in *The first part of the contention* (1600). Huntington library. *Bulletin,* no. 2, pp. 87–89, 1931.

DORAN, MADELEINE. Henry VI, parts II and III, their relation to the contention and true tragedy. Iowa City, University of Iowa, 1928. (University of Iowa. *Studies, humanistic series,* 4, no. 4.)

Julius Caesar.

BRADY, K. *Julius Caesar* goes to press. *English journal,* 20: 834–36, 1931.

The first translation of *Julius Caesar* into German. *Shakespeare Jahrbuch,* 66: 211, 1930.

L. Cardin's translation of *Julius Caesar* into Portuguese. *Times literary supplement,* March 18, 1926, p. 218.

MAGGS BROTHERS. Catalogue no. 493. Shakespeare and Shakespeareana. London, 1927. Facsimile of first German edition, Berlin, 1741, opp. p. 40.

WILSON, J. DOVER, *ed.* Julius Caesar, (a facsimile of the first folio text). Introduction and list of modern readings. London, Faber & Gwyer, 1929.

King Lear.

DORAN, MADELEINE. The text of *King Lear*. *Journal of English and Germanic philology,* 31: 296–99, 1932.

DORAN, MADELEINE. The text of *King Lear.* Stanford university, Stanford university press, 1931.

WILSON, J. DOVER, *ed.* King Lear, (a facsimile of the first folio text). Introduction and list of modern readings. London, Faber & Faber, 1931.

Locrine, 1595.

AMERICAN ART ASSOCIATION. Sales catalogue. Rare books from the library of the late Willis Vickery. New York, 1933. Facsimile of title-page, p. 23.

Macbeth.

KNIGHT, G. W. A Shakespeare problem: an early *Macbeth. Times literary supplement,* August 2, 1928, p. 568.

MAGGS BROTHERS. Catalogue no. 493. Shakespeare and Shakespeareana. London, 1927. Facsimile of title-page of the first edition of Sir William Davenant's version, opp. p. 29.

MANCHESTER, P. T. *Macbeth* in the hands of French and Spanish translators. *Modern language journal,* 16: 1–13, 1932.

TANNENBAUM, SAMUEL A. Another Shakespeare forgery. (*Macbeth* and Collier.) *Modern language notes,* 44: 13–15, 1929.

WILSON, J. DOVER, *ed.* Macbeth, (a facsimile of the first folio text). Introduction with a list of modern readings. London, Faber & Gwyer, 1928.

Measure for measure.

BUDD, FREDERICK E. Material for a study of the sources of Shakespeare's *Measure for measure. Revue de littérature comparée,* 11: [711]–36, 1931.

Midsommer night's dreame, 1600.

SAWYER and DARTON. English books, v. 1, p. [154]. Facsimile of title-page.

SAWYER and DARTON. English books, v. 1, p. 156. Facsimile of title-page of Pavier's edition antedated 1600 for 1619.

Shakespeare, William (*Continued*)

Much ado about nothing, 1600.

AMERICAN ART ASSOCIATION. Sales catalogue. Rare books from the library of the late Willis Vickery. New York, 1933. Facsimile of title-page.

Passionate pilgrim, 1599.

SAWYER and DARTON. English books, v. 1, p. 159. Facsimile of title-page.

Sir John Oldcastle.

MAGGS BROTHERS. Catalogue no. 493. Shakespeare and Shakespeareana. London, 1927. Facsimile of title-page of second issue of first edition, opp. p. 28.

Sir Thomas Moore.

TANNENBAUM, SAMUEL A. Shakespeare and *Sir Thomas Moore.* New York, Tenny press, 1929. 64 pp., 12 facsimiles.

Sonnets.

FORT, J. A. Further notes on Shakespeare's *Sonnets. Library,* s. 4, 9: [305]–25, 1929.

SAWYER and DARTON. English books, v. 1, p. 160. Facsimile of title-page (London, 1609).

TANNENBAUM, SAMUEL A. The "copy" for Shakespeare's *Sonnets. Philological quarterly,* 10: 393–95, 1931.

Taming of the shrew.

R., J. *Taming of a shrew.* Facsimile of a rare broadside, London, 1635. Maggs brothers. Catalogue no. 550. London, 1931.

Tempest.

WILSON, J. DOVER, *ed.* Tempest (a facsimile of the first folio text). Introduction and a list of modern readings. London, Faber & Gwyer, 1928.

Troilus and Cressida.

ALEXANDER, PETER. *Troilus and Cressida,* 1609. *Library,* s. 4, 9: [267]–86, 1929.

Twelfth night.

Wilson, J. Dover, *ed.* Twelfth night (a facsimile of the first folio text). Introduction and list of modern readings. London, Faber & Faber, 1931.

Two noble kinsmen.

Maggs Brothers. Catalogue no. 493. Shakespeare and Shakespeareana. London, 1927. Facsimile of title-page of first edition, opp. p. 29.

Venus and Adonis.

Chambers, Edmund K. The printing of *Venus and Adonis. Year's work in English studies,* 8: 145, 1929.

Currie, Barton. Fishers of books. Boston, Little, Brown and co., 1931. Facsimile of title-page (London, 1593), opp. p. 196.

Sawyer and Darton. English books, v. 1, p. [7]. Facsimile of title-page (London, 1593).

Winter's tale.

Wilson, J. Dover, *ed.* Winter's tale (a facsimile of the first folio text). Introduction with list of modern readings. London, Faber & Gwyer, 1929.

Shaw, George Bernard, 1856——

American Art Association. Sales catalogue. First editions & autograph letters by George Bernard Shaw, the property of Dr. Archibald Henderson . . . New York, 1933. 204 items. "The letters, manuscripts, and books described in this catalogue are a selection from one of the most important and extensive collections of Shaviana in the world."—Foreword by Francesco M. Bianco.

American Art Association. Sales catalogue. First editions, letters, and mss. of Barrie, Dickens, Galsworthy, Shaw, Trollope . . . from the library of Thomas Hatton. New York, 1929.

Braybrooke, Patrick. The subtlety of George Bernard Shaw . . . [London]. C. Palmer, [1930]. Bibliography, pp. 242–43.

Shaw, George Bernard (*Continued*)

Broad, C. Lewis, and Broad, Violet M. Dictionary to the plays and novels of Bernard Shaw, with a bibliography of his works and of the literature concerning him, with a record of the principal Shavian play productions. London, Black, 1929. 244 pp. *Ibid.,* New York, Macmillan, 1929. 231 pp.

Cutler and Stiles. Modern British authors, pp. 125–31.

Ellehauge, Martin. The position of Bernard Shaw in European drama and philosophy. Copenhagen, Levin & Munksgaard, 1931. (Thesis, University of Copenhagen.) Bibliographical appendix, pp. ⌊384⌋–90.

First Edition Club. A bibliographical catalogue, pp. 102–5.

Holmes, Maurice. Some bibliographical notes on the novels of George Bernard Shaw. With some comments by George Bernard Shaw. London, Dulau, 1929. 20 pp.

Shanks, Edward B. Bernard Shaw. London, Nisbet, ⌊1924⌋. Bibliography of Shaw's principal writings, pp. 119–22; American bibliography, pp. 123–25.

Wagenknecht, Edward. A guide to Bernard Shaw. London, Appleton, 1929. xi+128 pp.

Wells, Geoffrey H. A bibliography of the books and pamphlets of George Bernard Shaw. *Bookman's journal, supplement,* pp. 1–46, 1928.

Press cuttings, 1909.

Sawyer and Darton. English books, v. 1, pp. 18–19.

Shaw, Henry Wheeler, 1818–1885

Clemens, Cyril. John Billings, Yankee humorist . . . with an introduction by Rupert Hughes . . . Webster Groves, Mo., 1932. Bibliography, pp. 184–88.

Fullerton, Bradford M. Selective bibliography, pp. 243–44.

Shelley, Harriet

See Shelley, Percy Bysshe.

Shelley, Mary Wollstonecraft Godwin, 1797–1851

Church, Richard. Mary Shelley. New York, Viking, 1929. Bibliography, p. [92]. *Ibid.,* London, Howe, [1928].

See also Shelley, Percy Bysshe.

Shelley, Percy Bysshe, 1792–1822

Granniss, Ruth S. A descriptive catalogue of the first editions in book form of Percy Bysshe Shelley. New York, Grolier club, 1923. xx+133 pp., facsimiles.

Hill, R. H., *ed.* Letters of Percy Bysshe Shelley and others, mainly unpublished, from the collection presented to the library by Lady Shelley in 1892. With a chronological table of the collection and a list of other Shelley manuscripts and relics in the library. Oxford, Bodleian library, 1926.

Peck, Walter E. Shelley's reviews written for *The examiner. Modern language notes,* 39: 118–19, 1924.

Pottle, Frederick A. Shelley and Browning; a myth and some facts ... with a foreword by William Lyon Phelps. Chicago, Pembroke press, 1923. List of books referred to, pp. [91]–94.

Ricci, Seymour de. A bibliography of Shelley's letters, published and unpublished. Paris, privately printed, 1927. 296 pp. Review, *Library,* s. 4, 9: 425–26, 1929.

Sawyer and Darton. English books, v. 1, p. 18; v. 2, pp. 38, 49–61, 67–68, 76, 241, 380–81.

A Shelley discovery. *Book-notes,* 5: 111, 1927. Refers to a recently discovered crayon portrait of Shelley.

Wise, Thomas J. A Shelley library, a catalogue of printed books, manuscripts, and autograph letters by Percy Bysshe Shelley and Mary Wollstonecraft Shelley ... London, privately printed, 1924. xvii+164 pp., facsimiles.

Shelley, Percy Bysshe (*Continued*)

WOODBERRY, GEORGE E., *ed.* The Shelley notebook in the Harvard library. Reproduced with notes and a postscript ... Cambridge, Harvard university press, 1930. 23 pp.

Adonais, 1821.

AMERICAN ART ASSOCIATION. Sales catalogue. Rare books from the library of the late Willis Vickery. New York, 1933. Facsimile of title-page, p. 35.

CARLTON, W. N. C. Shelley's *Adonais,* 1821. *American collector,* 5 : 25–31, 1928. Bibliography.

SAWYER and DARTON. English books, v. 2, p. 58. Facsimile of title-page.

Epipsychidion, 1821.

AMERICAN ART ASSOCIATION. Sales catalogue. Rare books from the library of the late Willis Vickery. New York, 1933. Facsimile of title-page, p. 36.

Original poetry by Victor and Cazire, 1810.

SAWYER and DARTON. English books, v. 2, p. 51. Facsimile of title-page.

Posthumous fragments of Margaret Nicholson, 1810.

SAWYER and DARTON. English books, v. 2, p. 55. Facsimile of title-page.

Posthumous poems.

BABINGTON, PERCY L. The "errata" leaf in Shelley's *Posthumous poems. Library,* s. 4, 5 : [365], 1925.

Queen Mab, 1813.

AMERICAN ART ASSOCIATION. Sales catalogue. Rare books from the library of the late Willis Vickery. New York, 1933. Facsimile of title-page, p. 33.

SAWYER and DARTON. English books, v. 2, p. [60]. Facsimile of title-page.

STARRETT, VINCENT. Pennywise and book foolish. New York, Covici Friede, 1929. Facsimile of title-page, opp. p. 54.

Shenstone, William, 1714–1763

Bond, Richmond P. Shenstone's heroi-comical poem. *Studies in philology,* 28: 742–49, 1931. Relates to an unpublished manuscript, *The snuff box,* in the British museum.

Fullington, J. F. Some early versions of William Shenstone's letters. *Modern philology,* 29: 323–24, 1932.

Purkis, E. Monro. William Shenstone, poet and landscape gardener. Wolverhampton, Whitehead brothers, [1931]. Bibliographical notes, pp. [139]–43.

Williams, Iolo A. Seven XVIIIth century bibliographies. London, Dulau, 1924, pp. 41–71.

School-mistress, 1742.

Maggs Brothers. Catalogue no. 550. London, 1931. Facsimile of title-page, opp. p. 616.

Sheridan, Richard Brinsley Butler, 1751–1816

Panter, George W. Early editions of Sheridan. *Times literary supplement,* April 15, 1926, p. 283.

Rhodes, R. Crompton. Sheridan: a study in theatrical bibliography. *London Mercury,* 15: 381–90, 1927.

Rhodes, R. Crompton, *ed.* The plays & poems of Richard Sheridan. Oxford, Blackwell, 1928. 3 v. The bibliographies record every discoverable edition of the plays and poems.

Rhodes, R. Crompton. Sheridan apocrypha. *Times literary supplement,* August 26, 1926, p. 564.

Rhodes, R. Crompton. Sheridan bibliography. *Times literary supplement,* June 17, 1926, p. 414.

Rhodes, R. Crompton. Some aspects of Sheridan bibliography. *Library,* s. 4, 9: [233]–59, 1929.

Williams, Iolo A. Seven XVIIIth century bibliographies. London, Dulau, 1924, pp. 210–39.

Sheridan, Richard Brinsley Butler (*Continued*)

Duenna, 1794.

RHODES, R. CROMPTON. The early editions of Sheridan. I. *The Duenna. Times literary supplement,* September 17, 1925.

School for scandal.

CURRIE, BARTON. Fishers of books. Boston, Little, Brown and co., 1931. Facsimile of title-page of edition of 1780, p. [115].

RHODES, R. CROMPTON. The early editions of Sheridan. II. *The school for scandal. Times literary supplement,* September 24, 1925. Cf. W. Roberts, *ibid.,* October 15, 1925.

Sherman, Frank Dempster, 1860–1916

FULLERTON, BRADFORD M. Selective bibliography, p. 244.

Shiel, Matthew Phipps, 1865——

GAWSWORTH, JOHN, *pseud.,* (T. Fytton Armstrong). Ten contemporaries: notes toward their definitive bibliography. First series. London, Benn, 1932.

VAN VECHTEN, CARL. Excavations. New York, Knopf, 1926. List of Shiel's works, pp. 160–61.

Shillaber, Benjamin Penhallow, 1814–1890

FULLERTON, BRADFORD M. Selective bibliography, pp. 244–45.

Shorter, Clement King, 1857–1926

BULLOCH, JOHN M., *ed.* C. K. S., an autobiography: a fragment by himself. [Edinburgh], privately printed, 1927. Bibliography of Shorter's works, pp. 153–68.

Shorthouse, Joseph Henry, 1834–1903

FIRST EDITION CLUB. A bibliographical catalogue, p. 106.

Sidney, Margaret, *pseud.*

See Lothrop, Harriet Mulford (Stone).

Sidney, Philip, (*Sir*), 1554–1586

OSBORN, ALBERT W. Sir Philip Sidney en France . . . Paris, Champion, 1932. Bibliography, pp. [165]–71.

SAWYER and DARTON. English books, v. 1, pp. 86–87.

Countesse of Pembroke's Arcadia, 1590.

SAWYER and DARTON. English books, v. 1, p. [88]. Facsimile of title-page.

ZANDVOORT, REINHARD W. Sidney's *Arcadia,* a comparison between two versions. Amsterdam, 1929. Bibliography, pp. 200–215.

Countesse of Pembroke's Arcadia, 1605.

MAGGS BROTHERS. Catalogue no. 550. London, 1931. Facsimile of title-page, opp. p. 632.

Sigourney, Lydia (Huntley), 1791–1865

FULLERTON, BRADFORD M. Selective bibliography, p. 245.

Sill, Edward Rowland, 1841–1887

FULLERTON, BRADFORD M. Selective bibliography, pp. 245–46.

Silliman, Benjamin, 1779–1864

DANA, MARIA T. Benjamin Silliman manuscripts. Yale university library. *Gazette,* 6: 74–75, 1932.

Sime, Sidney H.

FIRST EDITION CLUB. A bibliographical catalogue, p. 107.

Simms, William Gilmore, 1806–1870

FULLERTON, BRADFORD M. Selective bibliography, pp. 246–49.

Sinclair, Upton Beall, 1878——

SINCLAIR, UPTON. The books of Upton Sinclair in translations & foreign editions. Pasadena, California, 1931. 525 titles. Review, *American Mercury,* 22: xxxviii, (April) 1931.

Sitwell, Edith, 1887——

BALSTON, THOMAS. Sitwelliana, 1915–1927 . . . London, Duckworth, 1928. x+24 pp.

GAWSWORTH, JOHN, *pseud.,* (T. Fytton Armstrong). Ten contemporaries: notes toward their definitive bibliography. First series. London, Benn, 1932.

MÉGROZ, RODOLPHE L. The three Sitwells, a biographical and critical study. London, Richards press, 1927. Bibliographical list of books by the Sitwells, p. 333.

Sitwell, Osbert, 1892——

See Sitwell, Edith.

Sitwell, Sacheverell, 1897——

See Sitwell, Edith.

Skelton, John, 1460(?)–1529

HENDERSON, PHILIP, *ed.* The complete poems of John Skelton, laureate. London, Dent, 1931. "Useful bibliography of editions, early and modern, of manuscripts, and of some critical articles."—*Year's work in English studies,* 12: 139, 1931.

SAWYER and DARTON. English books, v. 1, pp. 56–59.

Colyn Cloute, 1545.

SAWYER and DARTON. English books, v. 1, p. [57]. Facsimile of title-page.

Why come ye nat to courte? ca. 1483.

SAWYER and DARTON. English books, v. 1, p. [57]. Facsimile of title-page.

Sladen, Douglas Brooke Wheelton, 1856——

SERLE, PERCIVAL. Bibliography of Australasian poetry, p. 183.

Slick, Sam, *pseud.*
See Haliburton, Thomas Chandler.

Smith, Adam, 1723–1790
Wealth of nations, 1776.
American Art Association. Sales catalogue. Library of Frank Irving Fletcher. New York, 1932. Facsimile of title-page, p. 160.

Smith, Charles Henry, 1826–1903
Fullerton, Bradford M. Selective bibliography, p. 249.

Smith, Francis Hopkinson, 1838–1915
Fullerton, Bradford M. Selective bibliography, pp. 249–50.
Johnson, Merle. American first editions, pp. 202–3 (328–30). The check-list in the 1929 edition was compiled by George E. Schilling.

Smith, John, 1580–1631
Waldman, Milton. Americana. New York, Holt, 1925, pp. 120–33.
Generall historie, 1624.
Waldman, Milton. Americana. New York, Holt, 1925, p. 130. Facsimile of title-page.

Smith, John Frederick, 1804(?)–1890
A Victorian best-seller. *Times literary supplement,* December 25, 1930, p. 1104.

Smith, Percy
First Edition Club. A bibliographical catalogue, p. 108.

Smith, Samuel Francis, 1808–1895
Fullerton, Bradford M. Selective bibliography, pp. 250–51.

Smith, Seba, 1798–1868
Fullerton, Bradford M. Selective bibliography, pp. 251–52.

Smith, William Russell, 1815–1896

EASBY-SMITH, ANNE. William Russell Smith of Alabama, his life and works, including the entire text of *The uses of solitude* . . . foreword by George H. Denny. Philadelphia, Dolphin press, 1931.

Smollett, Tobias George, 1721–1771

KNAPP, LEWIS M. A rare satire on Smollett. *Times literary supplement,* October 8, 1931, p. 778.

KNAPP, LEWIS M. Smollett's early years in London. *Journal of English and Germanic philology,* 31 : 224–25, 1925.

KNAPP, LEWIS M. Smollett's works as printed by William Strahan, with an unpublished letter of Smollett to Strahan. *Library,* s. 4, 13 : [282]–91, 1933.

Peregrine Pickle, 1758.

BUCK, HOWARD S. A study in Smollett, chiefly *Peregrine Pickle,* with a complete collation of the first and second editions. New Haven, Yale university press, 1925. xii+216 pp.

ELKIN MATHEWS, LTD. Catalogue no. 23. London, 1929. Facsimile of title-page, p. 31.

Roderick Random, 1748.

KNAPP, LEWIS M. Smollett's *Roderick Random. Times literary supplement,* January 8, 1931, p. 28.

Smythe, A. E. S., 1861——

PIERCE, LORNE. Outline of Canadian literature, p. 94.

Snaith, John Collis, 1876——

OVERTON, GRANT. Cargoes for Crusoes. New York, Appleton, [1924], p. 372.

Snelling, William Joseph, 1804–1848

FULLERTON, BRADFORD M. Selective bibliography, p. 252.

Southerne, Thomas, 1660–1746

DODDS, JOHN W. Thomas Southerne, dramatist . . . New Haven, Yale university press, 1933. (Thesis, Yale university.) Bibliography, pp. [220]–27.

Southey, Robert, 1774–1843

HAVENS, RAYMOND D. Southey's contributions to the *Foreign review. Review of English studies,* 8: 210–11, 1932.

Southwell, Robert, 1561(?)–1595

SAWYER and DARTON. English books, v. 1, pp. 92–93.

Southworth, Emma Dorothy Elizabeth Nevitte, 1819–1899

FULLERTON, BRADFORD M. Selective bibliography, pp. 252–53.

Spenser, Edmund, 1552(?)–1599

CARPENTER, FREDERICK I. A reference guide to Spenser. Chicago, University of Chicago press, 1923. vi+333 pp.

JONES, HARRIE S. V. A Spenser handbook. New York, Crofts, 1930. x+419 pp. Reading lists at end of chapters. Reviews, *Modern language review,* 26: 496, 1931; *Review of English studies,* 8: 94–95, 1932.

MCMURPHY, SUSANNAH J. Spenser's use of Ariosto for allegory. Seattle, Wash., 1924. (University of Washington. *Publications in language and literature,* v. 2.) (Thesis, University of Washington.) Bibliography, pp. 50–52.

PARROTT, ALICE. A critical bibliography of Spenser from 1923–1928. *Studies in philology,* 25: 468–90, 1928.

SAWYER and DARTON. English books, v. 1, pp. 75–80.

Faerie queene, 1590.

SAWYER and DARTON. English books, v. 1, p. 77. Facsimile of title-page.

View of the state of Ireland, 1633.

COLE, GEORGE W. Bibliographical pitfalls — linked books. Bibliographical society of America. *Papers,* 18: 12–30, 1924.

Spofford, Harriet Elizabeth (Prescott), 1835–1921
FULLERTON, BRADFORD M. Selective bibliography, pp. 253–54.

Sprague, Charles, 1791–1875
FULLERTON, BRADFORD M. Selective bibliography, p. 254.

Stanley, William, (*Sixth Earl of Derby*), *d.* 1642
GREG, WALTER W. Derby, his hand and soul. *Library,* s. 4, 7: [39]–45, 1927.

Stansbury, Joseph, 1750–1809
FULLERTON, BRADFORD M. Selective bibliography, pp. 254–55.

Stedman, Edmund Clarence, 1833–1908
FULLERTON, BRADFORD M. Selective bibliography, pp. 255–56.

Steele, Richard, 1672–1729
Christian hero.
BLANCHARD, RAE. *The Christian hero,* by Richard Steele: a bibliography. *Library,* s. 4, 10: [61]–72, 1930.
BLANCHARD, RAE, *ed.* The Christian hero. Edited with an introduction and bibliography . . . London, Oxford university press, 1932.

Steendam, Jacob, *b.* 1616
New York city's first poet. *New York times magazine,* November 3, 1929, p. 16.

Steere, Richard
Daniel catcher, 1713.
[*Daniel catcher.*] *The month at Goodspeed's,* 1: 168–71, 1930. Facsimile of title-page.

Stephens, Alfred George
SERLE, PERCIVAL. Bibliography of Australasian poetry, pp. 189–90.

Stephens, James, 1882——
CUTLER and STILES. Modern British authors, pp. 132–33.

Stephens, James Brunton, 1835–1902
SERLE, PERCIVAL. Bibliography of Australasian poetry, pp. 189–90.

Sterling, George, 1869–1926
JOHNSON, CECIL. A bibliography of the writings of George Sterling. San Francisco, Windsor press, 1931. viii+64 pp. Review, *Books,* 7: 31, April 12, 1931.
JOHNSON, MERLE. American first editions, pp. (331–32).
JOHNSON, MERLE. American first editions: George Sterling (1869–1926). *Publishers' weekly,* 119: 2023–24, 1931.
STERLING, GEORGE. George Sterling check-list compiled by Sterling himself in 1925, and here first published and now brought up to date. *Hesperian,* summer issue, 1930. 3 pp.

Sterne, Laurence, 1713–1768
CROSS, WILBUR L. Life and times of Laurence Sterne . . . New Haven, Yale university press, 1925. 2 v. Bibliography, v. 2, pp. [265]–98.
A facsimile reproduction of a unique catalogue of Laurence Sterne's library. Preface by C. Whibley. London, Tregaskis, 1930. 108 pp.
SAWYER and DARTON. English books, v. 1, pp. 278–81.

Sentimental journey, 1748.
SAWYER and DARTON. English books, v. 1, p. [279]. Facsimile of title-page.

Tristram Shandy, 1760.
SAWYER and DARTON. English books, v. 1, p. [279]. Facsimile of title-page.

Steven, Alexander Gordon, 1885–1923
SERLE, PERCIVAL. Bibliography of Australasian poetry, p. 191.

Stevens, Bertram, 1872——

Serle, Percival. Bibliography of Australasian poetry, pp. 191–92.

Stevenson, Robert Louis, 1850–1894

American Art Association. Sales catalogue. First editions of Thomas Hardy, Rudyard Kipling, Robert Louis Stevenson. The renowned collection of George Barr McCutcheon. New York, 1925.

Anderson Galleries. Sales catalogue. The Stevenson library of Henry A. Colgate. New York, 1928.

Carter, John. Binding variants in English publishing, 1820–1900. London, Constable, 1932.

Cutler and Stiles. Modern British authors, pp. 134–44.

Ford, R. Clyde. Modestine's shoes: a bit of Stevensoniana. *Atlantic monthly,* 137: 527–31, 1926.

Swinnerton, Frank A. R. L. Stevenson: a critical study. New York, Doran, [1923]. Bibliography, pp. 193–95.

Records of a family of engineers, 1912.

Stevenson's *Records of a family of engineers. Times literary supplement,* August 4, 1927, p. 536.

Stewart, Donald Ogden, 1894——

Overton, Grant. American nights entertainment. New York, Appleton, 1923, pp. 246–47.

Overton, Grant. Authors of the day. New York, Doran, [1924], pp. 136–37.

Stimson, Frederick Jesup, 1855——

Fullerton, Bradford M. Selective bibliography, p. 256.

Stockton, Frank R. (Francis Richard), 1834–1902

Fullerton, Bradford M. Selective bibliography, p. 257.

Johnson, Merle. American first editions, pp. 204–6 (333–36). The check-list in the 1929 edition was compiled by Vrest Orton.

Rudder grange, 1879.

Curle, Richard. Collecting American first editions, p. 204.

Stoddard, Charles Warren, 1843–1909
FULLERTON, BRADFORD M. Selective bibliography, p. 258.

Stoddard, Elizabeth Drew (Barstow), 1823–1902
FULLERTON, BRADFORD M. Selective bibliography, pp. 258–59.

Stoddard, Theodore Lothrop, 1883——
OVERTON, GRANT. American nights entertainment. New York, Appleton, 1923, p. 386.
OVERTON, GRANT. Authors of the day. New York, Doran, [1924], p. 226.

Stopes, Marie Charlotte (Carmichael), 1880——
MURPHY, GWENDOLEN A. A bibliographical list of the writings of Charlotte Carmichael Stopes. Royal society of literature. *Essays by divers hands,* v. 10, 1931, pp. [95]–107.

Story, William Wetmore, 1819–1895
FULLERTON, BRADFORD M. Selective bibliography, p. 260.

Stowe, Harriet Elizabeth (Beecher), 1811–1896
FULLERTON, BRADFORD M. Selective bibliography, pp. 261–62.
JOHNSON, MERLE. American first editions, pp. (337–40).
JOHNSON, MERLE. American first editions: Harriet (Elizabeth) Beecher Stowe, 1811–1896. *Publishers' weekly,* 120: 1738–39, 1932.

Uncle Tom's cabin, 1852.
CURLE, RICHARD. Collecting American first editions, pp. 105, 126, 149, 204.
Uncle Tom's cabin. Bibliography. *Times literary supplement,* July 8, 1926, p. 468.
WINTERICH, JOHN T. Books and the man. New York, Greenberg, 1929, pp. 79–101. Facsimile of title-page, p. 87.

Stratton-Porter, Gene, 1868–1924

OVERTON, GRANT. American nights entertainment. New York, Appleton, 1923, pp. 291–92.

OVERTON, GRANT. Authors of the day. New York, Doran, [1924], pp. 165–66.

Strecche, John

TAYLOR, FRANK. The chronicle of John Strecche for the reign of Henry V (1414–1422). John Rylands library. *Bulletin,* 16: 137–87, 1932. Bibliographical footnotes.

Street, Alfred Billings, 1811–1881

FULLERTON, BRADFORD M. Selective bibliography, p. 262.

Stretton, Arthur

FIRST EDITION CLUB. A bibliographical catalogue, p. 109.

Stringer, Arthur John Arbuthnott, 1874——

PIERCE, LORNE. Outline of Canadian literature, p. 101.

Strong, Leonard Alfred George, 1896——

GAWSWORTH, JOHN, *pseud.,* (T. Fytton Armstrong). Ten contemporaries: notes toward their definitive bibliography. Second series. London, Joiner & Steele, 1932.

Stuart, Ruth (Mc Enery), 1856–1917

FULLERTON, BRADFORD M. Selective bibliography, p. 263.

Sullivan, Arthur Seymour, (*Sir*)

See Gilbert, William Schwenck, (*Sir*).

Surtees, Robert Smith, 1805–1864

SAWYER and DARTON. English books, v. 2, pp. 223, 227–34.

Handley cross, 1854.

SAWYER and DARTON. English books, v. 2, p. [231]. Facsimile of title-page.

Swift, Jonathan, 1667–1745

SAWYER and DARTON. English books, v. 1, pp. 17–18, 260–64.

VAN DOREN, CARL. Swift. New York, Viking press, 1930. Bibliographical note, pp. 269–72.

WHITE, NEWPORT B. Bibliography of Dean Swift. *Times literary supplement,* June 9, 1927, p. 408.

Directions to servants, 1745.

BRADLEY, L. J. H. Swift's *Directions to servants. Times literary supplement,* February 11, 1926, p. 99.

Gulliver's travels, 1726.

CURRIE, BARTON. Fishers of books. Boston, Little, Brown and co., 1931. Facsimile of title-page of first edition.

Gulliver's travels. Bibliographical problems. *Times literary supplement,* November 11, 1926, p. 804.

SAWYER and DARTON. English books, v. 1, p. 261. Facsimile of title-page of first edition.

TAYLOR, RUPERT, *ed.* Gulliver's travels, by Dean Swift; with an introduction by ... New York, Macmillan, 1927. Facsimiles of title-pages of first edition, general title-page of v. 1 and special title-pages of parts 1, 2, and 4; second edition, parts 3 and 4.

VAN DOREN, CARL, *ed.* Gulliver's travels, A tale of a tub, The battle of the books. Introduction by ... New York, Modern library, [1931]. Facsimiles of original title-pages including the special title-pages of the parts.

WILLIAMS, HAROLD. The Motte editions of *Gulliver's travels. Library,* s. 4, 6: [229]–63, 1926. Facsimiles.

WILLIAMS, HAROLD, *ed.* Gulliver's travels. The text of the first edition, with an introduction, bibliography, and notes by ... London, First edition club, 1926. Review by Henry C. Hutchins, *Times literary supplement,* February 10, 1927, p. 88.

Swift, Jonathan (*Continued*)

WILLIAMS, HAROLD. *Gulliver's travels:* further notes. *Library,* s. 4, 6: [229]–63, 1926.

WILLIAMS, HAROLD. *Gulliver's travels:* further notes. *Library,* s. 4, 9: [187]–96, 1929.

History of John Bull, 1712.

TEERINK, HERMAN. The history of John Bull, for the first time faithfully reissued from the original pamphlets, 1712, together with an investigation into its composition, publication, and authorship ... Amsterdam, Paris, 1925. 250 pp.

Life and genuine character of Dr. Swift, 1733.

DAVIS, HERBERT. Verses on the death of Dr. Swift. *Book-collector's quarterly,* no. 2, March–May, 1931, pp. 57–73.

London tale, 1710.

[*London tale,* 1710, a broadside.] *The month at Goodspeed's,* 2: 132–37, 1931.

Tale of a nettle, 1710.

[*Tale of a nettle,* 1710, a broadside.] *The month at Goodspeed's,* 2: 132–37, 1931.

Swinburne, Algernon Charles, 1837–1909

FIRST EDITION CLUB. A bibliographical catalogue, p. 110.

LAFOURCADE, GEORGES. ... La jeunesse de Swinburne (1837–1867). Paris, 1928. 2 v. Bibliography, v. 2, pp. 583–600. (Université de Strasbourg, Faculté des lettres, *publications.*)

PRAZ, MARIO. Swinburniana con una nota sul tipo letterario dell'inglese sadico. *La cultura* (January): 11–23, 1930.

RUTLAND, WILLIAM R. Swinburne, a nineteenth-century Hellene ... Oxford, Blackwell, 1931. Bibliography, pp. 401–6.

SYMONS, ARTHUR. Notes on two manuscripts. *English review,* 54: 514–20, 1932. Refers to the manuscript of *Cleopatra.*

WELBY, THOMAS E. A study of Swinburne. New York, Doran, [1926]. Bibliographical note, pp. 283–89.

WELBY, THOMAS E. A Swinburne library. *Saturday review,* 140: 306–7, 1925.

WISE, THOMAS J. The Ashley library. A catalogue of printed books, manuscripts, and autograph letters. London, privately printed, 1926. v. 7. Swinburne and Tennyson. xiv+220 pp. Review, *Times literary supplement,* April 29, 1926, p. 319.

Swinnerton, Frank, 1884——

OVERTON, GRANT. Authors of the day. New York, Doran, [1924], pp. 342–43.

Symonds, John Addington, 1840–1893

BABINGTON, PERCY L. Bibliography of the writings of John Addington Symonds. London, Castle, 1925. xi+244 pp. Review, *Library,* s. 4, 6: 397–98, 1926.

CUTLER and STILES. Modern British authors, pp. 145–48.

FIRST EDITION CLUB. A bibliographical catalogue, pp. 111–12.

Symons, Arthur, 1865——

FIRST EDITION CLUB. A bibliographical catalogue, p. 113.

WELBY, THOMAS E. Arthur Symons: a critical study. London, Philpot, 1925. Bibliographical note, pp. 141–48.

Tabb, John Bannister, 1845–1909

JOHNSON, MERLE. American first editions, pp. 207 (341).

JOHNSON, MERLE. American first editions: John Bannister Tabb, 1845–1909. *Publishers' weekly,* 104: 21, 1923.

LITZ, FRANCIS E. A. Father Tabb; a study of his life and works . . . Baltimore, Johns Hopkins press, 1923. Bibliography, pp. 289–91.

Tagore, Rabindranath, (*Sir*), 1861——

THOMPSON, EDWARD J. Rabindranath Tagore, poet and dramatist. London, Oxford university press, 1926. Bibliography, pp. 310–18.

Taine, Hippolyte Adolphe, 1828–1893

SMITH, HORATIO. The Taine centennial: comment and bibliography. *Modern langauge notes,* 44: 437–45, 1929.

Tarkington, Newton Booth, 1878——

CURRIE, BARTON. Booth Tarkington. Bibliography. New York, 1932.

FULLERTON, BRADFORD M. Selective bibliography, p. 264.

JOHNSON, MERLE. American first editions, pp. 208–10 (342–47). The check-list in the 1929 edition was compiled by Henry C. Quinby.

OVERTON, GRANT. American nights entertainment. New York, Appleton, 1923, pp. 236–38.

OVERTON, GRANT. Authors of the day. New York, Doran, [1924], pp. 128–30.

Taylor, James Bayard, 1825–1878

FULLERTON, BRADFORD M. Selective bibliography, pp. 264–65.

Taylor, Jeremy, 1613–1667

GATHORNE-HARDY, ROBERT. Bibliography of Jeremy Taylor. *Times literary supplement,* October 2, 1930, p. 782.

KEYNES, GEOFFREY. Bibliography of Jeremy Taylor. *Times literary supplement,* October 9, 1930, p. 810.

SMITH, LOGAN P., *ed.* The golden grove. London, Oxford university press, 1930. Bibliography by Robert Gathorne-Hardy.

WHITE, NEWPORT B. Bibliography of Jeremy Taylor. *Times literary supplement,* September 18, 1930, p. 758.

Taylor, John, 1580–1653

RUSHFORTH, MARJORIE. Two John Taylor manuscripts at Leonard Lichfield's press. *Library,* s. 4, 11 : [179]–92, 1931.

SAWYER and DARTON. English books, v. 1, pp. 196–97.

Verbum sempiternum, 1616.

STONE, WILBUR M. The *Verbum sempiternum* of John Taylor. *American collector,* 5 : 46–59, 1928.

Teasdale, Sara, 1884–1933

JOHNSON, MERLE. American first editions, pp. 211 (348). The check-list in the 1929 edition was compiled by Mildred C. Smith.

SMITH, MILDRED C. American first editions: Sara Teasdale, 1884——. *Publishers' weekly,* 103 : 1380, 1923.

Temple, William, (*Sir*), 1628–1699

MARBURG, CLARA. Sir William Temple, a seventeenth century "libertin." New Haven, Yale university press, 1932. "An appendix gives the details of the composition and publication of the *Miscellanea.*"—Review, *Studies in philology,* 29 : 512, 1932.

Tenny, Tabitha, 1762–1837

FULLERTON, BRADFORD M. Selective bibliography, pp. 265–66.

Tennyson, Alfred, (*First Baron*), 1809–1892

Tennyson manuscripts. *Times literary supplement,* July 17, 1930, p. 596.

WILLIAMS, IOLO A. [Tennyson first editions.] *London Mercury,* 19 : 640, 1929.

WISE, THOMAS J. An apocryphal Tennyson poem. *Times literary supplement,* March 27, 1930, p. 274.

Tennyson, Alfred (*Continued*)

WISE, THOMAS J. The Ashley library. A catalogue of printed books, manuscripts, and autograph letters. London, privately printed, 1926. v. 7. Swinburne and Tennyson. xiv+220 pp. Review, *Times literary supplement,* April 29, 1926, p. 319.

Death of Oenone, 1892.

ELKIN MATHEWS, LTD. Catalogue no. 35. Bibliographical notes concerning two different advance issues and variations therein from the text of the first published version, p. 92.

Tiresias and other poems, 1885.

ELKIN MATHEWS, LTD. Catalogue no. 35, Bibliographical notes concerning advance issues and variations therein from the text of the first published version.

Terhune, Mary Virginia (Hawes), 1830–1922

FULLERTON, BRADFORD M. Selective bibliography, p. 266.

Teuffel, Blanche Willis (Howard), 1847–1898

FULLERTON, BRADFORD M. Selective bibliography, p. 283.

Thackeray, William Makepeace, 1811–1863

AMERICAN ART ASSOCIATION. Sales catalogue. The renowned collection of first editions of Charles Dickens and William Makepeace Thackeray formed by George Barr McCutcheon. New York, 1926.

ELWIN, MALCOLM. Thackeray, a personality . . . London, Cape, [1932]. Bibliography including published books, novels in numbers, contributions to newspapers and periodicals, contributions to almanacks, annuals, etc., pp. 372–92.

FIRST EDITION CLUB. A bibliographical catalogue, pp. 114–15.

NEWTON, A. EDWARD. This book-collecting game, pp. 95, 363–65, 367, 373.

SAWYER and DARTON. English books, v. 1, pp. 229, 276; v. 2, pp. 138, 240, 269, 291, 295–306, 308, 312, 328.

Exquisites, 1839.

SAWYER and DARTON. English books, v. 2, p. [302]. Facsimile of title-page and frontispiece.

King Glumpus, 1837.

SAWYER and DARTON. English books, v. 2, p. [304]. Facsimile of title-page and frontispiece.

Second funeral of Napoleon, 1841.

STARRETT, VINCENT. Pennywise and book foolish. New York, Covici Friede, 1929. Facsimile of title-page, p. 24.

Vanity fair, 1847.

SAWYER and DARTON. English books, v. 2, p. [294]. Facsimile of the wrapper of Part I.

WINTERICH, JOHN T. Books and the man. New York, Greenberg, 1929, pp. 357–74. Facsimile of the wrapper of Part I.

Thanet, Octave, ***pseud.***

See French, Alice.

Thatcher, Charles Robert

SERLE, PERCIVAL. Bibliography of Australasian poetry, p. 199.

Thaxter, Celia (Leighton), 1835–1894

FULLERTON, BRADFORD M. Selective bibliography, pp. 266–67.

Thomas, Edith Matilda, 1854——

FULLERTON, BRADFORD M. Selective bibliography, p. 267.

Thomas, Edward, 1878–1917

MURPHY, GWENDOLEN. Bibliographies of modern authors. No. 2. Edward Thomas. *London Mercury,* 16: 71–75, 193–98, 525–30, 1927; 17: 76, 1928.

Thomas, Frederick William, 1808 (or 1810)–1866

Fullerton, Bradford M. Selective bibliography, pp. 267–68.

Thompson, Daniel Pierce, 1795–1868

Flitcroft, John E. The novelist of Vermont: a biographical and critical study of Daniel Pierce Thompson. Cambridge, Harvard university press, 1929. List of published writings, pp. [321]–24; list of references, pp. 325–29.

Fullerton, Bradford M. Selective bibliography, pp. 268–69.

Johnson, Merle. American first editions, p. (349).

Thompson, Francis, 1859–1907

Cutler and Stiles. Modern British authors, pp. 149–50.

First Edition Club. A bibliographical catalogue, p. 116.

Mégroz, Rodolphe L. Francis Thompson: the poet of earth in heaven ... London, Faber & Gwyer, [1927]. Bibliography of first editions, pp. 276–79.

Stonehill, C. A., and Stonehill, H. W. Bibliographies of modern authors. Second series. London, Castle, [1925].

Thompson, J. Maurice, 1844–1901

Fullerton, Bradford M. Selective bibliography, p. 269.

Thompson, Vance, 1863–1925

Hanighen, Frank C. Vance Thompson and *M'lle New York*. *Bookman* (New York), 75: 472–81, 1932.

Thompson, William Tappan, 1812–1882

Fullerton, Bradford M. Selective bibliography, pp. 269–70.

Thomson, Edward William, 1849–1924

Pierce, Lorne. Outline of Canadian literature, p. 89.

Thomson, Hugh, 1860–1920

FIRST EDITION CLUB. A bibliographical catalogue, pp. [117]–26.

Thomson, Mortimer, 1831–1865

FULLERTON, BRADFORD M. Selective bibliography, p. 270.

Thoreau, Henry David, 1817–1862

AMERICAN ART ASSOCIATION. Sales catalogue. Stephen H. Wakeman collection. New York, 1924. Items 972–1075.

FULLERTON, BRADFORD M. Selective bibliography, pp. 271–72.

JOHNSON, MERLE. American first editions, pp. 212–14 (350–53). The check-list in the 1929 edition was compiled by Francis H. Allen.

Cape Cod, 1865.

CURLE, RICHARD. Collecting American first editions, p. 145.

Excursions, 1863.

CURLE, RICHARD. Collecting American first editions, pp. 62–63.

Maine woods, 1864.

CURLE, RICHARD. Collecting American first editions, pp. 13–14, 90.

Walden, 1854.

ADAMS, RAYMOND. A bibliographical note on *Walden. American literature,* 2: 166–68, 1931.

AMERICAN ART ASSOCIATION. Sales catalogue. Stephen H. Wakeman collection. New York, 1924. Item 1005. Facsimile of title-page.

CURLE, RICHARD. Collecting American first editions, pp. 18–19, 26, 63.

WINTERICH, JOHN T. Romantic stories of books: *Walden. Publishers' weekly,* 116: 1363–68, 1929.

Thoreau, Henry David (*Continued*)

Week on the Concord, 1849 and 1862.

Curle, Richard. Collecting American first editions, pp. 77–78, 86–87, 195. Facsimile of title-page, opp. p. 76.

Yankee in Canada, 1866.

Curle, Richard. Collecting American first editions, p. 210.

Thorpe, Thomas Bangs, 1815–1878

Fullerton, Bradford M. Selective bibliography, pp. 272–73.

Thrale, Hester (Lynch), 1741–1821

Silk, Edmund T. A critical bibliography of Hester Lynch Thrale, Mrs. Piozzi. (Thesis, Yale university.)

Zamick, M., *ed.* Three dialogues . . . from the hitherto unpublished original manuscript in the John Rylands library. John Rylands library. *Bulletin,* 16: 77–114, 1932. Introduction with bibliographical footnotes, pp. 77–96.

Thynne, Francis, 1545(?)–1608

Case is altered, 1604.

American Art Association. Sales catalogue. Rare books from the library of the late Willis Vickery. New York, 1933. Facsimile of title-page, p. 40. (This work is also attributed to Nicholas Breton.)

Tickell, Thomas, 1688–1740

Colin and Lucy, 1725.

Butt, J. E. A first edition of Tickell's *Colin and Lucy. Bodleian quarterly record,* 6: 103–4, 1931.

Ticknor, Francis Orray, 1822–1874

Fullerton, Bradford M. Selective bibliography, pp. 273–74.

Tiernan, Mary Spear (Nicholas)
FULLERTON, BRADFORD M. Selective bibliography, p. 274.

Timrod, Henry, 1829–1867
FULLERTON, BRADFORD M. Selective bibliography, pp. 274–75.
THOMPSON, HENRY T. Henry Timrod, laureate of the Confederacy. Columbia, S.C., State co., 1929. Bibliographical lists.

Tomlinson, Everett Titsworth, 1859——
OVERTON, GRANT. Cargoes for Crusoes. New York, Appleton, [1924], p. 250.

Torrance, Joan
See Kerr, Joan (Torrance).

Tottell, Richard, *d.* 1594
BYROM, H. J. Richard Tottell—his life and work. *Library,* s. 4, 8: [199]–232, 1928.

Touchet, Eleanor
WRIGHT, S. G. Dougle fooleries. *Bodleian quarterly record,* 7: 95–98, 1932.

Tourgee, Albion Winegar, 1838–1905
FULLERTON, BRADFORD M. Selective bibliography, pp. 275–76.

Traherne, Thomas, *fl.* 1673–1699
WADE, GLADYS I. The manuscripts of the poems of Thomas Traherne. *Modern language review,* 26: 401–7, 1931.

Train, Arthur Cheney, 1875——
OVERTON, GRANT. American nights entertainment. New York, Appleton, 1923, p. 101.
OVERTON, GRANT. Authors of the day. New York, Doran, [1924], p. 65.

Trollope, Anthony, 1815–1882

American Art Association. Sales catalogue. First editions, letters, and mss. of Barrie, Dickens, Galsworthy, Shaw, Trollope . . . from the library of Thomas Hatton . . . New York, 1929.

Irwin, Mary L. Anthony Trollope, a bibliography. *Bulletin of bibliography,* 12: 71–73, 92–96, 114–16, 150–55, 1924–1925.

Irwin, Mary L. Anthony Trollope, a bibliography. New York, Wilson, 1926. 97 pp.

Sadleir, Michael. Anthony Trollope and his publishers. A chapter in the history of nineteenth-century authorship. *Library,* s. 4, 5: [215]–42, 1925.

Sadleir, Michael. Trollope: a bibliography; an analysis of the history and the structure of the works of Anthony Trollope and a general survey of the effect of original publishing on a book's subsequent rarity. London, Constable, 1928. xvi+320 pp.

Sadleir, Michael. Trollope, a commentary. London, Constable, 1927. ix+432 pp. Appendix contains a bibliography of Anthony Trollope and one of Frances Trollope. *Ibid.* with an introduction by A. Edward Newton. Boston, Houghton Mifflin co., 1927. ix+xi+432 pp.

Trollope, Frances (Milton), 1780–1863

See Trollope, Anthony.

Troubetzkoy, Amélie (Rivers, Chanler), 1863——

Fullerton, Bradford M. Selective bibliography, pp. 276–77.

Trowbridge, John Townsend, 1827–1916

Fullerton, Bradford M. Selective bibliography, p. 278.

Trumbull, John, 1750–1831

Fullerton, Bradford M. Selective bibliography, pp. 278–79.

Tucker, George, 1775–1861
FULLERTON, BRADFORD M. Selective bibliography, pp. 279–80.

Tucker, Nathaniel Beverly, 1784–1851
FULLERTON, BRADFORD M. Selective bibliography, pp. 280–81.

Tuckerman, Henry Theodore, 1813–1871
FULLERTON, BRADFORD M. Selective bibliography, p. 281.

Tufts, Henry, 1748–1831
A Yankee Casanova. *The month at Goodspeed's,* 3 : 99–102, 1931.

Tully, Michael Joseph
SERLE, PERCIVAL. Bibliography of Australasian poetry, p. 204.

Turner, Walter James
SERLE, PERCIVAL. Bibliography of Australasian poetry, pp. 204–5.

Twain, Mark, *pseud.*
See Clemens, Samuel Langhorne.

Twamley, Louisa Anne (Meredith)
SERLE, PERCIVAL. Bibliography of Australasian poetry, pp. 135–36.

Tyler, Royall, 1757–1826
FULLERTON, BRADFORD M. Selective bibliography, pp. 281–82.

Tyrie, James, 1543–1597
Refutation of ane answer made by Schir Johne Knox, 1573.
MAGGS BROTHERS. Catalogue no. 550. London, 1931. Facsimile of title-page, p. 665.

Udall, Nicholas, 1505–1556

MOON, A. R. Was Nicholas Udall the author of *Thersites*? *Library,* s. 4, 7: [184]–93, 1927.

SAWYER and DARTON. English books, v. 1, pp. 117–18.

Umphraville, Angus

PLEADWELL, F. L. Who was Angus Umphraville? (Author of the *Siege of Baltimore and the battle of La Tranche,* Baltimore, 1817.) New York public library. *Bulletin,* 28: 552–53, 1924.

Updike, Daniel Berkeley, 1860——

WINSHIP, GEORGE P. The Merrymount press of Boston. An account of the work of D. B. Updike, with a list of one hundred and fifty Merrymount press books. Vienna, Reichner, 1929. 176 pp., 60 plates.

Van Vechten, Carl, 1880——

CUNNINGHAM, SCOTT. A bibliography of the writings of Carl van Vechten. Philadelphia, Centaur bookshop, 1924. 52+[10] pp.

JOHNSON, MERLE. American first editions, pp. 219–20 (354–56). The check-list in the 1929 edition was compiled by James H. Drake.

Viner, Charles, 1678–1756

GIBSON, STRICKLAND, and HOLDSWORTH, WILLIAM, (*Sir*). Charles Viner's *General abridgment of law and equity.* Oxford bibliographical society. *Proceedings and papers,* 2: [227]–325, 1930.

Waite, Arthur Edward, 1857——

VOORHIS, HAROLD V. B. Arthur Waite. A check-list of his writings. Red Bank, N.J., privately printed, 1932. 16 pp.

Wakefield Author, The

CAREY, MILLICENT. The Wakefield group in the Towneley cycle, a study to determine the conventional and original elements in four plays commonly ascribed to the Wakefield author. Göttingen, Vandenhoeck & Ruprecht, 1930. Bibliography, pp. 245–51.

Walch, Garnet

Serle, Percival. Bibliography of Australasian poetry, p. 207.

Walker, Francis Amasa, 1840–1897

Munroe, James P. A life of Francis Amasa Walker. New York, Holt, 1923. Bibliography, pp. 420–39.

Walkley, Thomas

Greg, Walter W. Thomas Walkley and the Ben Jonson *Works* of 1640. *Library,* s. 4, 11 : [461]–65, 1931.

Marcham, Frank. Thomas Walkley and the Ben Jonson *Works* of 1640. *Library,* s. 4, 11 : [225]–29, 1931.

Wall, Arnold, 1869——

Serle, Percival. Bibliography of Australasian poetry, p. 208.

Wallace, Lew, 1827–1905

Fullerton, Bradford M. Selective bibliography, p. 284.

Johnson, Merle. American first editions, pp. 221 (357).

Ben Hur, 1880.

Curle, Richard. Collecting American first editions, pp. 38–39, 52, 204.

Waller, Edmond, 1606–1687

De Beer, E. S. An uncollected poem by Waller. *Review of English studies,* 8: 203–5, 1932.

Walpole, Horace, 1717–1797

Lewis, Wilmarth S. Forlorn printer, being notes on Horace Walpole's alleged neglect of Thomas Kirgate. Farmington, Conn., 1931.

Sawyer and Darton. English books, v. 1, pp. 32, 312; v. 2, pp. 9, 12, 15, 241, 381.

Toynbee, Paget, *ed.* Journal of the printing office at Strawberry Hill. London, Constable, 1923.

Walpole, Horace (*Continued*)

WALPOLE, HORACE. On modern gardening. With a bibliographical note by W. S. Lewis. New York, Young, 1932.

WALPOLE, HORACE. Strawberry Hill accounts. Oxford, Clarendon press, 1927.

Walpole, Hugh, 1884——

OVERTON, GRANT. Authors of the day. New York, Doran, [1924], pp. 241–42.

Walton, Izaak, 1593–1683

BUTT, J. E. Bibliography of Izaac Walton's *Lives*. Oxford bibliographical society. *Proceedings and papers,* 2: [327]–40, 1930.

Compleat angler, 1658.

[Census of existing copies.] *Fishing gazette* (London), December 22, 1928.

SAWYER and DARTON. English books, v. 1, p. 216. Facsimile of title-page.

WINTERICH, JOHN T. Books and the man. New York, Greenberg, 1929, pp. 62–76. Facsimile of title-page, p. 70.

Universal angler, 1676.

WINTERICH, JOHN T. Books and the man. New York, Greenberg, 1929. Facsimile of title-page, p. 73.

Ward, Adolphus William, (*Sir*), 1837–1924

BARTHOLOMEW, A. T. A bibliography of Sir Adolphus William Ward, 1837–1924. With a memoir by T. F. Tout. London, Cambridge university press, 1926. xxxiv+99 pp. Review, *Library,* s. 4, 7: 433, 1927.

Ward, Artemus, *pseud.*

See Browne, Charles Farrar.

Ward, Elizabeth Stuart (Phelps), 1844–1911

FULLERTON, BRADFORD M. Selective bibliography, p. 285.

Ware, Eugene Fitch, 1841–1911

FULLERTON, BRADFORD M. Selective bibliography, pp. 285–86.

Ware, William, 1797–1852

FULLERTON, BRADFORD M. Selective bibliography, pp. 286–87.

Warner, Charles Dudley, 1829–1900

FULLERTON, BRADFORD M. Selective bibliography, pp. 287–88.

Warner, William, 1558(?)–1609

SAWYER and DARTON. English books, v. 1, p. 115.

Albion's England, 1586.

SAWYER and DARTON. English books, v. 1, p. [116]. Facsimile of title-page.

Warren, Caroline Matilda

FULLERTON, BRADFORD M. Selective bibliography, p. 288.

Warton, Thomas, 1728–1790

MARTIN, BURNS. Some unpublished Wartoniana. *Studies in philology,* 29: 53–67, 1932.

PARTRIDGE, ERIC, *ed.* The three Wartons: a choice of their verse . . . edited with notes and select bibliography. London, Scholartis press, 1927. Bibliography, pp. 19–35.

Washington, George, 1732–1799

CONNECTICUT HISTORICAL SOCIETY. Washington letters in the library of the Connecticut historical society. Hartford, 1932. 53 pp.

HARASZTI, Z. A notable bequest of Washingtoniana. *More books,* 7: 49–57, 1932. Refers to the gift of the collection of Walter U. Lewisson to the Boston public library.

HARASZTI, Z. Washington bicentennial exhibit [at the Boston public library]. *More books,* 7: 79–97, 1932.

Washington, George (*Continued*)

HARASZTI, Z. Washington letters in this library [Boston public library]. *More books,* 7 : 43–55, 1932.

HART, ALFRED B. A study of Washington biography. *Publishers' weekly,* 119 : 820–22, 1932.

HAY, J., JR. George Washington : literary man. *Publishers' weekly,* 121 : 934–44, 1932.

HAYWARD, RUTH P., *comp.* George Washington, 1732–1799 : a list of manuscripts, books, and portraits in the library of the society [State historical society of Wisconsin]. Madison, 1932. 70 pp.

HEARTMAN, CHARLES F. Sales catalogue. Important Washingtoniana and rare Americana . . . including the fine collection formed by Foster Stearns . . . Metuchen, N.J., 1932.

HENKELS, STAN V., JR. Sales catalogue. Americana, Washingtoniana . . . New York, 1932.

HUNTINGTON LIBRARY (San Marino, California). Catalogue of a Washington exhibition. San Marino, California, 1932. 25 pp.

MCCOMBS, CHARLES F. The Washington bicentennial exhibition. New York public library. *Bulletin,* 36 : 207–17, 1932.

RITTER, HALSTEAD L. Washington as a business man. New York, Sears, [1931]. Bibliography, pp. 291–95.

RHODE ISLAND. STATE BUREAU OF INFORMATION. Autograph letters and documents of George Washington now in Rhode Island collections. Providence, 1932. (*Historical publications,* no. 6.) 171 pp.

WOODWARD, WILLIAM E. George Washington, the image and the man. New York, Boni, 1926. Bibliography, pp. xiii–xxvi.

Watson, Albert Durrant, 1859–1926

PIERCE, LORNE. Outline of Canadian literature, pp. 91–93.

Watson, Michael Joseph

SERLE, PERCIVAL. Bibliography of Australasian poetry, pp. 209–10.

Watton

Speculum Christiani, 1480.

SAWYER and DARTON. English books, v. 1, p. 36. Facsimile of a page.

Watts, Alfred

SERLE, PERCIVAL. Bibliography of Australasian poetry, pp. 209–10.

Wayland, John

BYROM, H. J. John Wayland—printer, scrivener, and litigant. *Library,* s. 4, 11 : [312]–49, 1931.

Webber, Charles Wilkins, 1819–1856

FULLERTON, BRADFORD M. Selective bibliography, pp. 289–90.

Webster, Daniel, 1782–1852

CAREY, ROBERT L. Daniel Webster as an economist. New York, Columbia university press, 1929. Brief bibliography.

CLAPP, CLIFFORD B. Analytical methods in bibliography applied to Daniel Webster's speech at Worcester in 1832. Bibliographical essays: a tribute to Wilberforce Eames. Cambridge, Harvard university press, 1924.

FUESS, CLAUDE M. Daniel Webster ... Boston, Little, Brown and co., 1930. 2 v. Bibliography, v. 2, pp. [419]–30.

KENNEDY, ELIJAH R. The real Daniel Webster. New York, Revell, [1924]. Authorities, pp. 262–66.

Webster, Noah, 1758–1853

FULLERTON, BRADFORD M. Selective bibliography, pp. 290–91.

Weems, Mason Locke, 1759–1825

A brief for Parson Weems. New York public library. *Bulletin,* 33: 139–45, 1929.

Ford, Paul L. Mason Locke Weems, his work and ways ... Part I. A bibliography left unfinished by Paul Leicester Ford. Edited by Emily Ellsworth Ford Skeel. New York, 1929.

Skeel, Emily E. F. A further note on Mason Locke Weems. New York public library. *Bulletin,* 33: 220, 1929.

Two lives. *The month at Goodspeed's,* 3: 173–75, 1932.

Life of Washington the great, 1806.

[*Life of Washington the great,* Augusta, 1806.] New York public library. *Bulletin,* 36, opp. p. 211, 1932. Facsimile of title-page.

Weever, John, 1576–1632

Faunus and milliflora, 1600.

A newly discovered copy of *Faunus and milliflora. Times literary supplement,* June 12, 1924, p. 376.

Welby, Amelia B. (Coppuck), 1821–1852

Fullerton, Bradford M. Selective bibliography, p. 291.

Wellesley, Arthur, (*First Duke of Wellington*), 1762–1852

Ardagh, John. A bibliography of the Duke of Wellington. (Additions to the list compiled by J. Paine.) *Notes and queries,* 152: 266–67, 1927.

B., J. F. A bibliography of the Duke of Wellington. (Additions to the list compiled by J. Paine.) *Notes and queries,* 152: 302, 1927.

H., A. J. A bibliography of the Duke of Wellington. (Additions to the list compiled by J. Paine.) *Notes and queries,* 152: 267, 1927.

Paine, J. A bibliography of the Duke of Wellington. *Notes and queries,* 152: 222–24, 226, 1927.

Wells, Herbert George, 1866——

BROWN, IVOR J. C. H. G. Wells. New York, Holt, 1924. Bibliographies, pp. 120–25.

CHAPPELL, FRED. A bibliography of H. G. Wells; with a prologue introducing Mr. Wells to the future. Chicago, Covici-McGee, 1924. xviii+51 pp.

CUTLER and STILES. Modern British authors, pp. 153–60.

FIRST EDITION CLUB. A bibliographical catalogue, pp. [131]–77.

WELLS, GEOFFREY H. A bibliography of the works of H. G. Wells, 1893–1925. With some notes and comments. London, Routledge, 1925. xiii+72 pp. Review, *London Mercury,* 12: 415, 1925.

Wendell, Barrett, 1855–1921

HOWE, M. A. D. Barrett Wendell and his letters. Boston, Atlantic monthly press, [1924]. Bibliography, pp. [335]–39.

West, Rebecca, 1892——

OVERTON, GRANT. Authors of the day. New York, Doran, [1924], pp. 260–61.

Westcott, Edward Noyes, 1847–1898

FULLERTON, BRADFORD M. Selective bibliography, pp. 291–92.

Wetherald, Ethelwyn, 1857——

FULLERTON, BRADFORD M. Selective bibliography, pp. 292–93.

Wharton, Edith (Newbold Jones), 1862——

DAVIS, LAVINIA. A bibliography of the writings of Edith Wharton. Portland, Maine, Southworth press, 1933. x+62 pp.

JOHNSON, MERLE. American first editions, pp. 222–23 (360–62). The check-list in the 1929 edition was compiled by Laurence Gomme.

Wharton, Edith (*Continued*)

JOHNSON, MERLE. American first editions: Edith Wharton, 1862——. *Publishers' weekly,* 103:796, 1923.

LOVETT, ROBERT M. Edith Wharton. New York, McBride, 1925. Bibliography, pp. 89–91.

MELISH, LAWSON McC. A bibliography of the collected writings of Edith Wharton. New York, Brick row bookshop, 1927. xi+87 pp.

OVERTON, GRANT. American nights entertainment. New York, Appleton, 1923, pp. 361–62.

OVERTON, GRANT. Authors of the day. New York, Doran, [1924], pp. 203–4.

Wheatley, Phillis, 1753(?)–1784

MATTHEWS, A. The writings of Phillis Wheatley. *Notes and queries,* 159:30–31, 1930.

Whipple, Edwin Percy, 1819–1886

FULLERTON, BRADFORD M. Selective bibliography, pp. 293–94.

Whistler, James Abbott McNeill, 1834–1903

FULLERTON, BRADFORD M. Selective bibliography, p. 294.

JOHNSON, MERLE. American first editions, pp. 224–25 (363–64). The check-list in the 1929 edition was compiled by Don C. Seitz.

LAVER, JAMES. Whistler. Cosmopolitan book co., 1930. Bibliographical note, pp. 305–8. *Ibid.,* London, Faber & Faber, [1930]. Bibliographical note, pp. 295–98.

Whitcher, Frances Miriam (Berry), 1811–1852

FULLERTON, BRADFORD M. Selective bibliography, pp. 294–95.

White, Gilbert

SERLE, PERCIVAL. Bibliography of Australasian poetry, p. 213.

White, Harry John

SERLE, PERCIVAL. Bibliography of Australasian poetry, p. 213.

White, Stewart Edward, 1873——

JOHNSON, MERLE. American first editions, pp. 226–27 (366–67). The check-list in the 1929 edition was compiled by O. L. Griffith.

OVERTON, GRANT. Authors of the day. New York, Doran, [1924], pp. 252–53.

White, William Allen, 1868——

JOHNSON, MERLE. American first editions, pp. 233–36 (368–69).

JOHNSON, MERLE. American first editions: William Allen White, 1868——. *Publishers' weekly,* 103: 519, 1923.

White, William Hale, 1831–1913

SMITH, SIMON M. Mark Rutherford: a short bibliography of the first editions. Bibliographies of modern authors. Third series. London, Bookman's journal, 1931. 23 pp.

Whitman, Walt(er), 1819–1892

ANDERSON GALLERIES. Sales catalogue. Rare books, manuscripts, and autograph letters, including the Walt Whitman collection of Bayard Wyman ... New York, 1928.

BIRSS, JOHN H. Notes on Whitman. *Notes and queries,* 163: 311–12, 1932. Reprints a bibliographical note from the front end-paper of an advance copy of Isaac Hull Platt's biography of Whitman.

BRESLOW, M. M. American first editions: Walt Whitman, 1819–1892. *Publishers' weekly,* 104: 1929–30, 1923.

CATEL, JEAN. Walt Whitman; la naissance du poète ... Paris, Rieder, 1929. Bibliography, pp. [471]–79.

FULLERTON, BRADFORD M. Selective bibliography, pp. 295–97.

Whitman, Walt (*Continued*)

Furness, Clifton J., *ed.* Walt Whitman's workshop. A collection of unpublished manuscripts. Cambridge, Harvard university press, 1928.

Glicksberg, Charles I. Walt Whitman and the civil war . . . Philadelphia, 1933. (Thesis, University of Pennsylvania.) List of newspaper clippings, pp. 183–92; bibliography, p. xiii.

Holloway, Emory. The Walt Whitman exhibition. New York public library. *Bulletin,* 29: 763–66, 1925.

Holloway, Emory. Whitman: an interpretation in narrative. New York, Knopf, 1927. Brief bibliography.

Hungerford, Edward. Walt Whitman and his chart of bumps. *American literature,* 2: 350–84, 1931. Relates to Whitman and the works of various phrenologists.

Johnson, Merle. American first editions, pp. 233–36 (370–74). The check-list in the 1929 edition was compiled by M. M. Breslow.

Kennedy, William S. The fights of a book for the world . . . Stonecroft press, 1926. Bibliography of Whitman's writings, pp. 237–72.

Monroe, Will S. Recent Walt Whitman literature in America. *Revue Anglo-Américaine,* 8: 138–41, 1931.

Sparke, Archibald. Collection of Whitmaniana in the reference library, Bolton (England). Bolton, 1931. 28 pp.

Drum-taps, 1865.

Curle, Richard. Collecting American first editions, pp. 44–45.

Franklin Evans, 1842.

Curle, Richard. Collecting American first editions, pp. 158–59.

Mabbott, Thomas O. Notes on Whitman's *Franklin Evans. Notes and queries,* 149: 419–20, 1925.

Leaves of grass, 1855.

CURLE, RICHARD. Collecting American first editions, pp. 20–22, 32, 43–44, 89, 143, 159, 166, 172–73, 196–97, 203. Facsimile of title-page of first edition (Brooklyn, 1855).

CURRIE, BARTON. Fishers of books. Boston, Little, Brown and co., 1931. Facsimile of title-page, p. 239.

WINTERICH, JOHN T. Books and the man. New York, Greenberg, 1929, pp. 1–17. Facsimile of title-page, p. 7.

WINTERICH, JOHN T. Romantic stories of books: I, *Leaves of grass. Publishers' weekly,* 112: 1869–73, 1927.

Leaves of grass imprints, 1860.

"One's self I sing" (*Leaves of grass imprints,* Boston, 1860). *The month at Goodspeed's,* 2: 91–96, 1930. Facsimile of front cover.

Memoranda during the war, 1875–1876.

CURLE, RICHARD. Collecting American first editions, p. 208.

November boughs, 1888.

CURLE, RICHARD. Collecting American first editions, p. 210.

Specimen days, 1882–1883.

CURLE, RICHARD. Collecting American first editions, p. 210.

Two rivulets, 1876.

CURLE, RICHARD. Collecting American first editions, p. 171.

[*Two rivulets.*] *The month at Goodspeed's,* 3: 26–27, 1931.

See also Burroughs, John.

Whittier, John Greenleaf, 1807–1892

AMERICAN ART ASSOCIATION. Sales catalogue. Stephen H. Wakeman collection. Items 1076–1279.

FORSYTHE, ROBERT S. An uncollected poem by Whittier. *American literature,* 4: 194–95, 1933. Refers to "To Alice and Phoebe Cary" in James C. Derby's *Fifty years among authors, books and publishers.*

Whittier, John Greenleaf (*Continued*)

FULLERTON, BRADFORD M. Selective bibliography, pp. 298–301.

JOHNSON, MERLE. American first editions, pp. 230–32 (375–79).

PRAY, FRANCES M. A study of Whittier's apprenticeship as a poet; dealing with poems written between 1825 and 1835 not available in the poet's collected works . . . [Bristol, N.H.], 1930. (Thesis, Pennsylvania state college.) Bibliography, pp. [245]–54, 261–62.

T., H. S. John Greenleaf Whittier manuscripts: the Oak Knoll collection. Essex institute. *Historical collections,* 67: 113–18, 1931.

Among the hills, 1869.

CURLE, RICHARD. Collecting American first editions, pp. 136–37, 149, 175.

Ballads and other poems, 1844.

CURLE, RICHARD. Collecting American first editions, pp. 118–19.

Bay of seven islands, 1883.

CURLE, RICHARD. Collecting American first editions, pp. 19–20, 136–37.

Chapel of the hermits, 1853.

CURLE, RICHARD. Collecting American first editions, p. 210.

Hazel-blossoms, 1875.

CURLE, RICHARD. Collecting American first editions, pp. 145–46, 175.

History of Haverhill, 1832.

CURLE, RICHARD. Collecting American first editions, p. 30.

In war time, 1864.

CURLE, RICHARD. Collecting American first editions, pp. 11–12, 15, 128–29, 143–44, 183.

Jack in the pulpit, 1884.
CURLE, RICHARD. Collecting American first editions, p. 137.

James Williams, 1838.
CURLE, RICHARD. Collecting American first editions, pp. 112–14.

Justice and expediency, 1833.
AMERICAN ART ASSOCIATION. Sales catalogue. Stephen H. Wakeman collection. Item 1087. Facsimile of title-page.
CURLE, RICHARD. Collecting American first editions, pp. 194–95.

King's missive, 1881.
CURLE, RICHARD. Collecting American first editions, p. 176.

Lays of my home, 1843.
CURLE, RICHARD. Collecting American first editions, pp. 58, 116.

Legends of New-England, 1831.
CURLE, RICHARD. Collecting American first editions, pp. 71–74, 100. Facsimile of title-page, opp. p. 72.

Letters from John Quincy Adams, 1837.
CURLE, RICHARD. Collecting American first editions, p. 28.

Literary recreations, 1854.
CURLE, RICHARD. Collecting American first editions, p. 210.

Mabel Martin, 1876.
CURLE, RICHARD. Collecting American first editions, p. 148.

Margaret Smith's journal, 1849.
CURLE, RICHARD. Collecting American first editions, pp. 89–90, 114–16.

Maud Muller, 1854.
CURLE, RICHARD. Collecting American first editions, p. 172.

Minstrel girl, 1840.
CURLE, RICHARD. Collecting American first editions, p. 111.

Whittier, John Greenleaf (*Continued*)

Miriam, 1871.

Curle, Richard. Collecting American first editions, pp. 146–47, 175.

Mogg Megone, 1836.

Curle, Richard. Collecting American first editions, pp. 60, 110–11, 143.

Moll Pitcher, 1832.

American Art Association. Sales catalogue. Stephen H. Wakeman collection. Item 1084. Facsimile of title-page.

Curle, Richard. Collecting American first editions, pp. 110–11.

Old portraits, 1850.

Curle, Richard. Collecting American first editions, p. 90.

Our countrymen in chains, 1837.

Curle, Richard. Collecting American first editions, p. 172.

Panorama, 1856.

Curle, Richard. Collecting American first editions, p. 183.

Pennsylvania pilgrim, 1872.

Curle, Richard. Collecting American first editions, p. 175.

Poems, 1838.

Curle, Richard. Collecting American first editions, pp. 106, 118.

Poems written during the progress of the abolition question, 1837.

Curle, Richard. Collecting American first editions, pp. 27–29, 31, 39–41.

Snow-bound, 1866.

Curle, Richard. Collecting American first editions, pp. 37–38.

Song of the Vermonters, 1833.

AMERICAN ART ASSOCIATION. Sales catalogue. Stephen H. Wakeman collection. New York, 1924. Item 1091. Facsimile of title-page.

CURLE, RICHARD. Collecting American first editions, p. 207.

Songs of labor, 1850.

CURLE, RICHARD. Collecting American first editions, p. 17.

Stranger in Lowell, 1845.

CURLE, RICHARD. Collecting American first editions, p. 156.

Supernaturalism of New England, 1847.

CURLE, RICHARD. Collecting American first editions, p. 156. Facsimile of title-page, opp. p. 158.

Sycamores, 1857.

AMERICAN ART ASSOCIATION. Sales catalogue. Stephen H. Wakeman collection. New York, 1924. Item 1141. Facsimile of title-page.

CURLE, RICHARD. Collecting American first editions, p. 209.

Tent on the beach, 1867.

CURLE, RICHARD. Collecting American first editions, pp. 91–92, 95–96.

Tract for the times! 1850.

CURLE, RICHARD. Collecting American first editions, p. 172.

Vision of Echard, 1878.

CURLE, RICHARD. Collecting American first editions, pp. 174–75.

Voices of freedom, 1846.

CURLE, RICHARD. Collecting American first editions, pp. 116–20, 158. Facsimile of title-page, opp. p. 116.

Wiggin, Kate Douglas (Smith), 1859–1926

FULLERTON, BRADFORD M. Selective bibliography, p. 301.

Wigglesworth, Michael, 1631–1705

Day of doom, 1752.

NEWTON, A. EDWARD. This book-collecting game. Boston, Little, Brown and co., 1928. Facsimile of title-page, p. 74.

Meat out of the eater, 1670.

Michael Wigglesworth's *Meat out of the eater.* Yale university library. *Gazette,* 5 : 45–47, 1931.

Notes for a bibliography of Michael Wigglesworth's *Day of doom* and *Meat out of the eater.* American antiquarian society. *Proceedings,* 39, part 1, 77–84, 1929.

Wilcox, Carlos, 1794–1827

FULLERTON, BRADFORD M. Selective bibliography, pp. 301–2.

Wilcox, Ella (Wheeler), 1855–1920

FULLERTON, BRADFORD M. Selective bibliography, p. 302.

Wilcox, Thomas, 1549(?)–1608

Glasse for gamesters, 1581.

MAGGS BROTHERS. Catalogue no. 550. London, 1931. Facsimile of title-page, opp. p. 687.

Wilde, Oscar, 1854–1900

COWAN, ROBERT E., and CLARK, WILLIAM A., JR. The library of William Andrews Clark, jr. Wilde and Wildeiana. Volume IV. The miscellaneous writings of Oscar Wilde. With critical and historical notes by William Andrews Clark, jr. San Francisco, privately printed, 1931. 122 pp.

COWAN, ROBERT E., and CLARK, WILLIAM A., JR. The library of William Andrews Clark, jr. Wilde and Wildeiana. Volume V. Miscellaneous writings, writings of the Wildes and Wildeiana. With critical and historical notes by William Andrews Clark, jr. San Francisco, privately printed, 1931. 121 pp.

DAVRAY, HENRY D. Les apocryphes d'Oscar Wilde. *Mercure de France,* 183 : 104–17, 1925 ; 185 : 790–91, 1926 ; 186 : 308–17, 1926 ; 193 : 246–48, 1927.

DAVRAY, HENRY D. De quelques "poèmes en prose" inédits d'Oscar Wilde. *Mercure de France,* 189 : 257–77, 1926.

FIRST EDITION CLUB. A bibliographical catalogue, p. 178.

Wilde, Richard Henry, 1789–1847

FULLERTON, BRADFORD M. Selective bibliography, pp. 302–3.

Wilder, Thornton Niven, 1897——

JOHNSON, MERLE. American first editions, p. (382).

Willard, Edward Smith

HARTING, HUGH. Edward Smith Willard bibliography. *Notes and queries,* 163 : 402–4, 1932.

Willard, Emma C. (Hart), 1787–1870

FULLERTON, BRADFORD M. Selective bibliography, pp. 303–4.

LUTZ, ALMA. Emma Willard: daughter of democracy. Boston, Houghton Mifflin co., 1929. Bibliography, pp. [273]–79.

Williams, George Phipps

SERLE, PERCIVAL. Bibliography of Australasian poetry, p. 215.

Williams, Roger, 1608–1683

EASTON, EMILY. Roger Williams: prophet and pioneer. Boston, Houghton Mifflin co., 1930. Sources, pp. [379]–80.

Williamson, Henry, 1897——

GIRVAN, I. WAVENEY. A bibliography and critical survey of the works of Henry Williamson. Together with authentic bibliographical annotations by another hand. Chipping Campden, Gloucester, Alcuin press, 1931. 56 pp.

Willis, Nathaniel, 1806–1867

FULLERTON, BRADFORD M. Selective bibliography, pp. 304–5.

Willobie, Henry, 1574(?)–1596(?)

Willobie his avisa, 1594.

SAWYER and DARTON. English books, v. 1, p. [64]. Facsimile of title-page.

Wills, W. R.

SERLE, PERCIVAL. Bibliography of Australasian poetry, pp. 216–17.

Willson, Forceythe, 1837–1867

FULLERTON, BRADFORD M. Selective bibliography, p. 306.

Wilmer, George

SERLE, PERCIVAL. Bibliography of Australasian poetry, p. 216.

Wilmot, Frank Leslie Thompson, 1881——

SERLE, PERCIVAL. Bibliography of Australasian poetry, p. 217.

Wilmot, John, (*Second Earl of Rochester*), 1647–1680

PRINZ, J. John Wilmot, Earl of Rochester, his life and work. Leipzig, Mayer and Müller, 1927. Bibliography, pp. [305]–443. Reviews: "One of the most important sections . . . is the bibliography of Rochester's writings." —A. Nicoll, *Modern language review,* 23:358–59, 1928; "Weiter gibt er noch einegehende Rochester-Bibliographie mit genauer Angabe der Buchtitel, so dass man die einzelnen Ausgaben nun bequem vergleichen kann, was bei der Ähnlichkeit der Titel zahlreicher Ausgaben sehr wertvoll ist. Auch die Angabe der wichtigsten Bibliotheken, in denen sich die Bücher befinden, ist sehr dankenswert."—K. Brunner, *Archiv für das Studium der neueren Sprachen und Literaturen,* 156:129, 1929.

Wilson, Alexander, 1766–1813
FULLERTON, BRADFORD M. Selective bibliography, pp. 306–7.

Wilson, Harry Leon, 1867——
JOHNSON, MERLE. American first editions, pp. 237–38 (383–84).

Wilson, John, 1785–1850
COLBY, RALPH. John Wilson; a study of his writings. Urbana, Ill., 1931. (Abstract of thesis, University of Illinois.)

Wilson, Robert Burns, 1850–1916
FULLERTON, BRADFORD M. Selective bibliography, pp. 307–8.

Wilson, Thomas, 1525(?)–1581
Arte of rhetorique, 1553.
WAGNER, RUSSELL H. The text and editions of Wilson's *Arte of Rhetorique. Modern language notes,* 44:421–28, 1929.
Rule of reason, 1567.
MAGGS BROTHERS. Catalogue no. 550. London, 1931. Facsimile of title-page, opp. p. 702.

Wilson, Thomas Woodrow, 1756–1924
ANNIN, ROBERT E. Woodrow Wilson; a character study. New York, Dodd, Mead and co., 1924. Bibliography, pp. vii–viii.
FULLERTON, BRADFORD M. Selective bibliography, p. 308.
JOHNSON, MERLE. American first editions, pp. 239–40 (385–86).

Winter, William, 1836–1917
FULLERTON, BRADFORD M. Selective bibliography, p. 309.

Winthrop, Theodore, 1828–1861
FULLERTON, BRADFORD M. Selective bibliography, pp. 309–10.

Wirt, William, 1772–1834
FULLERTON, BRADFORD M. Selective bibliography, pp. 310–11.

Wise, Henry Augustus, 1819–1869
FULLERTON, BRADFORD M. Selective bibliography, p. 311.

Wister, Owen, 1860——
JOHNSON, MERLE. American first editions, pp. 241–42 (387–88).
JOHNSON, MERLE. American first editions: Owen Wister, 1860——. *Publishers' weekly,* 103: 1068, 1923.

Wither, George, 1588–1667
SAWYER and DARTON. English books, v. 1, pp. 203–5.
SIMPSON, PERCY. Walkley's piracy of Wither's poems in 1620. *Library,* s. 4, 6: [271]–77, 1926.

Fidelia, 1615.
SAWYER and DARTON. English books, v. 1, p. [204]. Facsimile of title-page.

Great assises, 1645.
MAGGS BROTHERS. Catalogue no. 550. Facsimile of title-page, opp. p. 703.

Wood, Sally Sayward (Barrell, Keating), 1759–1855
FULLERTON, BRADFORD M. Selective bibliography, pp. 311–12.

Woodberry, George Edward, 1855–1930
ERSKINE, JOHN. George Edward Woodberry, 1855–1930. An appreciation. New York public library. *Bulletin,* 34: 275–79, 1930.
FULLERTON, BRADFORD M. Selective bibliography, pp. 312–13.
HAWKINS, R. R. A list of writings by and about George Edward Woodberry. New York public library. *Bulletin,* 34: 279–96, 1930.

Woodworth, Samuel, 1785–1842

FULLERTON, BRADFORD M. Selective bibliography, p. 313.

Woolf, Virginia (Stephen), 1882——

DELATTRE, FLORIS. Le roman psychologique de Virginie Woolf. Paris, Vrin, 1932. "Esquisse d'une bibliographie de Virginie Woolf," pp. 259–66.

Woolls, William

SERLE, PERCIVAL. Bibliography of Australasian poetry, p. 221.

Woolsey, Sarah Chauncey, 1835–1905

FULLERTON, BRADFORD M. Selective bibliography, pp. 313–14.

Woolson, Constance Fenimore, 1838–1894

FULLERTON, BRADFORD M. Selective bibliography, pp. 314–15.

Worde, Wynkyn De

See De Worde, Wynkyn.

Wordsworth, William, 1770–1850

BROUGHTON, LESLIE N. The Wordsworth collection formed by Cynthia Morgan St. John and given to Cornell university by Victor Emanuel. A catalogue compiled by . . . Ithaca, N.Y., Cornell university library, 1931. xii+124 pp. Review, *Books,* 7 : 15, July 5, 1931.

READ, HERBERT. Wordsworth. London, Cape, 1930. *Ibid.,* New York, Cape & Smith, [1931]. List of works, pp. [261]–64.

SAWYER and DARTON. English books, v. 2, pp. 26, 38–46, 67, 76, 101, 103.

SMITH, ELSIE, *ed.* Estimate of William Wordsworth by his contemporaries, 1793–1822. London, Blackwell, 1932. 379 pp.

Wordsworth, William (*Continued*)

Wise, Thomas J. Two Lake poets. A catalogue of printed books, manuscripts, and autograph letters. (William Wordsworth and Samuel Taylor Coleridge.) London, privately printed, 1927. xxi+135 pp., facsimiles.

Borderers, 1842.

McGillivray, James R. Wordsworth's *The borderers. Times literary supplement,* December 25, 1930, p. 1101.

Lyrical ballads, 1798.

Sawyer and Darton. English books, v. 2, p. [41]. Facsimile of title-page.

Lyrical ballads, 1800.

Chapman, Robert W. *Lyrical ballads,* 1800. *Book-collector's quarterly,* no. 6, pp. 25–26, April–June, 1932.

Prelude, 1850.

De Selincourt, Ernest, *ed.* The prelude, by William Wordsworth. Edited from the manuscripts, with introduction, textual and critical notes by . . . Oxford, Clarendon press, 1926.

Wright, David McKee, 1869——

Serle, Percival. Bibliography of Australasian poetry, p. 222.

Wright, Frances

See D'Arusmont, Frances (Wright).

Wright, Harold Bell, 1872——

Overton, Grant. American nights entertainment. New York, Appleton, 1923, p. 138.

Overton, Grant. Authors of the day. New York, Doran, [1924], pp. 98–99.

Wyatt, Thomas, (*Sir*), 1503(?)–1542

Sawyer and Darton. English books, v. 1, p. 80.

Wycherley, William, 1640(?)–1716
SAWYER and DARTON. English books, v. 1, pp. 209–10.

Wyclif, John, *d.* 1384
WORKMAN, HERBERT B. John Wyclif: a study of the medieval church. Oxford, Clarendon press, 1926. 2 v. Bibliographical footnotes.

Wylie, Elinor (Hoyt), 1886–1928
JOHNSON, MERLE. American first editions, pp. (389–90).
JOHNSON, MERLE. American first editions: Elinor Wylie, 1886–1928. *Publishers' weekly,* 116:2845–46, 1929.

Wynne, John Huddlestone, 1743–1788
SPARKE, ARCHIBALD. John Huddlestone Wynn. *Notes and queries,* 153:411–12, 1927.

Yarrington, William Henry Hazell
SERLE, PERCIVAL. Bibliography of Australasian poetry, pp. 222–23.

Yeager, Joseph
WEISS, HARRY B. Joseph Yeager, early American engraver, publisher of children's books ... New York public library. *Bulletin,* 36:611–16, 1932.

Yeats, William Butler, 1865——
CUTLER and STILES. Modern British authors, pp. 166–67.
SYMONS, A. J. A. A bibliography of the first editions of books by William Butler Yeats. London, First edition club, 1924. 54 pp.

Young, Brigham, 1801–1877
WERNER, MORRIS R. Brigham Young. New York, Harcourt, [1925]. Bibliography, pp. 463–69.

Zillman, John Herman Leopold
SERLE, PERCIVAL. Bibliography of Australasian poetry, p. 224.

SUPPLEMENT

Bates, Herbert Ernest, 1905——

SCHWARTZ, H. WARREN. Check-lists of twentieth-century authors. First series. Milwaukee, Wis., Casanova booksellers, 1931.

Blunden, Edmund Charles, 1896——

GASWORTH, A. J., and SCHWARTZ, JACOB. Bibliography of Edmund Blunden, with preface and copious notes by Edmund Blunden. London, Ulysses bookshop, 1931.

Browne, John Ross, 1821–1875

LONE, EMMA M. Check-list of first editions of the work of John Ross Browne . . . New York, Lathrop C. Harper, 1931. 16 pp.

Chaucer, Geoffrey, 1340–1400

BOND, R. P., *et al.* A collection of Chaucer allusions. *Studies in philology,* 28 : 481–512, 1929.

RUUD, MARTIN B. Chaucer studies. *Modern language notes,* 45 : 288–95, 1929; *Philological quarterly,* 8 : 296–306, 1929.

Cooper, James Fenimore, 1789–1851

SPILLER, ROBERT E. A Cooper bibliography (announced). *Saturday review of literature,* 8 : 607, 1932.

Coppard, Alfred Edgar, 1878——

FABES, GILBERT H. The first editions of A. E. Coppard, A. P. Herbert, and Charles Morgan. With points and values. London, Myers, 1933. 154 pp.

Davies, Rhys, 1903——

SCHWARTZ, H. WARREN. Check-lists of twentieth-century authors. First series. Milwaukee, Wis., Casanova booksellers, 1931.

Dickens, Charles, 1812–1870

DARTON, F. J. HARVEY. Dickens: positively the first appearance. A centenary review, with a bibliography of *Sketches by Boz.* London, Argonaut press, 1933.

Eliot, Thomas Stearns, 1888——

NICHOLLS, NORAH. A bibliography of T. S. Eliot. *Bookman* (London), 82: 309, 1932.

Faulkner, William, 1897——

SCHWARTZ, H. WARREN. Check-lists of twentieth-century authors. First series. Milwaukee, Wis., Casanova booksellers, 1931.

Foster, Stephen Collins, 1826–1864

Foster Hall bulletin. Issued occasionally and presented to collectors of and dealers in Fosteriana . . . Indianapolis, Josiah K. Lilly, 1933. Nos. 1–7 were mimeographed, no. 8 printed.

Frost, Robert Lee, 1875——

BOUTELL, H. S. A bibliography of Robert Frost. *Colophon,* part II, 1930. 3 pp.

MELCHER, FREDERIC. Robert Frost and his books. *Colophon,* part II, 1930. 7 pp.

Hardy, Thomas, 1840–1928

FOWLER, J. H. The novels of Thomas Hardy. London, Oxford university press, 1928. 18 pp. (English association. *Pamphlets,* no. 71.)

Hemingway, Ernest, 1898——

SCHWARTZ, H. WARREN. Check-lists of twentieth-century authors. First series. Milwaukee, Wis., Casanova booksellers, 1931.

Herbert, Allen Patrick, 1890——

FABES, GILBERT H. The first editions of A. E. Coppard, A. P. Herbert, and Charles Morgan. With points and values. London, Myers, 1933. 154 pp.

Johnson, Samuel, 1709–1784

Taxation no tyranny, 1775.

STILES, ROBERT E. Doctor Samuel Johnson's *Taxation no tyranny* and its half-title. *American book collector,* 1: 155–56, 1932.

Morgan, Charles, 1894——

FABES, GILBERT H. The first editions of A. E. Coppard, A. P. Herbert, and Charles Morgan. With points and values. London, Myers, 1933. 154 pp.

O'Flaherty, Liam, 1897——

SCHWARTZ, H. WARREN. Check-lists of twentieth-century authors. First series. Milwaukee, Wis., Casanova booksellers, 1931.

Pickthall, Marjorie Lowery Christie, 1883–1922

PIERCE, LORNE. Marjorie Pickthall, a book of remembrance. Toronto, Ryerson, 1925. Bibliography, pp. 201–17.

Sassoon, Siegfried Lorraine, 1886——

SCHWARTZ, H. WARREN. Check-lists of twentieth-century authors. First series. Milwaukee, Wis., Casanova booksellers, 1931.

Shelley, Percy Bysshe, 1792–1822

BODLEIAN LIBRARY. The Shelley correspondence in the Bodleian library. Letters of Percy Bysshe Shelley and others, mainly unpublished, from the collection presented to the library by Lady Shelley in 1892. Edited by R. H. Hill . . . With a chronological table and a list of other Shelley manuscripts and relics in the library. Oxford, printed for the Bodleian library, 1926. Review by R. Ingpen, Library association. *Record,* n.s., 4: 96–98, 1926.

SWANN, ARTHUR. A rare Shelley pamphlet. *American book collector,* 1: 352–56, 1932.

Webster, Daniel, 1782–1852

HARASZTI, Z. A Webster exhibit. *More books,* 7: 3–10, 1932.

Wilson, Alexander, 1766–1813

WEISS, HARRY B. Alexander Wilson as a chapbook author. *American book collector,* 2: 218–19, 1932.

APPENDIX

During the decade with which the *Index to Bibliographies* is concerned many books have been published which are so comprehensive that it is impractical to analyze each one for the purpose of indicating whether or not its record of the works of an individual author is more complete than the account given in separately published books and journal contributions.

Such works are of considerable supplementary value in connection with the material included in the *Index* and for this reason the more important of such publications are recorded in the Appendix. A selected list of general works relating to bibliography, literary history, and book-collecting published between 1923–1932 is also included.

The national bibliographies, concerning which full information may be found in the bibliographical handbooks of Schneider and Van Hoesen and Walter, together with the catalogues of the great national libraries, are obviously useful in any inquiry concerning the works of a particular author.

The catalogue cards issued by the Library of Congress are available for consultation in the larger libraries of the United States and at research centers abroad. These cards often are combined with similar cards from other libraries to form "union-catalogues."

The printed catalogue of the British Museum, of which a new series is now in progress, is similarly available. The printed catalogues of the Bibliotheque Nationale and of the German libraries are of less value as sources of information concerning English and American books, although frequently useful, particularly for the earlier writers.

The three publications in English devoted to an annual record of auction prices paid for rare books (*Book prices current,* London; *Book auction records,* London; *American book prices current,* New York) are continually referred to. These may be consulted in many of the larger American and English libraries.

ALDRED, THOMAS. Sequel stories, English and American. London, Association of assistant librarians, 1928. Second edition. 91 pp.

AMERICAN ART ASSOCIATION. Sales catalogues. New York, 1923–1932. A list of the sales for each season will be found in the corresponding volume of *American book prices current.*

American book prices current. New York, Bowker, 1923–1932. An annual record of sales at the principal American auction houses.

ANGOFF, CHARLES. A literary history of the American people ... New York, Knopf, 1931. 2 v. V. 1, 1607–1749; v. 2, 1750–1815.

ARNOLD, WILLIAM H. Ventures in book-collecting. New York, Scribner, 1923. xvii+356 pp.

BAKER, ERNEST A., and PACKMAN, JAMES. A guide to the best fiction, English and American ... London, Routledge, 1932. viii+634 pp.

BAKER, ERNEST A. The history of the English novel. The age of romance; from the beginnings to the renaissance. London, Witherby, 1924. 336 pp.

BINGHAM, CLIVE. The Roxburghe club, its history and its members, 1812–1927. London, 1928. With a full list of the Roxburghe club books.

BLOCK, ANDREW. The book-collector's vade mecum. London, Archer, 1932. viii+375 pp. Includes check-lists of Scott, Leigh Hunt, Shelley, Keats, Byron, Dickens, Thackeray, Ainsworth, Browning, and Tennyson.

BLOCK, ANDREW. Key books of British authors, 1600–1932. London, Archer, 1933. 384 pp.

Book auction records. London, Henry Stevens, son & Stiles, 1923–1932. A record of sales at the principal English auction houses.

Book prices current. London, Witherby, 1923–1932. A record of sales at the principal English auction houses.

BOUTELL, H. S. First editions of to-day and how to tell them. London, Elkin Mathews & Marrot, 1928; Philadelphia, Lippincott, 1929. 62 pp.

BOWYER, W. Publishers' binding cloth. *Book-collectors' quarterly,* no. 6, April–June 1932, pp. 57–59.

BREBNER, JOHN B., and NEFF, E. EDWARD. Bibliography of English literature and history ... New York, Columbia university press, 1932. 20 pp.

BREWER, LUTHER A. Joys and sorrows of a book-collector. Cedar Rapids, privately printed, 1929. 65 pp.

BRIGGS, MORRIS H. Buying and selling rare books. New York, Bowker, 1927. 91 pp.

BROWN UNIVERSITY. John Carter Brown library. Bibliotheca americana: catalogue. Providence, R.I., 1919+ (v. 3, 1659–1674, 1931).

Cambridge history of American literature, edited by William P. Trent [*et al.*]. New York, Macmillan, 1931. 4 v.

Cambridge history of English literature, edited by A. W. Ward and A. R. Waller. London, Cambridge university press; New York, Macmillan, 1932. 15 v.

CARTER, JOHN. Binding variants, 1820–1900. London, Constable, 1932. xviii+172 pp.

CARTER, JOHN. Notes on the early years of cloth binding. *Book-collectors' quarterly,* no. 6, April–June 1932, pp. 45–46.

CHAMBERS, EDMUND K. (*Sir*). The Elizabethan stage. Oxford, Clarendon press, 1923. 4 v.

CHAPMAN, ROBERT W. Cancels. London, Constable, 1930. 70 pp.

COWLING, GEORGE H. English bibliography: being a short list of books recommended to students of English language and literature. Melbourne, Melbourne university press, 1931. 49 pp.

CRANE, RONALD S., and KAYE, FREDERICK B. A census of British newspapers and periodicals, 1620–1820. *Studies in philology,* 24, no. 1, 1927. 205 pp.

CROSS, TOM P. List of books and articles, chiefly bibliographical, designed to serve as an introduction to the bibliography and methods of English literary history ... Chicago, University of Chicago press, 1932. viii+58 pp.

CURLE, RICHARD. Collecting American first editions. Its pitfalls and its pleasures. Indianapolis, Bobbs-Merrill, 1930. xviii+221 pp. Analyzed in the *Index.*

CURRIE, BARTON. Fishers of books. Boston, Little, Brown and co., 1931. xiv+350 pp. Facsimiles of title-pages noted in the *Index.*

Cutler, Bradley D., and Stiles, Villa. Modern British authors. Their first editions. New York, Greenberg, 1930. xi+171 pp. Analyzed in the *Index*.

Englisch, Paul. Geschichte der erotischen Literatur. Stuttgart, Puttmann, 1927. Part 6 relates to the English literature, pp. 611–62.

Esdaile, Arundell. The sources of English literature: a guide for students. (Sandars lectures, 1926.) Cambridge, Cambridge university press, 1928. vii+131 pp.

Esdaile, Arundell. Student's manual of bibliography. London, G. Allen & Unwin, 1931; New York, Scribner, 1931. 383 pp. Second edition, London, G. Allen & Unwin, 1932.

Evans, Arthur W. A century of famous title-pages. London, Elkin Mathews, 1931. One hundred facsimiles.

Evans, Charles. American bibliography. A chronological dictionary of all books, pamphlets, and periodical publications printed in the United States of America from the genesis of printing in 1639 down to and including the year 1820. Chicago, 1903——.

Fabes, Gilbert H. The autobiography of a book. London, Elzevir press, 1926. 204 pp. A fanciful work on book-collecting.

Fabes, Gilbert H. Modern first editions: points and values. First series. London, Foyle, 1929. xi+83 pp.

Fabes, Gilbert H., and Foyle, William H. Modern first editions: points and values. Second series. London, Foyle, 1931. xx+94 pp.

Fabes, Gilbert H. Modern first editions: points and values. Third series. London, Foyle, 1932. 128 pp.

Fullerton, Bradford M. Selective bibliography of American literature. 1775–1900 . . . New York, Payson, 1932. vii+327 pp. Analyzed in the *Index*.

Garnett, Robert S. Odd memories: more book-hunting adventures. London, Blackwood, 1932. vi+319 pp.

Garnett, Robert S. Some book-hunting adventures. London, Blackwood, 1931. x+318 pp.

Gasamtkatalog der Wiegendrucke. Leipzig, Hiersemann, 1925——. A complete catalog of all known incunabula. When completed this work will contain descriptions of about 38,000 editions.

Greg, Walter W. Dramatic documents from the Elizabethan playhouses: stage plots, actors' parts, prompt books. London,

Oxford university press, 1931–1932. 2 v. Volume 1, commentary; volume 2, reproductions and transcripts.

HALSALLE, HENRY DE. Treasure trove in bookland: the romance of modern first editions. London, Laurie, [1931]. xv+200 pp. Same with title: The romance of modern first editions. Philadelphia, Lippincott, 1931. xv+192 pp.

HART, HORACE. Bibliotheca typographica: in usum eorum qui libros amant. A list of books about books and printing. Rochester, N.Y., Leo Hart, 1933. xi+142 pp.

HENDERSON, JAMES D. Miniature books. Leipzig, Tondeur & Säuberlich, 1930. 34 pp.

HOBSON, G. D. A bibliography of book-binding. *Book-collectors' quarterly,* no. 7, July–September 1932, pp. 70–84.

HOBSON, G. D. English binding before 1500. (Sandars lectures, 1927.) Cambridge, Cambridge university press, 1929. vii+58 pp.

ISAAC, FRANK. English and Scottish printing types, 1501–1536 and 1508–1541. London, Bibliographical society, 1931.

JACKSON, GUY A. Primer of rare books and first editions ... Boston, Guy A. Jackson, 1930. xv, 17–106 pp.

JACKSON, HOLBROOK. The anatomy of bibliomania. London, Soncino press, 1930. 2 v. Also in 1 v., New York, Scribner, 1932. 869 pp.

JACKSON, HOLBROOK. The fear of books. New York, Scribner, 1932. x+199 pp.

JOHNSON, MERLE. American first editions. Bibliographic check lists of the works of one hundred and five American authors. New York, Bowker, 1929. viii+242 pp. Analyzed in the *Index.*

JOHNSON, MERLE. American first editions. Bibliographic check lists of the works of 146 American authors. Revised and enlarged. New York, Bowker, 1932. x+390 pp. Analyzed in the *Index.*

KENNEDY, ARTHUR G. A bibliography of writings on the English language from the beginning of printing to the end of 1922. Cambridge, Harvard university press [etc.], 1927. 17+517 pp.

KENT, VIOLET. The players' library and bibliography of the theatre. London, Gollancz, 1930. xvi+401 pp. A catalog of the library of the British drama league.

KLETSCH, ERNEST. A union catalog of photo facsimiles in North American libraries . . . Washington, D.C., 1929.

LEISY, ERNEST E., and HUBBEL, JAY B. Doctoral dissertations in American literature. *American literature,* 4:419–65, 1933. Part 1, completed dissertations; part 2, dissertations in progress.

LIBRARY OF CONGRESS. List of American doctoral dissertations printed in 1923, etc. Washington, D.C., 1923–1932.

MCANALLY, HENRY (*Sir*). Book-wrappers. *Book-collectors' quarterly,* no. 4, April–June 1932, pp. 10–17.

MCCUTCHEON, GEORGE B. Books once were men. An essay for booklovers . . . with an introduction by William Dana Orcutt . . . New York, Dodd, Mead & co., 1931. x+61 pp.

MCKERROW, RONALD B. An introduction to bibliography for literary students. Oxford, Clarendon press, 1928. xv+359 pp.

MCKERROW, RONALD B., and FERGUSON, F. S. Title-page borders used in England and Scotland, 1485–1640. Oxford, Clarendon press, 1932.

MATHESON, CYRIL. A catalogue of the publications of Scottish historical and kindred clubs and societies . . . 1908–1927. Aberdeen, Milne & Hutchinson, 1928. 240 pp.

MODERN HUMANITIES ASSOCIATION. Annual bibliography of English language and literature. London, Bowes & Bowes, 1923–1932.

MODERN HUMANITIES ASSOCIATION. Year's work in modern language studies . . . edited by William J. Entwistle. London, Oxford university press, 1930——.

MODERN LANGUAGE ASSOCIATION OF AMERICA. Bibliography of critical Arthurian legend. 1922–1929. New York, Modern language association of America, 1931. 59 pp.

MORLEY, CHRISTOPHER. Ex libris carissimis. Philadelphia, University of Pennsylvania press, 1932. x+134 pp.

MUIR, PERCY H. Points, 1874–1930: being extracts from a bibliographer's note book. London, Constable, 1931. xvii+167 pp.

MUMBY, FRANK A. Publishing and bookselling: a history from the earliest times to the present day: with a bibliography by W. H. Peet. London, Cape, 1930. 480 pp.

MUMEY, NOLIE. Study of rare books: with special reference to colophons, press devices and title-pages of interest to bibliophiles and the student of literature. Denver, Colo., Clason, 1930. xvii+572 pp.

Newton, A. Edward. The format of the English novel: with reproductions of title-pages from books in the author's library. Cleveland, Rowfant club, 1928. 41 pp.

Newton, A. Edward. The greatest book in the world . . . Boston, Little, Brown and co., 1925. xvii+451 pp.

Newton, A. Edward. This book-collecting game. Boston, Little, Brown and co., 1928. 410 pp.

Nield, Jonathan. A guide to the best historical novels and tales. London, Elkin Mathews & Marrot, 1929. 452 pp.

Northup, Clark S. A register of bibliographies of the English language and literature . . . with contributions by Joseph Q. Adams and Andrew Keogh. New Haven, Yale university press, 1925. 507 pp.

O'Leary, John G. English literary history and bibliography. London, Grafton, 1928. xii+192 pp.

Orcutt, William D. In quest of the perfect book: reminiscences and reflections of a bookman. Boston, Little, Brown and co., 1926. 316 pp.

Orcutt, William D. Kingdom of books. Boston, Little, Brown and co., 1927. xii+290 pp.

Orcutt, William D. Magic of the book: more reminiscences and reflections of a bookman. Boston, Little, Brown and co., 1930. vii+314 pp.

Pierce, Lorne. Outline of Canadian literature . . . Toronto, Ryerson press, 1927. 251 pp. Analyzed in the *Index*.

Plomer, Henry R., *et al.* Dictionary of booksellers and printers who were at work in England, Scotland, and Ireland from 1726 to 1775. London, Bibliographical society, 1932. xxi+432 pp.

Plomer, Henry R. English printers' ornaments. London, 1924.

Plomer, Henry R. Wynkyn de Worde and his contemporaries from the death of Caxton to 1535. London, Grafton, 1925. 253 pp.

Pollard, Alfred W. Cobden-Sanderson and the Doves press. The history of the press and the story of its types told by . . . and a list of the Doves press printings. San Francisco, Nash, 1929.

POLLARD, ALFRED W., REDGRAVE, G. R., *et al.* Short-title catalogue of books printed in England, Scotland, and Ireland, and of English books printed abroad, 1475–1640. London, Bibliographical society, 1926. xvi+609 pp.

RANSOM, WILL. Private presses and their books. New York, Bowker, 1929. 493 pp. The history of the private press movement with detailed check-lists of nearly 3,000 titles issued by over 300 presses.

REID, FOREST. Illustrators of the sixties. 1928. With a list of first editions of books illustrated by artists of the sixties. London, Faber & Faber, 1928. 312 pp.

ROSENBACH, A. S. W. Books and bidders: adventures of a bibliophile. Boston, Little, Brown and co., 1927. xiv+311 pp.

ROSENBACH, A. S. W. Early American children's books, 1682–1840 ... New York, New York public library, 1927. 15 pp.

ROSENBACH, A. S. W. The unpublishable memoirs. London, Castle, 1924. 151 pp.

ROSENBACH COMPANY. Catalogue of an exhibition of two hundred famous first editions ... New York, Rosenbach, [1931]. x+47 pp.

SADLEIR, MICHAEL. The evolution of publishers' binding styles, 1770–1900. London, Constable, 1930. 106 pp.

SARGENT, GEORGE H. A busted bibliophile and his books: being a most delectable history of the diverting adventures of that renowned book-collector, A. Edward Newton ... Boston, Little, Brown and co., 1928. 49 pp.

SAWYER, CHARLES J., and DARTON, FREDERICK J. H. English books, 1745–1900: a signpost for collectors. London, Sawyer; New York, Dutton, 1927. 2 v. Volume 1, Caxton to Johnson; volume 2, Gray to Kipling. Partly analyzed in the *Index*.

SCHNEIDER, GEORG. Handbuch der Bibliographie. Leipzig, Hiersemann, 1930. Fourth edition. ix+674 pp.

SCHWARTZ, JACOB. 1,100 obscure points. The bibliography of 25 English and American authors. London, Simpkin, Marshall, 1931. 95 pp.

SERLE, PERCIVAL. Bibliography of Australasian poetry and verse, Australia and New Zealand. Melbourne, Melbourne university press, 1925. xiv+235 pp.

SMITH, HARRY B. First nights and first editions. Boston, Little, Brown and co., 1931. x+325 pp.

STARRETT, VINCENT. Penny wise and book foolish. New York, Covici, 1929. 199 pp.

STILWELL, MARGARET B. Incunabula and Americana, 1450–1800: a key to bibliographical study. New York, Columbia university press, 1931. xviii+483 pp.

STONEHILL, CHARLES A., JR., BLOCK, ANDREW, and STONEHILL, H. WINTHROP. Anonyma and pseudonyma. London, Stonehill, 1926–1927. 4 v.

TOMKINSON, G. S. Select bibliography of the principal modern presses . . . in Great Britain and Ireland. London, First edition club, 1928. 264 pp.

VAN HOESEN, HENRY B., and WALTER, FRANK K. Bibliography, practical, enumerative, historical: an introductory manual. New York, Scribner, 1928. xiii+519 pp.

WARD, A. C. The nineteen-twenties . . . London, Methuen, 1930. 222 pp. A valuable work for collectors of English first editions.

WARD, A. C. Twentieth century literature . . . 1901–1925. London, Methuen, 1928. 242 pp.

WEGELIN, OSCAR. Early American fiction, 1774–1830: a compilation of the titles of works of fiction, by writers born or residing in North America . . . New York, Peter Smith, 1929. Third edition. 37 pp.

WEGELIN, OSCAR. Early American poetry, 1650–1820: a compilation of the titles of volumes of verse and broadsides by writers born or residing in North America . . . New York, Peter Smith, 1930. Second edition. 254 pp.

WHEELER, H. A. A short catalogue of books printed in England and English books printed abroad before 1641 in the library of Wadham college, Oxford. London, Longmans, 1929. xv+101 pp.

WILLIAMS, HAROLD. Book clubs and printing societies of Great Britain and Ireland. London, First edition club, 1929. x+126 pp.

WILLIAMS, IOLO A. Books on book-collecting. (A bibliography.) *Book-collectors' quarterly,* no. 5, January–March 1932, pp. 92–103.

WILLIAMS, IOLO A. The elements of book-collecting. London, Elkin Mathews & Marrot; New York, Stokes, 1928. 171 pp.

WINTERICH, JOHN T. Books and the man ... New York, Greenberg, 1929; London, G. Allen & Unwin, 1930. xiv+374 pp.

WINTERICH, JOHN T. Collector's choice. New York, Greenberg, 1928. 211 pp.

WINTERICH, JOHN T. A primer of book-collecting. New York, Greenberg, 1927. vii+206 pp.

WISE, THOMAS J. Ashley library. Catalogue of printed books, manuscripts, and autograph letters collected by ... London, privately printed, 1922–1932. 10 v. Collations from Nashe, Ben Jonson, Shirley, and Milton to Wordsworth, Shelley, Keats, Swinburne, and Conrad. Facsimiles of title-pages, manuscripts, etc.

INDEX

(Arranged by authors and compilers of bibliographies and bibliographical contributions)